Advance Praise for: *Prison: The Inside Story*

"This is a gripping and powerful book, but one that is not for the faint of heart. Jack Myette has pulled back the curtain on a segment of our society that many of us would pretend does not exist. As angry and cruel as many inmates are, Jack has painted a picture of individuals who may need our compassion and mercy more than any of our human brethren."
Dr. Seth Epstein – retired economics professor at DePaul University

"From the despair of many inmates to the indifference of staff, Jack tried to bring about change. The reader will be appalled and disgusted at times but will come away knowing inmates are just people like the rest of us."
Dr. Michael Wells – retired research associate, University of Colorado

"The author's compelling first-hand narratives draw you in and keep you fascinated with real prison situations and personalities. The inmates' accounts of their pre-prison environment and perspectives on 'justice' are astounding."
Mark Pulice – retired General Motors executive

"This story is not delicately nuanced but rather a character-driven tale of dignity and compassion for the most vulnerable in our prison system. Myette handles the harsh elements with sensitivity and truth, weaving a chronicle that will find a place in your soul, and will stay there."
Linda J Hulton, PhD, RN – Faculty Emeritus, School of Nursing, James Madison University

"Think you know prisons? You don't know Jack. Jack Myette, that is. This book will take you there. It ain't pretty, but it is gripping. Get a close look inside from someone who's been there. You'll see the guys you don't want to meet and the ones changing their lives."
Jackie Payne – retired fundraiser for WKAR at Michigan State University

Readers are encouraged to go to www.MissionPointPress.com to contact the author or to find information on how to buy this book in bulk at a discounted rate.

Mission Point Press

Published by Mission Point Press
2554 Chandler Rd.
Traverse City, MI 49696
(231) 421-9513
MissionPointPress.com

Design by Sarah Meiers

Softcover ISBN: 978-1-965278-41-3
Hardcover ISBN: 978-1-965278-40-6
Library of Congress Control Number: 2025900808

Printed in the United States of America

PRISON:
THE INSIDE STORY

TRANSFORMING LIVES AS
AN OFFICER AND EDUCATOR

JACK MYETTE

MISSION POINT PRESS

*To the men and women who risk their lives
by working in jails and prisons across our nation.
Also to my father, an avid reader and writer,
and my mother, who continually asked,
"When are you going to be done with your book?"*

*"Prison has a universal fascination.
It's a real-life horror story because,
given the right set of circumstances,
anyone could find themselves behind bars."*

—Wentworth Miller

Table of Contents

Author's Note XII

Prologue 1

I: Correctional Medical Aide
at Riverside Correctional Facility 5

    Chapter 1: Starting My Prison Career 7

    Chapter 2: A Red Tag No More 12

    Chapter 3: Jumping in with Both Feet 20

    Chapter 4: Incompetence Strikes Again and Again 32

    Chapter 5: Officers Over the Top 41

    Chapter 6: Swallowers, Cutters, Biters and More 47

    Chapter 7: The Games People Play 54

    Chapter 8: Mayhem and Mischief 61

    Chapter 9: My Introduction to 10 Building 74

    Chapter 10: A Couple of Heavy Hitters 84

II: Corrections Officer
at Mid Michigan Correctional Facility 95

Chapter 11: New Prison, New Position 97

Chapter 12: Learning From the Past 104

Chapter 13: About Drugs 112

Chapter 14: Escapes: Successful and Otherwise 119

III: Adult Basic Education Teacher
at St. Louis Correctional Facility......................... 129

Chapter 15: Early Teaching Days........................ 131

Chapter 16: Low-Level Students in a High-Level Prison.... 138

Chapter 17: My First Three Inmate Tutors................ 145

Chapter 18: Dealin' Drugs and Sellin' Guns 155

Chapter 19: The Language of Prison 163

Chapter 20: Disputes and Misunderstandings 169

Chapter 21: Black on Black 173

IV: Learning About a Different World..................... 181

Chapter 22: Southern Time 183

Chapter 23: A Taste of Jackson Prison 192

Chapter 24: Of the Caucasian Persuasion................. 196

Chapter 25: More Europeans 201

Chapter 26: Crime and Corruption
in the United Mexican States............................ 207

Chapter 27: The Gangs Are All Here 216

Chapter 28: Problems with Gangs 227

Chapter 29: Papa Smurf 233

**V: General Educational Development Teacher
at Pugsley Correctional Facility** 243

Chapter 30: Crusade Against Education
and Inmates' Success 245

Chapter 31: Graduation 254

VI: Thoughts About My Time in Prison and Retirement 261

Chapter 32: A Couple of the Best 263

Chapter 33: Prison Reform 270

Chapter 34: "A purpose to fulfill" 275

Glossary 279

Acknowledgments 285

About the Author 286

Author's Note

To protect the privacy of individuals in the book, I have changed most people's names. At work, I addressed staff and inmates by their last names to maintain a professional relationship and avoid overfamiliarity. Although I sometimes refer to prisoners by their nicknames in the book, I adhered to protocol when working.

The book is organized chronologically, but sometimes I have included flashbacks or rearranged sections by subject to make related topics more straightforward. It is important to note that any opinions shared about the people and the situations I encountered are solely my own and do not reflect the views of the Michigan Department of Corrections.

Prologue

In 1989, I moved to Lansing, Michigan, from Cancun, Mexico. Although the 80-degree year-round temperature and the 100-foot underwater visibility were amazing, I needed to return to reality and find work with benefits and a pension. After hearing the State of Michigan was hiring corrections officers, I applied and was offered a job working with the criminally insane at Riverside Correctional Facility, a psychiatric prison in Ionia, Michigan. I was about to depart on a Nantucket sleigh ride.

After working only a few days, I experienced one of the most bizarre incidents I had ever seen. I told the other three officers in the psychiatric ward, "Someone needs to write a book about this place. We are in a world that most people will never see." They looked at each other, and then the alpha officer said, "You're the only college boy here; you write the book."

I took that as a challenge and picked up a stack of pocket-sized notebooks, which I brought into work every day for 25 years. I recorded the names, dates, and times associated with the events that profoundly impacted me. When a notebook was full, I tossed it into a shoebox in my closet and started another.

No wonder the inmates call life on the outside "the real world." On the inside, things seem backward. Politeness and congeniality are appreciated on the outside, but those characteristics are a sign of weakness in prison. I observed the personalities of the staff and inmates and found they played by a different set of rules. They were cut from a different cloth than most, and they saw things from a different perspective. I learned about this alternate universe from the inmates and the staff at each prison where I was employed.

At Riverside, I was selected as a treatment team member who reported the patients' progress. Part of my job was to interact with inmates who had mental conditions such as paranoid schizophrenia, bipolar disorder, antisocial personality disorder, and borderline personality disorder. The majority of my time at Riverside was spent in 11 Building. According to the Corrections Academy's martial arts instructor, there were more critical incidents (fights, stabbings, and physical altercations) in 11 Building than in any other place in the Michigan Department of Corrections.

When Riverside Correctional Facility psychiatric units closed in the mid-1990s, I accepted a corrections officer (CO) position at the Mid-Michigan Correctional Facility, a Level I general population prison in St. Louis, Michigan. While there, I worked in various positions: the control center, kitchen, yard, and as a regular unit officer.

After working for 10 years as an officer, I decided I could better serve the Michigan Department of Corrections as a teacher. I recertified my teaching certificate by adding a minor as a Reading Specialist and later earned a Master of Arts in Educational Administration. My first teaching job was in Adult Basic Education at St. Louis Correctional Facility, a Level IV prison, for six years.

My new position in the department was quite satisfying; however, I had other aspirations that would make me feel more complete. One day when I came into work, a fellow teacher said, "Jack, there is a GED teacher opening at Pugsley Correctional Facility in Grand Traverse County." I secured that job and spent my last nine years teaching in northwestern Michigan. It was fulfilling knowing that by educating inmates, I was slowing the revolving door in the prison system.

As I approached retirement, I sifted through the quarter-century of notebooks I kept and began to organize them. This book is a hybrid memoir, a blend of my experiences as an officer and a teacher, numerous inmates' experiences in and out of prison, and some Michigan prison history. I want to share a different world that I hope others will never have to experience on their own. Let me take you inside the razor-wire ranches of the Michigan prison system. My career made for a long, fascinating, and often dangerous ride. I was frustrated and satisfied, angry and calm, happy and despondent throughout my employment. I learned much about people and life that I would never have known otherwise. My 25 years in the Michigan prison system changed me in profound and lasting ways. As an officer and prison teacher, I hoped to make a positive change in others. This is the story of those years.

I:

CORRECTIONAL MEDICAL AIDE AT RIVERSIDE CORRECTIONAL FACILITY

CHAPTER 1

Starting My Prison Career

The Fish Gets His Fins Wet

*"We're here to put a dent in the universe.
Otherwise, why even be here?"*
—Steve Jobs

On January 8, 1990, I started my officer training at the Corrections Academy in Lansing, Michigan. My fellow trainees and I were each issued three white shirts with epaulets and green and gold State of Michigan patches on the shoulders, three pairs of black pants, a green blazer, a green baseball cap with a State of Michigan patch on the front, two black clip-on ties, a green winter coat, a green Elmer Fudd-type winter hat with fuzzy ear flaps, and black leather shoes made by the prisoners. The green blazers made us look like golfers who had just won the Masters Tournament. Years later, the white shirts were replaced with gray ones that mercifully camouflaged our sweat stains and made us look like proper corrections officers or COs instead of CEOs. On my first training day, I woke up at home, put on my uniform, and stepped into the bathroom to look in the mirror. I thought, *Who decided on* this *getup?*

After marching in formation on my first day, the backs of my heels were raw and bloody. Then, I found out we would be marching *every* day. Going to the Foot Locker store in the mall, I purchased some military-style black leather lace-up boots, tossing my state-issued shoes.

We took classes in Taekwondo, Corrections Policy and Procedure, Sexual Harassment, The Anatomy of a Setup (which covered how inmates manipulate prison employees), and many other subjects. We learned how to take inmates down, apply cuffs and leg irons, and escort them to the Hole, a one-man cell where a prisoner who has committed a serious rule infraction is kept in isolation without privileges. In addition, we trained in fire rescue procedures, firearms, and de-escalation techniques.

We were informed that a third of us would not make it through the academy. Some would quit, while others would be fired for abusing sick time, having improper relationships with inmates or staff, or using various illegal substances. I attended the academy for four weeks, then reported to my assigned prison, Riverside Correctional Facility, for eight weeks of on-the-job training. I finally returned to the academy for another four weeks of classes before graduating.

The Michigan Asylum for Insane Criminals opened in Ionia in 1885. It was later the site of the Michigan Reformatory (a home for wayward boys) and a multi-level men's prison, which closed on November 13, 2022. Part of the old Ionia asylum was a farm where the mentally ill patients would work the fields and orchards and feed the livestock. The hospital was initially called North Branch, and the farm on Riverside Drive was known as the South Branch. The asylum's farm was transferred to the Michigan Department of Corrections in 1972 and became a prison: the Riverside Correctional Facility. Riverside housed general population and psychiatric prisoners in 9, 10, and 11 Buildings. It had been part of the prison system for 18 years before I started working there as a corrections medical aide, or CMA.

Unlike COs, CMAs were instructed to help the inmates/patients with socialization skills. Some of us were part of the psychological treatment team. This sounded interesting, and I wanted to participate. Maybe I could make a difference in some of their lives.

When we were new officers at the academy or in a prison during on-the-job training (OJT), we were known as Red Tags. This meant we wore red name tags, which indicated we were rookies. During this period, Red Tags had to follow behind seasoned officers, some of whom disliked mentoring rookies. The Red Tags were instructed to keep within arm's length of the senior officers.

Many fresh hires were pumped up about their new positions and embarked on instantaneous power trips. Some of them idolized and tried to emulate the behavior of the hard-nosed officers who hassled and demoralized convicts. In sub-zero weather, I observed guards and Healthcare workers make inmates stand in line outside for so long, waiting for their medications, that the inmates gave up and returned to their unit for fear of frostbite. The staff laughed and wrote the inmates tickets for being out of place. Senior staff would perform such childish, cruel acts in front of those they were supposed to be training, thus perpetuating problems in the department.

For a quarter of a century I observed the personalities of the staff and inmates, finding that many played by different rules and were cut from a different cloth than most people in the real world. Someone who applies for a job working inside a prison is an audacious adventurer.

Some inmates saw certain Red Tag and Green Tag (rookie) officers as easy prey, so they began their games of manipulation and intimidation. A target on the back of the new officers' shirts would have the same effect as the Red Tag or Green Tag on the front. Maybe others in the system eventually saw it the same way, because the colored-tag system was discontinued in Michigan shortly before I retired.

When I began training at the Corrections Academy, one of our instructors told us about Josephine McCallum, a 26-year-old female Red Tag. On March 24, 1987, she was found in an auditorium stairwell in Jackson State Prison. She was beaten, raped, and strangled to death by an inmate serving time for armed robbery, criminal sexual conduct, and kidnapping. Josephine had worked for the MDOC for four months; she left behind a husband and a young son, her murder sparking a major controversy about females working in male prisons and giving new officers certain dangerous assignments.

On my first day, my assigned mentor in 11 Building, CMA Geyer, told me about Penny, a petite, strawberry-blonde new-hire nurse who, to save herself a few steps at the end of her shift, regularly used an alternative stairway at the far end of the inmate's hallway to exit the building. At the time, a polite, burly inmate named Davis locked—the term we used for "resided"—next door to that stairwell. Davis observed Penny's routine night after night. One summer evening, for whatever reason, his door was not locked. He waited for Penny to put her key in the door, and as she did so shot out of his cell, pushed her into the stairwell, rushed in behind her, slammed the door shut, and brutally beat and raped her. Penny never returned for duty at our facility.

My mentor shared Penny's story to make several points, especially the importance of locking prisoners' doors at count time. He also wanted me to know the exit at the end of the hall was dangerous and to be aware of the female staff's whereabouts. These incidents made me wonder if working inside male prisons was a good idea for female staff.

Riverside Correctional Facility did not have security cameras, and unlike the newer prisons, there were no remote cell-door openers controlled from the office. In 11 Building, the officers had to walk down the block and open—or, as we said, "key"—the doors so the inmates could enter and exit their rooms.

The tragic assault on Penny crept into my mind when I conducted my hall checks. My questions were: who failed to lock Davis's door, and why was Penny allowed to use that exit at the end of the prisoner hallway? The examples the academy trainer and my Riverside mentor gave were forever etched in my memory banks. Everyone, not only the new hires or females, must be constantly alert. One simple slipup in prison could be your last.

When a prison employee is killed in the line of duty, the state names a training academy class after them. The Earl Demarse Training Academy was named after the first corrections officer murdered in a Michigan prison. On September 25, 1973—26 years into his career—Officer Demarse was stabbed to death in the Marquette Prison auditorium 15 minutes into his shift. His assailant, Richard Goodard, was on his third bit, serving time for felonious assault, burglary, arson, and auto theft. Goodard was subsequently sent to Marion Federal Prison in Illinois; shortly after arriving, he attempted to murder the warden. After this incident, Goodard was shipped back to Michigan, housed at Huron Valley Men's Facility, and placed on psychotropic drugs.

At Huron Valley Men's Facility, inmate Goodard was only allowed out of his cell to shower. Before leaving his cell, restraints were applied through his waist-high and ankle-low food slots. The full-body restraints comprise leg irons, belly chains, and a black box, a device secured with a padlock to keep the inmate from raising his arms. Although these precautions were taken, inmate Goodard still managed to assault staff through the slots in the door when they were opened. He was especially dangerous when he went off his medications. He pledged to "thin the MDOC's weak officers through survival of the fittest, in the name of Jesus Christ." Goodard is doing life without a chance of parole.

No one is safe in prison, so employees must have yearly training in self-defense, firearms, restraints, fire control, CPR, and more. Staff must learn from the past and prepare for the future. I was on an adventure, but did not know the route or the final destination.

CHAPTER 2

A Red Tag No More

Shorts vs. Boxers

*"Man can learn nothing except by going
from the known to the unknown."*
—Claude Bernard

After my on-the-job training at Riverside, I returned to the academy for additional instruction. In our final four weeks of training at the Demarse Academy, we were required to pass various written tests and do push-ups, sit-ups, and step tests, for which our heart rates had to fall within an acceptable range. The candidates who failed the written or physical tests were terminated while those who graduated started working in the prisons where they completed training.

When I graduated from the academy, I finally had a job with a steady income and benefits, not just another commission-only sales gig. I planned to make this my career and hoped to retire from the Michigan Department of Corrections in 2015.

I learned something new about how the prison operated every day. At the academy, the instructors told us how prison currency had changed. Inmates could no longer possess bills or coins. For a time they used tokens, but it was too easy for them to rob each other, so the tokens were discontinued. Now, the inmates' money is only on paper in an account, which holds deposits from family and friends and wages earned from prison jobs.

Although the prisoners have money in their accounts, they still need to create their financial standards to trade, gamble, and pay off debts. At one point, they used postal stamps. If an inmate were "running a store" (purchasing various products and selling them at inflated prices), his customers would accumulate stacks of stamps to pay him with. Inmates could also acquire large quantities of stamps by gambling or extorting other inmates.

Prisoners who collected hundreds of dollars of unused stamps would send them to their people on the outside. The U.S. Postal Service did not like it when an inmate's family members walked in demanding cash for a wad of stamps. The state eventually ended this monetary system, and the convicts had to create another one. Now inmates must purchase envelopes, which have an official mark recognized by the U.S. Post Office, made in the prison's mailroom. The inmates cannot use their personal envelopes or stamps.

More recently, Michigan inmates have used personal grooming products and food—the exact item does not matter—as currency. Ex-federal prisoners have told me that their capital consisted of cans of mackerel, with one can conveniently costing one dollar. Shampoo would have been the day's currency if a bottle of Head & Shoulders were a dollar.

At the academy, the instructors warned us about inmates running illegal stores. Indigent inmates often purchase items from someone running a store when they are broke. The inmate running the store fronts his customers with the commodities they want but demands double what the legitimate store would charge him. If the customer does not come through with the total amount on time, the store runner may make an example of him by hiring a thug to hurt him—or even taking care of business himself.

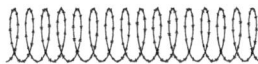

After completing my Red Tag period, I needed to take some paper-work to the administration offices up front. At count time, when every

prisoner's whereabouts are accounted for, I walked across the yard with an officer. He was bringing the count slips from the various psych units to the Control Center. The Control Center officer would ensure the number of inmates matched his record before clearing count and allowing prisoner movement.

I was no longer a Red Tag, so I had on my big boy pants. It was my first time crossing the yard without another officer escorting me. As I walked, I saw 9 and 10 Buildings a hundred-plus yards away at the other end of the track. While 11 housed the acute-care inmates, 9 and 10 were reserved for chronic care.

Suddenly, the doors of 9 and 10 burst open, and about 200 screaming inmates poured out, running in my direction and howling at the top of their lungs. My heart raced as I began to walk faster and faster. I wondered, *Should I keep up my brisk pace or haul ass and hope I make it into 11 before this stampede of maniacs tramples me into the ground?* I had little time, and my heart was about to explode.

Just as I passed in front of the prison store trailer, I was startled by a loud, ratchet-like sound and almost jumped out of my boots. The noise that startled me was benign—simply the storekeeper opening the rolling metal shutter window.

As my heart rate fell back to double digits, I watched the first 50 or so inmates excitedly file in line to purchase items at the prison store. I almost laughed aloud at how I assumed the very worst. But, in reality, the Control Center had just cleared the count and opened the yard to the 9 and 10 inmates so they could go to the store. I did not hear the announcement over my radio because it was turned off. Oops.

Because patients from 11 were not allowed in the main yard, their store orders were delivered to their unit. These patients could not deal with the social interaction inherent in the prison-store experience. Many of them were indigent because they were not competent to hold jobs even as unit porters (i.e., janitors)—also, giving them caustic cleaning supplies or mop wringers proved problematic. I cannot imagine what it would have been like if 11 Building patients had been part of that mad dash.

I was becoming familiar with the protocol in 11 but needed to learn the store program for 9 and 10. On this day, it felt like someone in this psycho squadron commanded, "Kill the Green Tag who dares to walk the yard on his own!" Control Center must have allowed the 9 and 10 Building patients to visit the store and return to their units before the general population (GP) inmates could come out and rip them off.

Over time, I learned that many prisoners only move fast when their unit is called to chow or the store. They are not supposed to run in the buildings or outside, and I never again saw inmates move as fast as they did that day. My fears could have been erased if I had made sure my mobile radio was on and the volume turned up.

After I graduated from the Corrections Academy, I had more freedom as a Green Tag. This meant I was no longer required to stay at arm's length from a Black Tag. Back when I smoked, I was having a cigarette on the airing porch one afternoon. It was just about count time (a roll call done several times a day), and all the patients had returned to their cells except for one. Inmate Stewart was a tall, thin, and pale man, who reminded me of Boo Radley (played by Robert Duvall) in *To Kill a Mockingbird*.

As I took a drag, Stewart crept closer and softly whispered, "Can I have your shorts?" then smiled creepily.

What a sicko! I thought. But all I said was, "No."

Stewart repeated, "Can I...have your shorts?"

I said, "No," and thought, *What's with this guy?* as I dropped my smoke and crushed it on the cement porch.

The inmate quickly picked up the butt and said, "Got a light?"

Reaching into my pocket, I handed him a pack of matches, trying not to touch his yellow-orange nicotine-stained fingers. He gave me a strange smirk, as if he had put one over on me. I walked off the airing porch, through the dayroom, past the poolroom and smoking room to enter the office, where three officers sat.

I said, "I was on the airing porch, and Stewart asked me for my shorts."

The officers all started laughing, and one said, "He wanted the end of your cigarette, not your tighty-whities."

I said, "Ah, that's why he looked so bummed when I crushed it. But he picked it up and asked for a light, so I gave him my matches."

"You can't give matches out!"

"Why not?"

Another officer explained, "Usually, you just light their cigarettes with a Zippo lighter. You can bring Zippos, but not Bics, because they can be explosive or turned into a torch. Regarding matches, you especially don't want Stewart to have any because he set his hair on fire last month."

"I guess I have some things to learn." This was an understatement. I immediately headed to Stewart's cell to retrieve the matches. I felt like a complete tenderfoot in a different world, inside the walls—or fence, as the case may be. Here, the officers and inmates spoke a language that was foreign to my ears.

During my Red Tag/Green Tag period at Riverside, the brass rarely placed me in the two geriatric units in 9 Building. I only occasionally worked in 10 Building's four chronic-care units. Most of the time I was assigned to the infamous acute-care units in 11 Building, usually in either the Admissions Unit on 11-1-East or upstairs on 11-2-East.

The inmate population in the 11 Building was often in transition. If an inmate was thought to be insane, they were transferred from other facilities to the 11 Building Admissions Unit. After their evaluation by the psychiatrist, they stayed in one of the four acute care units in 11 Building or were sent to one of the chronic care units in 9 or 10 Building. Only rarely did inmates improve enough to be placed in general population.

I felt fortunate to be a CMA rather than a CO. CMAs have the same responsibilities as COs; however, they receive additional training for their interaction with psych patients. I found an effective way to relate to the patients was to converse while playing card and table games. General population COs do not play games with inmates; that is not part of their job, and if they did, they would be written up for overfamiliarization. At Riverside, I was being paid to play. I enjoyed participating in these games and liked that they were provided to teach socialization skills to the patients.

With all the turnover in 11 Building, I continually sought competitive inmate Scrabble players. There were many reasons I liked to play Scrabble in prison. Sitting at a table allowed me to monitor the dayroom, get to know the inmates, keep entertained, and expand my mind.

One day, a new patient, Blake, was transferred upstairs from the Admissions Unit. He looked like a young Richard Gere, except for the gigantic deep-pink scar across his neck. I started to get to know him better during our daily pool games. Blake would make small talk and joke about politics, prison, and sports, but he never told me anything significant about his past life. Later, we began to play Scrabble regularly. Finally, after about a month, I felt that I could ask him about the origin of what looked to me like the result of a "Sicilian necktie," a brutal form of execution in which the victim's throat is slashed and the tongue pulled out of the front of the neck.

He said, "I haven't told anybody about that. So today, let's play Scrabble."

I replied, "No problem. Sorry I asked."

Several weeks later, Blake sat at the Scrabble table and said, "So let me tell you how I got my scar. I had a childhood without much parental influence. My father was hardly ever around, and when he was, I wished that he wasn't. My mother was there physically but couldn't be bothered with me between all her 'gentleman callers.' I did well in school but knew there was no money for college, so after high school I enlisted in the Marines.

"My MOS [Military Occupational Specialty] was in electronics maintenance. I did my four years, and when I got out met an older man who took me under his wing. He was an advanced electronics technician who taught me the tricks of the trade, soon becoming my best—really, only—friend. I was going to be certified as a master technician after his mentoring. I passed the test with flying colors, and we were both on top of the world. Now, we were ready to start a business together.

"My mentor and I drove down to Detroit so I could receive my certification. We stayed at a cheap motel in a rough neighborhood. We walked to a sleazy hole-in-the-wall bar nearby and got completely shit-faced. After doing lots of tequila shots and pounding beers, we started getting loud and obnoxious, pushing each other around until the bartender and some big bruiser threw us out. My friend then pulled out some money before handing me his wallet. He said, 'Hang onto my wallet. I'm going to get a hooker, and I don't want to get rolled.' Then he staggered away.

"I was worried about him, but I was more concerned about finding our motel. I had drunken double vision, so I closed one eye and tried to place one foot in front of the other. I managed to drag my intoxicated ass back to the No-Tell Motel, fell into our room, and passed out in my clothes.

"The next thing I know, I wake up because someone's beating the hell out of the door, and I've got a nuclear hangover. I figure it's my friend, so I open the door. Two cops burst in, screaming, 'Get down on the ground! Put your hands behind your back! Quit resisting!' I wasn't resisting, but didn't want to put my hands behind my back because I'd be left unprotected. I tried to cover up my head. So now, one cop's kicking me and the other's searching the room, and I have no fucking idea why all this is happening.

"My friend had not returned to our room; I didn't know that someone beat and kicked him to death while I was sleeping. The cops talked to the owner of the bar we had been drinking at the night before. He told them we were drunk and fighting before he kicked us out. When they checked my background, they found I was an ex-Marine trained in boxing and martial arts. They saw my prior arrest for assault and battery and found my friend's wallet in the motel room. That was enough cause for them to charge me with first-degree murder.

"I was broke, so I had no choice but to accept a court-appointed attorney. The jury was quick to convict me, and I got life without a chance of parole."

Blake was sent to the prison system Reception and Guidance Center (RG&C), where inmates are evaluated to determine which facility they will be assigned.

"When I got to RG&C," Blake continued, "I waited for the unit officer to make his rounds right before shift change, got my hands on a single-edged razor, and did my best to decapitate myself. That's how and why I got this nasty scar and ended up in the fucking acute care psych unit at Riverside."

At first, no words came to mind. Finally, I asked, "Is there any way you can seek an appeal?"

He said, "I'd love to, but there's this little matter of money. I ain't got none, and I don't have anyone to help me. My only friend in the world is dead, and the State of Michigan believes I killed him."

All I could muster was, "I'm sorry."

I could not help but think about the first line of Paul Simon's 1970 song "The Boxer" when I saw Blake on the unit. It begins, "I am just a poor boy though my story's seldom told…." In retrospect, I do not believe that Blake was insane. Instead, he was severely depressed—and for a good reason. There are plenty of inmates who are in similar situations. They have no one to bail them out and no money to obtain an attorney, so they are assigned a court-appointed lawyer and get convicted whether they are guilty or not.

Cases like Blake's made me think about how easily somebody's life can change. Suppose his buddy had just gone back to the motel after the bar. In that case, the two might have launched a successful business as electricians together, and he would not have been sitting in a Level IV psychiatric prison with a big scar across his neck, playing Scrabble with me. I can only hope his troubled soul has settled since I knew him. He was sentenced to life without parole; I wonder if he is still behind bars or if he decided to grant himself an early checkout.

CHAPTER 3

Jumping in with Both Feet

Scrabble as a Contact Sport

"Let me not pray to be sheltered from dangers,
but to be fearless in facing them."
—Rabindranath Tagore

ish is a term for new inmates and officers in the penal system. Even though I was still green or a fish, I was chosen as unit coordinator by default. The other officers on my unit were not interested in arriving early and assigning duties to their colleagues, so CMA Geyer, the alpha male on my unit, asked me if I would take the job.

I jumped at the opportunity because I always arrived early anyway, and the position meant I could custom-design my daily schedule. I scheduled myself for the first hall watch of the shift because I was already in the office with a view of both hallways while I filled out the daily schedule. All I had to do was walk up and down the halls about every 30 minutes to make sure no one was out of place, engaging in sex, or swinging from the end of a bed sheet. I would sporadically switch up my routine to make my rounds less predictable to the inmates, who carefully kept track of the officers' comings and goings.

Hall checks are required and essential, and I diligently performed them, making my rounds and noting them in the unit logbook. A sergeant would stop by to check the log, ensuring that assignments were carried out or recorded. In the department, they say, "If it isn't written, it didn't happen." Unfortunately, some officers did not always perform their hall checks but recorded them anyway, risking being written up for serious infractions such as inattention to duty or falsification of documentation.

On my rounds, it was "hide and go seek" time. Sexual activities among inmates take place whenever and wherever the inmates can get away with it. Hot spots include but are not limited to bathrooms, showers, storage closets, and walk-in kitchen coolers.

One of our daily assignments in the psych units was to run showers, which was jokingly called "bone hawking." It can be a bit uncomfortable for officers to look at naked men, let alone those with deranged minds, but it is just another job requirement. The procedure is quite simple in the psych units: Holler, "Showers are open!" and unlock the shower-room door…and occasionally check to see that no one is playing hide the bologna. An hour later, shout, "Showers are closed!" Once you've ensured all the inmates have left, lock the door.

In general population, sex in the shower is more common because there may not be a specific shower time or an officer assigned to that duty. A lower-level prison has community shower rooms with six to eight shower heads each. Officers need to check the shower room because it is where sexual and violent activities sometimes occur. The victims usually do not snitch out their attackers for fear of retaliation or being labeled a rat or a sissy. After receiving medical attention, a victim is generally returned to the same unit. When there are no consequences for their actions the perpetrators will attack again, forcing the victim to go on offense by carrying a shank or joining a gang. If an inmate cannot protect himself and does not have anyone else for backup, he is in danger of being punked out (becoming a sexual slave for other inmates). Some staff are more lax than others on their rounds, and prisoners take notice.

When the psychiatrist ordered a forced shower, a CMA sergeant would also be summoned to the unit. When an inmate did not shower for weeks, he would be locked in his cell and informed that he could only come out on the unit after he had showered. Two officers would escort him to the shower room if the inmate refused. If he did not get undressed, we would strip and handcuff him to a bar next to the showerhead. We would spray soap from a bottle and scrub him with a long-handled brush if he did not wash. On the fun scale, forced showers were right up there with booty duty (a strip search).

On prisoners' aromas, I am reminded of inmate Santos, a short Cuban refugee who was housed in 10 Building. He was walking in the main yard when he came upon a skunk that lived underneath the yard shack, where yard officers could go to escape the summer heat and winter cold. Apparently, Santos thought the animal was a cat, and when he picked it up received an odoriferous blast of stank at point-blank range.

The nurse called Dr. Leiberman, the psychiatrist, who ordered us to buy enough tomato juice to fill the one bathtub on the unit. CMA Bower purchased all the tomato juice cans in town, and we emptied them into the tub. When we stripped Santos and dragged him toward the tub, he went berserk; I believe he thought we would try to drown him in a tub full of blood. Because none of us spoke fluent Spanish, we could not convince Santos to step into the bath. Santos transformed into the Tasmanian Devil, scratching, kicking, and punching as he cussed us out in Spanish. We chased him around the shower room; he ran naked down the hall and back into his cell. I am unsure of the outcome of this situation, as I had only been pulled over to 10 Building to cover for a regular unit officer and assist with Santos's shower for a few fun hours.

Every time I ran showers at Riverside, I thought of Jack Budd, whose name I first heard while attending the Corrections Academy. Budd was a Jackson employee who posthumously had an academy class named after him. He was killed in the line of duty on December 27, 1987, only eight months after CO Josephine McCallum was murdered in the same facility.

Budd was helping another officer escort inmate James Lamont Miller to the showers when Miller broke free. Miller then ran down the block and located a homemade weapon: a sharpened mop handle. When Budd tried to subdue Miller, the convict fatally stabbed him. CO Jack Budd died four hours after he was admitted to the hospital. Miller had four other felony convictions and committed numerous assaults during his incarceration; he vowed to kill other guards if given a chance. James Lamont Miller was convicted of second-degree murder and sentenced to 80 to 120 years. He is commonly referred to by the staff as Killer Miller.

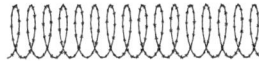

As the unit coordinator, I assigned myself to escort the unit to the chow hall in the basement for dinner. By doing so, I would be the first in line to eat; still, I needed more time to finish my meal before the next unit was summoned. The trek to and from chow was uncomfortable, since I was the lone officer in a cement stairwell with about 35 criminally insane inmates behind me. None of them ever thought about kicking a guard's ass down the stairs (yeah, right), but they could have done so at any time. The stairwell was an echo chamber with eerie resonance, and the patients took advantage by whooping, hollering, and chuckling creepily. The kitchen officers would encourage the inmates to inhale their food with lightning speed. Because I had always been a slow eater, I had to accelerate my intake and shovel in the grub. After a kitchen officer hollered, "Time's up!" I would get up from the officers' table and escort the inmates back to the unit.

The GP inmates at Riverside, except those locked in segregation (the punishment unit), shared one big kitchen and chow hall, but the psych units in 9, 10, and 11 each had their own smaller chow hall. General population kitchen workers transported food in carts from the kitchen to the psychiatric units. CMA kitchen officers led the GP kitchen workers through the catacomb-like tunnels under the prison complex. The tunnels provided a route for the food and laundry carts so the staff could avoid crossing the yard in Michigan's notoriously inclement weather. The tunnels were cool and damp, echoing loudly when the metal-wheeled food carts were pushed through them. This setup was logistically wise, but the tunnels had a dangerous ambiance, and I was a bit leery whenever I escorted the kitchen workers through them. I felt secluded and vulnerable among the nooks, crannies, and side passages that could easily conceal a malicious inmate. There were openings in the cement block walls. I did not know where they led. It smelled musty, and I could see the dirt floor, but I never went in to explore further. I reported the possible escape route to a sergeant and heard nothing more.

The rumor was that staff, inmates, and sometimes even a combination of the two used the tunnel tributaries for sexual encounters. On one occasion, several officers discovered a dirt tunnel off one of the main tunnel's branches. The inmates had been working on it for quite some time because their in-construction escape route stopped only a few yards short of the security fences surrounding the facility.

All the psychiatric units had a foul odor, but 11 Building was the worst; I constantly longed for relief from the stench. The first time I stepped into 11, I was hit with a sickening blend of urine, feces, body odor, and tobacco, instantly becoming nauseated. I tried to ignore this putrid, sour smell, but that was impossible. The best I could do was assign myself to take the inmates out to the small yard; this offered me a brief break from the enchanting fragrance, but it never seemed long enough.

The 11 Building patients did not care to stay outside for too long, partly because they were not provided with the recreational options of the GP inmates: a softball diamond, horseshoe pits, handball court, track, pull-up bars, and more. The building's small yard only offered a basketball court and a picnic table. After playing a game of Horse or Around the World, the few inmates who chose to spend time outside were ready to return to the familiar sights and sounds of 11 Building.

Psych patients from 11 Building were not permitted to go to the big yard with the GP inmates. It would not be a good idea to hand an acutely criminally insane inmate a baseball bat or a couple of horseshoes; it was dangerous enough to have pool tables on the psych units. After working at Riverside for a short while, I became concerned about the little wooden racks that held Scrabble tiles—it seemed anything that could be used as a weapon or for self-mutilation eventually would be.

New psychiatric patients at Riverside were initially placed in the 11-1-East Admissions Unit, where the powers that be decided to put me for my first four years. When a psychologist or psychiatrist in one of the general population prisons determined that an inmate had severe mental health issues, they wrote a referral stating that the inmate needed to be transferred to Riverside or the Forensic Center in Ypsilanti. Similarly, if inmates in 9 or 10 Building stopped taking their medications and began to decompensate, they were shipped over to 11 so they could be stabilized.

Playing games was an excellent way to discover where the patients' heads were. Once, over a game of pool, I asked inmate McDonald, "What are you in for?"

"Grave robbing," he replied.

I asked, "Why would you do that?"

McDonald said, "Besides being a demented devil worshiper, I guess it's because I usually found jewelry. And I liked to collect hands and skulls. You'd be surprised how many high-end coffins are switched out for cheap pine boxes after the family leaves the gravesite, and those are easy to get into."

Of course, I do not know if McDonald was speaking the gospel truth, but it made me wonder. Do funeral home staff switch out the expensive caskets for pine boxes? Do they sell the same coffin repeatedly for thousands of dollars? Who would ever know besides a grave robber, funeral home staff, or someone buying and fencing caskets? It is not something most of us would consider or talk about.

One afternoon, after finishing my hall duty, I saw inmates Brown, Strauss, and Sanchez standing in the poolroom in 11-2-East. I walked in and asked them if they wanted to play doubles. They exchanged uncertain glances and shrugged before Brown reluctantly nodded yes. I felt an ominous tension in the air as I grabbed a cue stick and said to Strauss and Sanchez, "Brown and I will take on you two." After Strauss broke and dropped a few balls, I could tell he and his companions were all on the lookout for something, which was not good.

Just then, inmates Cook, McDonald, and Grant entered through the back door of the poolroom. I could see by their expressions that they were not there to shoot a friendly game. Brown and Strauss flipped their sticks around, thick ends out, and Sanchez picked up a ball and smiled broadly at them.

I sternly declared, "Not tonight, gentlemen! Not on *my* shift!" Cook, McDonald, and Grant exchanged glances, said something I did not catch, slowly backed out of the room, and headed for the airing porch. As they departed, Brown shouted at them, "That's what I thought, you punk-ass bitches!"

After saying, "Sorry, I'm not in the mood for pool anymore, gentlemen—the poolroom is closed," I asked the three inmates to step out and locked the doors behind them. I entered the office to inform the other three officers of the trouble brewing. I also notified the unit officers next door and called downstairs to tell the CMAs something was amiss, so they should keep their ears tuned to their mobile radios.

I was relieved nothing jumped off, at least for the moment. Looking back at the situation, I am sure it was not just my words or presence that made Cook, McDonald, and Grant change their minds about starting a confrontation. Brown was sharp and likely figured that a game of pool was a legitimate way to arm himself, Strauss, and Sanchez. I can understand why the others quickly slipped out the back.

A couple of nights after the poolroom standoff, when the unit returned from chow I finished some paperwork, exited the office, and headed to the expansive dayroom. The dayroom had three tables for playing cards or Scrabble, a foosball table, a ping-pong table, numerous chairs, and a couch where inmates could sit and watch TV.

I looked forward to playing Scrabble with the inmates after chow as part of my daily routine. Today, I saw three criminally insane inmates—all doing "basketball numbers" (serving lengthy sentences) or life—waiting for me to play Scrabble with them. They were Dempsey, Hillman, and Sanchez.

Dempsey was spirited, a 6' 4" 220-pound 24-year-old with muscular arms that were severely scarred from years of self-mutilation. I saw numerous inmates with scars, but these were not just minor cuts; they were large gashes surgically stapled back together. In addition, his left forearm was covered with scar tissue from an incident in which he poured lighter fluid onto it and set himself on fire. Dempsey was a glutton for punishment and attention and probably had an audience for these disturbing acts.

He was in for stabbing his girlfriend numerous times with a butcher knife. Although his size was intimidating, he had a high-pitched voice, a feminine giggle, extremely animated gestures, and a Cheshire Cat grin. Still, you needed to be cautious because he was dreadfully dangerous and unpredictable. This inmate took everything to the extreme. He had to constantly be watched because he loved to screw with everyone impishly. Years later, I heard through the grapevine that Dempsey was locked in a maximum-security prison after stabbing an officer's eye out with a pen. I could imagine him nonchalantly asking a fish officer,

"Excuse me, sir; may I please borrow your pen?" just before plunging it into the rookie's eyeball.

Hillman was in his mid-20s, with a 5' 8" 185-pound bulldog frame, and was recently admitted to 11 Building. He told me the horrific crime story that led him to prison. One day on the street, he was spending some quality time with his brother, taking a leisurely ride on the southwest side of Detroit while freebasing cocaine and chugging vodka. The two spied an attractive young woman with her thumb out on the side of the road and brought the car to a screeching halt. After the hitchhiker climbed into the back seat the brothers sped off, continuing to ingest their coke and alcohol. Then, they abruptly attacked the woman as they drove, dowsing her in a flammable substance, laughingly setting her on fire and shoving her out of the moving vehicle.

When Hillman finished relating this gruesome tale, I asked him, "Why'd you torch her and toss her like a piece of trash?"

He replied, "'Cause she was a skanky-ass ho! The bitch had it coming!"

Later, I saw Hillman's victim interviewed on a popular daytime talk show. The once-gorgeous young woman was disfigured, scar tissue covering 90% of her body. When her beautiful "before" pictures were displayed on the screen, the contrast with her present appearance was staggering. It is hard to imagine that there are people with such little regard for human life as Hillman and his brother.

The last player at the Scrabble table was Sanchez, who had been in the poolroom when I narrowly averted a violent free-for-all. He looked like Billy Bear, the Native American criminal in the smash Eddie Murphy/Nick Nolte film *48 Hrs.*, and was doing life without parole for murder in the first degree. Sanchez never said much, but he treated Scrabble with intense seriousness and took great pleasure in a good game.

On this night, I saw that Dempsey had a big grin: He was tacitly challenging me by sitting in my "reserved" chair with his back to the wall. It was as if he were saying to me, "Now whatchoo gonna do?"

I gave Dempsey the skunk eye and said, "You're sitting in my seat!"

"Sorry, this seat is taken," he said with a smile and a shrug.

"We need to keep an eye on things," Hillman added.

Growing weary of Dempsey's casual defiance, I exclaimed, "Dempsey! Get up! I need my back to the wall to see what's happening." I always sat with my back to the wall when we played Scrabble or Euchre, and never had to kick anyone out of my seat before because it was understood it was reserved for me.

"We *all* need to see what's going on tonight," Sanchez replied.

I could see that the three men were unusually anxious about something. Dempsey reluctantly relinquished my seat and moved to my left. Now Hillman was across from me at the table, and Sanchez was to my right with his back toward the outside wall. After I bumped Dempsey out of my chair, he had the most vulnerable spot at the table. His back was to the poolroom, so he could not readily see if someone exited the smoking room—which, I am sure, is why he originally sat in my spot and was hesitant to move. Now, unlike Hillman and Sanchez, his back was exposed, and he was nervous about it. Someone could easily sneak up behind him if he were not paying attention.

In the joint, staff and prisoners constantly scan their surroundings and ask themselves, *Where are the escape routes? Is there anything that could be used as a weapon? What could I use as a barrier or shield? Who are these inmates? What are they in for? How are they acting? Where are the officers on the unit, and are they good backups?* These questions seemed especially material in a high-level psych prison. All four of us at the Scrabble table were contemplating them, but I did not know why.

My uncertainty was quickly dispelled when Hillman nodded to his right and softly said, "Look. There they are, conspiring in the poolroom."

Looking where he indicated, I saw the same three inmates who stepped into and backed out of the poolroom the other night. They talked and occasionally stole a glance in our direction. Then Cook and McDonald entered the dayroom and walked purposefully toward our table, stopping behind Hillman and Sanchez. Grant stood outside the poolroom beside a line of chairs, staring at us. I wondered why he stopped there until I realized he was waiting for a signal from Cook and McDonald.

The state had replaced our hard plastic and metal chairs, which had previously severely injured prisoners and staff. The chairs could be swung as they were or broken so the metal legs could be used as clubs or shanks. The new chairs had huge wooden frames with five-inch-thick plastic seats and backs. Whoever decided to replace the old chairs thought the new ones were so big and clumsy that no one could pick them up and use them as weapons. Once again, the bigwigs, who spent no real time in prison, were wrong.

There was a dense fog of ill ease, and the room was charged with nervous anticipation. In a loud, stern voice, I stood up from the table and said, "Not tonight, gentlemen! Not on *my* shift!" while praying this would cause the three inmates surrounding us to back off. These words had helped me in the past, but unfortunately, they did not work this time. Grant suddenly picked up one of the enormous chairs, hoisted it over his head, and came running at us.

We all jumped out of our seats. I had no idea which one of us Grant was planning to smash his chair down on. Hillman took a proactive approach; jumping up high, he got a grip on Grant's chair, slamming it back on the attacker's head with a pronounced *clunk*.

Grant bled profusely from the top of his shaved head as he stumbled backward, dazed. I grabbed him in a bear hug and carried him out of the dayroom, around the corner, and down the long hall to his cell, my adrenaline surging as he struggled to escape.

Arriving at Grant's cell, I found Sgt. Nicholes was shaking it down. I thought, *Maybe the word is out about the beef between the two groups, and Nicholes is acting on a tip from a snitch about a shank.* I barked, "Sarge, Grant tried to hit Hillman with a chair in the dayroom! It would be best if you locked him up. There's a mini-riot going on, so I'm heading back out there!" I spun around and left Grant in the cell with the sergeant, thinking he would secure the inmate as I asked. But, silly me, no one listens to the new guy—and the consequences of his ignoring my request would change how I moved through life.

I later learned that back in the dayroom, the inmates were still going at it with unbridled ferocity. Cook threw fists at Dempsey, who taunted him, chuckling as he said, "That's all you got, bitch?" before landing a powerhouse left to Cook's nose and a right uppercut to his chin. Meanwhile, Sanchez and Hillman were beating the living daylights out of McDonald. Since I removed Grant from the picture, it was now three on two, and my appreciative Scrabble partners were having fun.

Someone must have called for backup on the radio because Officer Geyer flew up the back stairwell, burst through the door to the airing porch, and entered the dayroom with CMAs Phillips, Bard, and Freeman in tow. Geyer bolted across the dayroom and executed a flying kick to Dempsey's back, sending him crashing into the outside wall of the smoking room. Then he cuffed Dempsey and helped CMA Bard cuff McDonald.

CMA Phillips tackled Cook like a pro linebacker and slapped on the cuffs, wrenching them tight as the two slid across the floor. Officers Bard and Freeman struggled to subdue Hillman, who was strong as a bear and relentless as a pit bull, having already shaken them loose several times. CMA Freeman got behind Hillman and grabbed hold of his hair, yanking it hard. Hillman arched back with his arms stretched behind him, as if he were crying uncle or howling at the moon. Once the CMAs had the other assailants under control, Sanchez ceased fighting and cooperated; the officers still cuffed him for his participation.

The 11 Building CMAs at Riverside were big, strong farm boys who knew how to take care of business. They did not hesitate when there was a distress call over the mobile radio; they seemed to get a high off it. Most of these officers were unafraid to mix it up in or out of the workplace. They were placed in 11 because they were damn good in volatile situations. In their high school years most of these fellows played football or wrestled, and in the summer many baled hay and drove tractors. I once talked to a high school football coach who told me that the big, round balers farmers use today hurt the football programs. He said there is nothing like good old-fashioned manual hay-baling in the hot fields, year after year, to boost strength and endurance. This activity increased one's ability to toss around not only bales but also pigs, calves, football opponents—or, as in this case, convicts.

At this time in the department, CMAs and COs wore white shirts. On the day of the mini-riot, the front of mine was crimson red with Grant's blood, so when the unit nurse saw me heading back to the dayroom from his cell, she shrieked, "Jack, have you been struck?"

Shaking my head and answering, "No," I continued down the hall.

Suddenly, CMA Carter yelled, "Jack! Watch out!"

Whipping around, I saw inmate Grant running straight at me. I grabbed and bear-hugged him again, his feet leaving the ground as he kicked and struggled to escape. Sgt. Nicholes ran up behind Grant and sandwiched him between us. I was struck from behind without warning, throwing the three of us to the floor. The bulldozer that hit me was one of our own, CMA Chadwick. The sight of me covered in blood and of Sgt. Nicholes and I struggling with Grant energized Chadwick, and he went into maniacal room-rush mode, striking with reckless abandon. I picked myself up off the floor and immediately felt a terrible pain in my back. It was later discovered that two of my discs were seriously damaged. My back has never been right since and has continued to get worse, necessitating surgery and causing numerous other problems over the years. But I knew what I was getting into when I joined the department. When you are in prison, you not only have to watch out for the prisoners. My back problems were due to friendly fire that I never saw coming.

Later, when I was filling out the critical incident report, I wrote, "I escorted inmate Grant from the dayroom to his cell." Sgt. Nicholes examined my report and said, "You were not escorting Grant. His feet were not touching the floor."

At the time, I did not remember carrying Grant. I just knew I had removed him from harm's way. It is incredible what strength people have that they are unaware of. In emergencies, it seems an unconscious power kicks in to protect ourselves and others. This phenomenon is known as hysterical strength and is activated by the body's fight-or-flight response. The nervous system supplies extra strength to get you through highly stressful situations.

CHAPTER 4

Incompetence Strikes Again and Again

My "Amazing" Backup Crew

"Fools rush in where angels fear to tread."
—Alexander Pope

I usually played Scrabble after supper with three inmates, but this evening it was just inmate Sanchez and me. We were seated at a card table, and we each chose our seven tiles. I was placing my first word on the board when I saw CMA Andrews, a Green Tag officer, walking our way.

I'd met this guy in the academy and worked with him in several Riverside units when we were both Red Tags. He believed he was a badass…and he was half-right. Unfortunately we were short-staffed that night, so he had been assigned to our unit for the shift. With his attitude and lack of discretion, it would only be a matter of time before he saw stars circling his head.

It was Sanchez's turn on the Scrabble board when Andrews walked up and stood in front of us, watching for a few seconds before demanding, "Let me in on this shit, Myette!"

"Andrews," I replied, "sorry, but we've already started the game."

"Come on! There's only one word on the board!"

I paused. "Okay, take seven letters and have a seat."

After Andrews pulled the tiles from the bag, he said, "I'll be back in a minute. I'm on hall duty, and I gotta do my rounds."

"How are you going to do that and play with us?" I questioned.

"I'm almost off halls, so chill, brah!" Andrews said with a sneer as he strutted away from the table. I did not have a good feeling about the upcoming game.

Sanchez took his turn, and we waited for Andrews. After quite some time elapsed, Andrews finally returned, stepped up to the table, looked at the board, and said with disgust, "Who put that shit down? Get that shit out of there!" as he pointed at Sanchez's word, which was perfectly okay—but evidently, Andrews did not know it.

Sanchez tensed and said, "Are you challenging my word?"

Andrews barked, "Get that shit off the board, now!"

"Are you challenging my word?" Sanchez repeated. "Because if you are, look it up in the dictionary, and if it's there, you'll lose your turn."

Andrews bent forward toward the board and turned to Sanchez, getting right up in his face. "I don't have to look up *shit*, boy!" he snarled. "Just get that crap off the board!"

As Andrews finished speaking, Sanchez popped him with a hard left to his nose, breaking his glasses in two. Andrews stumbled back, nose bleeding and eyes watering. I grabbed Sanchez's arm to escort him to the seclusion room; I did not bother cuffing him. Andrews stood there, dumbfounded and in tears, with his nose bleeding profusely and his broken glasses on the floor.

As I walked Sanchez away, he looked straight ahead and said, "I don't know why I do these things. I have to try to control myself."

I thought he was telling me what he thought I wanted to hear. I said, "Aren't you right-handed? Because that was a hell of a left, you didn't telegraph it a bit."

Sanchez smiled, but I was cool with that.

Officers like Andrews who try to play Rambo are dangerous to be around. Psych patients do not have anything to lose. Sanchez was, and probably is, still doing life in prison without a chance of parole. He was locked in 11 Building, meaning he could not catch a new bit or even a ticket, no matter whom he punched out. I might have popped the jackass myself if I were in his shoes. Staff who treat inmates as less than human find themselves in difficult situations and endanger others' lives. They sometimes get away with their super-macho behavior at Level I facilities, but not so much in higher levels, especially in the psych wards.

Some officers act tough, but most have some semblance of a conscience learned from someone who tried to teach them to do the right thing. Inept officers should be fired or placed in positions with minimal contact with inmates, but CMA Andrews was eventually promoted to a sergeant's job at another prison. I heard he ultimately retired as a captain. And so it goes.

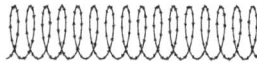

◊◊◊◊◊◊◊◊◊◊◊◊◊◊◊◊◊

It was not just the new hires that flirted with danger. Early in my Riverside experience, CMA Pittman was doing his routine hall checks on 11-1-East when he approached inmate Edwards's cell. From the office, I could hear the prisoner yelling, "Fuck the po-lice! Fuck you, punk-ass bitches! Come on in! I'm ready to fuck some motherfuckers up!" I thought, *Thanks for the invitation, but I'll take a rain check.*

On the other hand, CMA Pittman thought he would give the inmate a piece of his mind, so he unlocked Edwards's door. The inmate stepped out and hit Pittman's face as if it were a speed bag, getting in about eight good punches before Pittman knew what was happening and then retreated to his cell, pulling the door shut. Pittman said he had heard his neck snap on Edwards's first punch. With a broken neck, he found a vast difference between his small-town black-belt karate skills and the sheer power of an experienced street fighter who trained at Detroit's Kronk Gym. Unfortunately, Officer Pittman did not learn his lesson.

One evening after dinner, I sat in the dayroom, where inmate Curtain watched his favorite TV show, *Wheel of Fortune*, and lusted after Vanna White. Officer Pittman walked in, strolled up to the TV, and changed the channel to his favorite show—*Walker, Texas Ranger*, starring tough guy Chuck Norris—just as Vanna flipped the letters. Without warning, Curtain ran up to Pittman and belted him in the jaw. Curtain was in the dayroom every night at the same time with his eyes glued on Vanna. He lived at Riverside; Pittman just worked there.

I witnessed similar examples of cause-and-effect involving staff and inmates. Time and again, some officer would be called to an unfamiliar unit, stick out his chest, and say something obnoxiously derogatory and inconsiderate—then immediately get his wig blown back.

Staff and inmates alike are apprehensive of change, so new officers must ease into the prison environment before they will be trusted and accepted. Mentally ill prisoners are impetuous and unpredictable, so any changes must be explained—or staff may get a painful lesson in etiquette.

Officers must show respect to each prisoner in their unit, and inmate Curtain's assault on Pittman demonstrated that. Years later, I heard his neck was broken for a second time, and he was medically retired.

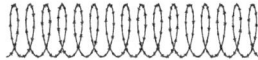

∞∞∞∞∞∞∞∞∞∞∞∞∞∞∞

A stocky inmate on 11-2-East, Caveman wore his beard long and full. In the real world, he was a homeless vagabond who rode the rails and wandered around random Michigan towns. His first name was Luke, but he liked being called Caveman.

Caveman was a twin born to a hardcore biker couple from southeast Michigan. When he was an infant, his mother and father tattooed a skull and crossbones on his forehead in a sloppy, drunken manner. Soon after the parents dropped off their twins, like a couple of barn cats, to live at their uncle's farm. The uncle locked the tikes in a coop occupied by egg-laying chickens. Neighbors heard the sound of babies crying day and night and eventually notified the authorities. Luke's twin was discovered malnourished and pecked to death. Protective services placed Luke in one foster home after another; not surprisingly, he became a problem child and habitual runaway.

Several decades later, after multiple run-ins with the law, Luke was passed out in a park in Saginaw. Some thirsty soul tried to steal the bottle of Mad Dog he was clutching, and Luke stabbed the thief, catching a case for attempted murder. When the staff realized he was unable to adjust to general population, Caveman was evaluated and eventually found himself in my unit in 11 Building.

I was still in training when, one morning, I was assigned to shadow

CMA Carter, a well-endowed 50-something bleach-bottle blonde. When the unit opened, I went to look for her in the dayroom. As I approached, I heard her screech: "Luke, sit up!"

Entering, I saw Caveman was the only inmate in the dayroom. He was lying peacefully on a couch, watching TV, and unless he was stone deaf he heard Carter's demand. But he refused to move a muscle.

Carter tried again. "Luke, I'm giving you a direct order to sit up—now!"

Caveman probably crept out to the dayroom, hoping to kick back on the new couch and watch a little TV before others arrived. CMA Carter's harassment was not part of his plan to chill.

Carter repeated her previous admonishment even more forcefully as I sat in a chair beside her. I thought, *Caveman isn't taking space away from anyone. Leave him alone. Give him this moment.* Carter turned to me and said, "Jack, aren't you going to back me up on this?"

I turned to Caveman and calmly said, "Hey, Caveman, would you sit up, please?" Luke sat up. "Thanks, Caveman," I said. Then, turning back to Carter I asked, "Happy now? We have compliance."

Caveman's lack of respect for Carter's demands and quick compliance with my request upset her. She howled, "Luke, you need to go to your friggin' cell *now*! If you don't, we'll escort you!" She was begging for a critical incident and trying to drag me in.

Caveman gave her her critical incident. With uncontrolled rage he stood up, hoisted one of the enormous new chairs over his head, and bolted toward Carter, screaming, "Fuck you, bitch!" The frightened woman rushed toward the office, and, wary of the chair, I ran behind her, thinking, *My sentiments exactly!* Carter slipped into the office, and I made it inside just as the chair Caveman meant for Carter careened off the door. Shutting the door behind me, I heard Caveman stomping to his cell, growling and barking obscenities.

Carter said, "We must report this insane behavior to the sergeant and nurse!"

I asked, "*Whose* behavior?" while I thought, *Yours or his?*

Because of her conduct, Carter was another officer I felt uncomfortable working with. I was still a Red Tag, and she was a Black Tag charged with breaking me in. She was dangerous and not sensitive to nuances like Luke's preference to be addressed as Caveman. He most likely would have complied with her requests if she had treated him respectfully. Now, he probably never would.

Like CMA Andrews, Carter was eventually promoted to sergeant, a typical example of prison management emptying its trash by promoting the most incompetent and malicious staff members. Officers with a macho mindset do not like to take orders but love to give them. Unfortunately, some of these imbeciles have helped promote officers with like minds and most likely are now retired with captains' pay.

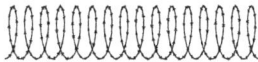

One night I was walking by the poolroom when I saw two inmates shooting pool and heard inmate Boyton snarl at inmate Garden, "I'll throw this fuckin' ball through your head, bitch!"

I thought, *Boyton, you said that to the wrong inmate. Garden was arrested for standing on a bridge and firing a shotgun at the drivers below. Now he has a cue stick in his hand, and you just threatened him.* I spun around to enter the poolroom, but by the time I got inside Garden had already struck Boyton several times with the stick, and Boyton's head was bleeding.

I hollered, "Garden, drop it!"

Garden turned and fixed a frightening stare on me. I heard a sudden *whoosh!* in front of my face as he swung the cue stick at me wildly. I leaped back, and with a second *whoosh!* he flipped my Green Tag off my shirt pocket.

Unbeknownst to me, one of the CMAs in the office announced over his mobile radio, "Fight on 11-2-East!" Officer Bard from 11-2-West must have been coming up the back stairwell when he heard this because he appeared on cue in the back door to the poolroom and tackled Garden from behind before the prisoner knew what hit him. I handcuffed Garden and took him to the seclusion room. On my way out, I saw Officer Dintz—a short, stocky, beer-bellied CMA—who emerged from the office after watching the incident but doing nothing. I asked him to cuff Boyton and put him in his cell for threatening inmate Garden, which started the whole incident.

Returning to the poolroom, I saw Dintz had not heeded my request, ignoring me in the same way Sgt. Nicholes had when I asked him to handcuff Grant before I got slammed to the floor. It was no surprise; I was still the Green Tag fish on the block.

Out of nowhere, in stepped Jackson, a large, scruffy inmate who had observed the fiasco. Jackson shouted at Boyton, "Bitch, you had that coming!" This infuriated Boyton, who ran straight at Jackson and jumped on him. Like a couple of alley cats, the two fell to the ground and rolled every which way. Jackson was clawing Boyton with his long fingernails and savagely bit his ear.

I pried the inmates apart and cuffed Jackson while CMA Bard cuffed Boyton. I did not notice that Jackson had clawed me until I completed the required Critical Incident Report and saw my arm bleeding. Like many 11 Building inmates, Jackson's hygiene left much to be desired, but what concerned me more was that he and Boyton were sexually promiscuous with other prisoners. I worried I might have been infected with HIV in the melee. I immediately headed to the hospital for an HIV test and was not informed of the negative results for several stressful weeks.

Although Riverside was designated a Level IV, unlike other IVs, the psychiatric units occasionally received Level V and VI prisoners. For example, inmate Williams, a massive individual with a humongous head, shoulders, and arms, was a gift from I-Max, a Level VI prison. The inmates at Level VI were by far the most dangerous in the system.

Officer Dintz was conducting his first hall check on 11-1-East when he came to Williams's cell. As Dintz peaked through the small door window, he heard, "What the fuck you looking at, you fat little peckerwood?" Dintz foolishly keyed open Williams's door to have a word, and the inmate rewarded him with a tremendous uppercut to his nose. Dintz was down and out, and Williams closed his cell door. The doctor who examined Dintz said he had seen similar breaks on victims who died because the nasal bones were driven so deep into their brains.

Dintz enjoyed geeking up prisoners, but, as in the Boyton incident, he was unaware of whom he was dealing with. Someone should have told him, "If you don't know the pond, don't dive in the water." Officer Dintz did not return to work for several months. He later applied for promotion to sergeant and landed a job at the Mound facility in Detroit.

Although it is easy to find fault in others, it is a good idea for everyone to contemplate how we could have done things differently. It is also important to look at why the inmates are in prison. We had an inmate in our unit whom everyone called Big Ben. He was a well-put-together 24-year-old kid, about 6' 3", with broad shoulders, bulging biceps, and a goofy grin.

One of the first signs of serious psychological problems for a child is the torturing of animals. While attempting to understand Ben's behavior, I looked at his file and saw several appalling incidents involving cats. He once tied two cats together by their tails and hung them over a clothesline so he could watch them fight—and as if that was not bad enough, he poured gas on them and set them on fire. His neighbor witnessed the incident and reported it to the police. The neighbor said Ben laughed hysterically as he watched the screaming animals burn.

Ben's violent behavior continued to escalate. Before he was incarcerated, he was at his girlfriend's trailer one day. She apparently did something to displease him because he smashed a six-pack of full Pepsi bottles—glass ones—on her head, one at a time, crushing her skull. Even with her dental records, a positive ID of his dead partner was difficult. So, the judge gave Ben "basketball numbers": 60 to 90 years.

Years later, I was playing Scrabble with inmates Brown and Sanchez in the dayroom. Big Ben strutted by us in a tank top and jeans, boom box in hand, as he headed for the airing porch. He plugged the box into an outlet just outside the airing porch door and set it on a card table. I watched him plunge his large hand into the pocket of his jeans and pull out a cassette tape. He held it up high and let out a loud, "Yeah, baby!" After shoving the tape into the boom box, he hit play, cranked it up, and started jumping up and down, pumping his fist into the air and hollering, "Woo-hooo!"

With Metallica blaring and Ben hollering, the unit's decibel level went up quite a few notches. Ben was the conductor of the "crazy train," which was picking up speed. No one could hear the TV, concentrate on their card games, board games, dominos, or even converse. My fellow Scrabble players and the other inmates glared at me as if to say, "Are you going to take control of this situation?"

The other officers were hanging out in the office as usual, so I handled this myself. I yelled, "Ben, turn it down!" He continued to jump up and down and to scream. I repeated, louder this time, "Ben, turn down the music!"

With the unit still agitated, I got up and walked toward the airing porch. I again ordered Ben to reduce the volume. He continued to hop and howl, so I bent down and yanked the boom box's plug from the outlet. Ben stopped jumping, landed with a thud, turned, looked me in the eyes, and started walking toward me like Frankenstein's monster on steroids. He stuck out his hand as if he were going to grab my throat. I intercepted it and tried to turn his attempted choke into a high hand-shake, but the painful grip of his giant iron mitt told me I was in a world of trouble. With a snarl on his face, he stiffened his arm and shoved me against the wall. As his hand tightly clutched mine, I pictured him waving his arm over his head this way and that with me in tow, as if we were cartoon characters, and smashing my head into the cement porch. I realized unplugging his boom box had been a massive mistake, and I needed to smooth over my blunder quickly.

"Ben! Metallica! *Master of Puppets*! Great album!"

Suddenly, Ben snapped out of his maniacal trance and smiled. "Dude! Officer Myette! I didn't know you were a heavy metal thrasher!"

"I can relate. I grew up with the British Invasion—The Beatles, The Stones, The Who. You younger folks have Ozzy, Rush, and Metallica. But we need to share the unit, so if you turn it down, everyone will be happy." At that, Ben finally let go of my hand.

As I walked away, I considered how I approached the situation. I should have made sure I had Ben's attention before asking him to turn down his boom box. I should have also thought about his horrifying history and monstrous sentence. I knew I was lucky to not be another of Ben's victims—and that I was as capable as the next officer at making blunders.

CHAPTER 5

Officers Over the Top

A Beautiful Backup

> *"If you don't look out for others,*
> *who will look out for you?"*
> —Whoopi Goldberg

Riverside had the most colorful people I have ever worked with— inmates and staff. Two of the most outrageous officers were Sgt. Gibson and his sidekick, Officer Kozak. The sarge was a West Virginia wild man who provided the male staff with high-quality marijuana and the female employees with another kind of joint. In the early 1990s, drug testing was not yet required. However, later drug testing would be used to weed (so to speak) some out. One of Gibson's aphorisms was, "Reality is for people who can't handle drugs."

Sgt. Gibson took sexual advantage of any willing female officer, nurse, or secretary he could get into the sack, closet, or back seat. He bragged about scheduling a fellow officer for overtime, going to the officer's house, and consorting with his wife. Gibson said, "Hey, the officer was happy to make time-and-a-half, and his wife and I were happy bumpin' uglies. It was a friggin' happiness trifecta."

Gibson carried a concealed weapon on the streets. When I asked him why, he replied, "I've pissed off a lot of convicts in my time. Most'll get out someday, so I'm just being proactive."

He was correct; most inmates will be released at some point. I always tried to treat everyone civilly. I did not want to give any of them a reason to knock on my door with a chip on their shoulder and a Glock in their pocket.

Kozak was a tall, wiry Flint boy and the king of handling critical incidents. He was also a frequent bar and street fighter and would often come to work sporting his battle scars.

Once, he came in with cuts and bruises on his face and hands.

"Kozak, rough night?" I asked him.

"I went back to Flint for the weekend. My two brothers and I each put away a fifth of Jack, and then we all got into it in the front yard, a real knockdown drag-out. I don't even remember what started it; it's just kind of a tradition with us. The next thing I know, four gangsta wannabes walk up, get all up in our faces and try to stop the fight. They picked the wrong family to mess with; I'm sure we hospitalized all of them, but the details are a bit hazy."

Another time, Kozak walked into the unit office with a serious knot on the left side of his forehead. I asked, "Who gave you that monster goose egg?"

"There was a little dispute over a pool game at the bar. Unfortunately, the other guy led with his stick, so I had to teach him a lesson."

"Any repercussions other than that lump on your head?"

"Hell, yeah, I'm banned from one of my favorite watering holes!"

I was starting to think that Kozak's life outside of prison could be wilder than it was inside, and this was confirmed when he came into work once with a black eye.

I asked him who gave him the shiner.

Mimicking a pirate, he replied, "That be me wife, matey." He chuckled and added, "Must have pissed her off. I passed out on the couch and woke up when she hit me in the eye with a frying pan."

At work, Kozak bumped heads with the nursing director numerous times. She questioned his actions in several critical incidents, saying he used excessive force. He shot back in TV lawyer mode: "Did you appoint your husband as the doctor to conduct all of the physicals for the thousand-plus inmates at Riverside? Did you further arrange for your husband to conduct these physicals in the other five prisons in town? If so, do the words 'conflict of interest' or 'monopoly' mean anything to you?"

Kozak's questions tripped her trigger. She snapped back, "You'd better mind your own business, or I'll put a Stop Order on you and have you fired before you know what happened!" Staff members never want to see their name and picture on a Stop Order, which documents serious rule violations; it is like a wanted poster at the post office. Termination often follows.

When people start threatening each other's livelihoods, things can get ugly, and they certainly did in this case. I'd heard a rumor that Kozak ran the nursing director off the road, so I asked him if that was true.

"Yeah," he said matter-of-factly.

"Was it premeditated?"

"Hell, no! I just got lucky. On my way to work, I saw her Maserati heading toward me. So we played chicken, and the bitch lost," Kozak said with a grin.

A couple of weeks later, as I walked into work I saw him and Sgt. Gibson standing in front of the Administration Building. Kozak was pointing at a giant hornet's nest looming in the back corner of the massive front porch, about 40 feet up.

Kozak said to Sgt. Gibson, "See that hornet's nest up there? Well, I'm about to stir those buzzin' bitches up!" He removed the heavy ring of prison keys from the clip on his belt and said, "Watch this, Sarge!"

He leaned back and threw the keys straight at the nest like a fastball. I could only assume he thought they would hit the top of the nest, dislodge it, and knock it to the ground, but the keys hit too low and got stuck deep in the middle of the massive nest. The three of us looked at each other in surprise. Kozak said, "Oops." A few hornets emerged from the nest and buzzed about for several seconds, but fortunately the entire thing did not dislodge, fall, and explode on the ground before us.

Key control, however, is a serious matter in prison, and Kozak was in deep dookie once again. I did not want to be called as a witness to the incident, so I walked toward the Administration Building to punch the time clock. I heard Sgt. Gibson say, "Kozak, in five minutes I'm supposed to represent your ass in a disciplinary conference! Now I have to open with, 'This yahoo, who's already under investigation, just lodged his prison keys into a hornet's nest 40 feet off the ground,' and then deal with the other charges." On and off all shift, I wondered how those keys would be recovered, but it was not my monkey or circus, and I never did find out.

There are plenty more Sgt. Gibson and Kozak tales, which I will not divulge. Unsurprisingly, I heard both yahoos were eventually dismissed from the department. Sgt. Gibson was terminated for sexual harassment and CMA Kozak for conduct unbecoming an officer. These two rogues could have been written up on those types of charges daily. Still, I must admit that I could forgive Kozak for his harebrained moments because he shone brightly in his dealings with dangerous convicts. The nursing director might have set up Kozak in this case, but he generally had no problem finding trouble in or outside of the joint. I would not have been shocked to see him or Gibson wearing prisoner blues.

When I was transferred upstairs from 11-1-East to 11-2-East, Nurse Elzada Chandler was in charge. She had a personality and appearance similar to Nurse Ratched's in the movie *One Flew Over the Cuckoo's Nest*. She was in her late 50s or early 60s, wore an all-white uniform from her orthopedic shoes to her nursing cap, and looked like she applied her makeup with a putty knife. She plucked out her eyebrows and sharply penciled in new ones in black. She always wore fire-engine-red lipstick, and her stiff black hair was streaked with gray and white wisps, giving her a Cruella de Vil vibe. Her bangs were permanently curled high in a "Tootsie Roll" style, and the back was curled under in a pageboy with military precision.

One afternoon on 11-2-East, Nurse Elzada Chandler and I began the daily routine of dispensing medications to the patients. I hollered, "Med lines!" and the inmates assembled in front of the office medication window, where she began passing out the pills through a small window. My job was to make sure the inmates swallowed their meds; I checked each one's hands and had him open his mouth, move his tongue around, and pull his cheeks out by hooking his pinkies at the corners of his mouth, confirming that he had swallowed his pills and was not "cheeking" his meds (hiding them between his cheeks and gums rather than swallowing them).

When inmate Robinson, a 6' 4" 300-pound young Black man, stepped up to the med window, he loudly stated, "Nurse Elzada, you ain't nothin' but a nasty ole White bitch that wants a big, hard, nigger dick up yo' ass!" All the inmates in the med line and anywhere within earshot laughed.

After his comment, inmate Robinson turned around and walked down to his cell, leaving Nurse Chandler with steam shooting out of her ears. When CMA Carnegie walked to the office to see why everyone was laughing hysterically, Chandler barked, "Put Robinson in the seclusion room, *now!*"

I was relieved that when Carnegie and I told Robinson he would be placed in seclusion, he smirked and shrugged as if to say, *Okay, I probably deserve a time out, but I enjoyed it.* He seemed to be cooperating, so we did not cuff him, each grabbing one of his massive arms so that we could lead him. Everything was going smoothly as we escorted the behemoth toward the seclusion room, but when we approached the unit office, Nurse Chandler stepped out in front of the inmate and screeched, "That will be the last time you shoot off your big mouth on my unit—sonny!"

This outburst caused Robinson to flex his arms, shake loose from our grips and lunge toward Nurse Chandler, screaming, "You fuckin' bitch!" Just then CMA Kozak appeared from the dayroom. He grabbed Robinson's T-shirt from the bottom in the back, pulled it over the convict's head, and tucked it under his chin, blinding him. Kozak then used the inmate's momentum against him; grabbing Robinson's right arm, he swung him around backward, slamming him into the jamb of the seclusion room's open door. Kozak finished his well-executed maneuver by side-kicking Robinson through the opening and shutting the door. I wanted to cheer, applaud, and hold up a 10-point card in appreciation of his feat. Kozak's moves looked as if Jackie Chan himself choreographed them. His poolroom brawls and Ultimate Fighting Championship matches with his brothers paid off.

Although Kozak was continually in boiling water, he was the kind of backup you wanted in a critical incident or perilous situation. If he had not stepped in at that moment, Nurse Chandler and several officers, including me, would have been injured by the burly inmate. Kozak was brilliantly inventive in a crisis, and his sharp instincts prevented serious injuries and saved lives on more than one occasion.

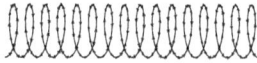

Because Riverside was a psychiatric hospital before it was a prison, some of the senior officers were left over from being mental health workers. Some of them had a unique way of handling critical incidents.

Old School Ollie was one of these. In 11 Building, we had a prisoner with an antisocial personality disorder whose handle was Teflon Juan. I figured Juan was given this moniker because he did not take responsibility for anything he did; guilt slid right off him. To build his macho street cred, he told everyone that he killed a cop, but the truth was that when he was a teenager he murdered his little brother. We had to watch out if Teflon did not get his way because he would throw a hissy fit to beat the band.

One night, something did not go Teflon's way, so he started hurling pool balls at other inmates in the room. Everyone scattered, but Juan just kept throwing the balls. Windows cracked, but wires embedded in the safety glass held them together. The officers shouted from the dayroom, hoping to make Juan stop, but he continued whipping balls.

As Teflon kept up his unrelenting onslaught, Old School Ollie, working overtime on the unit, walked in. I never knew why he always had a towel draped around his neck.

Ollie calmly approached Juan and said, "How's that pitching arm, pal?" He whipped his towel around the back of Juan's neck with his right hand, caught the loose end with his left, crossed it over, and gave the towel several quick twists. Juan's head turned red, and his eyes bugged out just before he dropped like a rag doll. Ollie dragged him to his cell as we followed, in awe of his mastery of towel martial arts. Once at his cell he took the towel off Juan's neck, and the inmate gasped for air.

Old School Ollie shoved him into his cell, flipped the towel back to its usual position on his shoulders, and said, "And that's how we did it in the old days, boys. We didn't have your fancy radios, handcuffs, or Taekwondo—just our trusty towels. Remember, it's all in the wrist."

CHAPTER 6

Swallowers, Cutters, Biters and More

Inmates Over the Edge

*"When we remember that we are all mad,
the mysteries disappear and life stands explained."*
—Mark Twain

The terrible incidents that happened in the psych units never ceased to amaze me. I was continually reminded of where I was. After returning from my weekend off, our second shift officers exchanged equipment with the first shift while Nurse Chandler informed us of the excitement of the previous shift. She said two unsuspecting CMAs, a Red Tag and his mentor, were doing routine hall checks after shift change. They made their way down the block, peering in each cell window to ensure all the inmates were present.

Before making their rounds, they failed to look at the notes the psychiatrists wrote in the logbook: "Inmate Bannon believes the devil has possessed his penis." When the two CMAs stopped and looked in Bannon's cell, he stood naked, one hand pulling on his manhood and the other holding a single-edged razor blade. When he had eye contact, Bannon dismembered himself and devoured his take. He was swiftly sent to the hospital, stitched up, and returned to our unit.

Bannon was one of many self-mutilators at Riverside. Before I was assigned to 11 Building I was told about a couple of Big Ben's unimaginable moves. One night in our unit, as he sat on his bed, he ripped his scrotum open with his bare hands, causing his testicles to drop out. He was rushed to the hospital. Apparently this act gave him some satisfaction, because after he was stitched up and starting to heal, he repeated his performance.

I was glad I was not there to witness or react to Bannon's or Big Ben's acts. I felt awful just imagining them, each of these incidents etched into my mind. My stomach would turn as my brain tried to comprehend the patients' actions. Self-mutilation was a common occurrence, especially in 11 Building.

Another bizarre gesture that we dealt with occasionally was inmates swallowing objects. Inmate Denslow was the king of the swallowing game. The psychiatrist said he went to the hospital so often that his trips cost Michigan taxpayers well over a million dollars. On one of his excursions, the staff accompanying him told Denslow they were tired of his attention-seeking antics. In retaliation, he tore up the state van by breaking the bench seat and denting the sidewalls. After this visit, the CMAs called the local police to transport him because the van was in such bad shape. Denslow proceeded to kick out the windows of the police car on the way back, further racking up the bills.

Inmate Boyton was another swallower, who was in and out of the hospital so many times the doctors eventually could not retrieve the objects via his throat. The excessive scar tissue that formed from previous retrievals forced them to go through his stomach. Even then, Boyton would rip his stitches out, which prompted the psychiatrist to order him to be four-pointed so he could not use his hands for this self-destructive behavior. Boyton did this once too often; his intestines finally ripped open, and fecal matter escaped, causing gangrene to set in. He died shortly thereafter.

Jumbo, an obese young man, was a swallower and self-mutilator. In the chow hall, the state did not supply metal spoons and forks; we had plastic "sporks," which are a combination of both. Jumbo would swallow sporks, batteries, screws, nails, glass, or whatever else he knew would require surgery to remove. Whenever he did so, he would inform the nurse, who would call the psychiatrist, who would have an armed officer take him to the hospital for an X-ray, after which a doctor would remove the offending item from his stomach because, like Denslow and Boyton, his throat was blocked with scar tissue. The doctors might as well have installed zippers on these patients' stomachs to make the retrieval easier. In addition to swallowing, Jumbo broke windows to obtain glass to cut himself with and shoved pens and pencils into his arms.

Cutting was another form of mutilation. When the unit's windows or TV screen were broken, inmates would scamper over to snag pieces of glass that they could use to cut themselves with later. For this reason, psych patients were prohibited from having their TVs in their rooms. We would shakedown the inmates and their cells if we suspected them of picking up the glass. This pastime was so popular that the Forensic Center in Ypsilanti had a "Cutters Unit" to house inmates obsessed with carving on themselves.

Inmates who self-mutilate have typically done so since childhood to gain attention. Most of their scars are superficial, and they should not be confused with genuinely suicidal inmates, who are more prone to cut their carotid or femoral arteries or hang themselves.

I once asked Jumbo, "Why do you cut yourself?"

His reply was disturbing. "Because when I see my blood, I know I'm alive."

Trying to make sense of mentally ill inmates' way of thinking was confusing. Surrounded by the sadistic mindset of some of the staff and the warped logic of the criminally insane, it could make ordinary people think they were going mad.

I wondered about the early lives of self-mutilators. How could a child's circumstances have been so dire that the only way he could gain attention was to do bodily harm to himself? In an attempt to understand Jumbo's mindset, I pulled his file. I flipped through the pages and read that he had broken out every window in his parents' house and set the place on fire. If you want attention from your parents, burning your house down might be one way to get it—not only from them but also from your neighbors, the fire and police departments, and the Department of Corrections.

After Jumbo was paroled from prison, the Control Center patched an outside call to our unit, and I was summoned to the office to take it. I answered the phone and was stunned to hear it was Jumbo, who quickly spewed several questions: "Officer Myette, how are you? Who else is working on the unit today? Does Smitty still lock there?"

I felt sorry for him, but I said, "Jumbo, it's against prison policy for me to accept any calls from ex-inmates on parole—or current inmates, for that matter. I'm jeopardizing my job by talking to you, so please don't call and ask for me or any other prison employee again. I wish you well. Goodbye." That was hard to do, but it had to be done.

Before working in prison, I never thought of the various forms of mutualization I encountered. When I met inmate Tinsley, I noticed he was missing some fingers. I assumed it was due to a woodshop accident. Most of his fingers were gone to the second knuckle, making his hands resemble cat paws. He was handsome, about 5' 7", and 22 years old, with wavy brown hair, blue eyes, and an outgoing personality.

I was a Green Tag, still adjusting to the surreal environment where I found myself. I had shot pool, played Euchre, and had plenty of conversations with Tinsley, so I was surprised the first time we caught him trying to bite off another finger. We first put him in handcuffs behind his back; then the psychiatrist ordered we four-point him (strapping his arms and legs to a bed with leather restraints). This was my first time four-pointing a patient/inmate.

Later, when I returned to check his restraints and bent over him, he tried to bite and head-butt me, so the psychiatrist directed us to five-point him. (This is the same as four-pointing, with the addition of immobilizing the head with a strap over the forehead.)

I was shocked at Tinsley's behavior because we talked daily—and he showed no signs of such compulsive or aggressive behavior. His obsession with removing his digits was not limited to his hands, but since he was not limber enough to put his foot in his mouth, he would tie strings around his toes to cut off the circulation. When the strings were tight enough and left there long enough, his toe would eventually fall off. It is hard to imagine why someone would want to rid themselves of something as precious as their fingers and toes; they help us maneuver through life.

This surreal, unpredictable, and dangerous behavior prompts

psychiatrists to order the CMAs to four- or five-point patients. The psychiatrist may also request a one-on-one, in underwear only. On a one-on-one, the CMA would have to sit outside the door of the inmate's cell to make sure he did not do anything to harm himself or others. The "underwear only" order ensures the inmate is not concealing weapons or contraband.

When staff first reported to their respective units at the beginning of a shift, the nurses from the previous shift would give reports. We would hear something like, "Smitty is four-pointed and on a one-on-one in room six. Jackson is in the seclusion room, in underwear only, on close observation, because of references to committing suicide. Brown appears agitated and is wearing boots and gloves, looking as if he is ready to fight. Dr. Lieberman is due at 6:00 p.m. to check on Smitty and Jackson. You all keep an eye on Brown."

One day, we received a new admission. After the doctor completed his evaluation, he ordered the patient to be four-pointed and placed on a one-on-one, and further ordered the CMA on the one-on-one to sit behind a plastic shield designed for room rushes.

When we asked Lieberman, "Why the shield?" he said, "This patient gets upset when he's four-pointed, and he has a history of projectile vomiting when he's upset, so the shield may be needed." My mind pictured a particular scene with Linda Blair in *The Exorcist*.

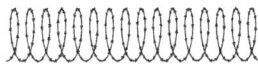

〰〰〰〰〰〰〰〰〰〰〰〰〰

Some mutilate themselves, seeking attention, and others enjoy pain. Then, some take it a step further. When I reported to the 10-2-East office during the shift change one afternoon, CMAs Millett, Bower, and I received our equipment from the previous shift's officers. Suddenly, we heard Officer Peters screaming as she ran up the hall, "I need help! Hogan's swinging!"

Bower shouted, "Quick, Peters—call Healthcare and the sergeant!"

If someone just walked by Hogan's cell, they would never have seen him hanging. Peters had to step into his cell to take in that macabre spectacle. On entering I saw inmate Hogan suspended like a steer on a meat hook, all 275 pounds. This was the first time I had seen someone hanging. He had tied his bedsheet to an air vent about eight feet up a wall.

At this point, we were unsure if Hogan was dead or alive. Although the former seemed the case at first glance, we had to proceed as if he were alive and try to keep him that way.

Bower hopped up on the small desk at the end of the bed, lifted Hogan's body to prevent the sheet from cutting off his air supply, and shouted, "I need a knife!"

Millett hopped up on the desk and started cutting the sheet with a jackknife, an awkward endeavor that caused the desk to rock back and forth with the weight of the officers and Hogan. It looked like something would give soon, so I spotted the trio in case the desk collapsed or tipped over.

When Millett finished cutting through the sheet, Hogan slipped out of Bower's arms and flopped down into mine, his weight forcing me back until I fell on the bed with Hogan's bulky, lifeless body on top of me.

Bower and Millett hopped off the desk; each grabbed Hogan under an arm and lifted him off me. They laid him down in the hallway outside his cell to give us space to start CPR. Healthcare called for an ambulance. Millett pulled out his CPR kit, donned his latex gloves, placed the plastic mask over Hogan's nose and mouth, and started administering CPR. Three Healthcare workers ran down the hall and took over until the paramedics arrived. When the ambulance pulled up in front of 10 Building, the paramedics loaded Hogan onto the gurney. Later, after I finished running chow lines, I asked the unit nurse about Hogan's status, and she said that he had been declared DOA at the Ionia hospital.

The administration sent a psychologist to our unit, who asked if anyone needed counseling. Peters welcomed the opportunity. After talking with the psychologist, she was off work on stress leave for a month.

The prison inspector investigated to determine who had been assigned hall duty at the time of Hogan's hanging, also checking if there was documentation of him exhibiting any unusual behavior that day. The logbook indicated Hogan had requested to talk to Dr. Leiberman, the head psychiatrist, on several occasions, so there was probably some investigation based on that alone.

Although I did not ask for time off like Officer Peters, seeing Hogan hanging was a dreadful experience, and having his dead body pin me to a bed was something I will never forget.

CHAPTER 7

The Games People Play

Sex, Cigs, and Foot Races with Inmates and Officers

"Even a good player will someday become a toy of a better player. It's called karma."

—Unknown

Prison provides ample time for devious minds to contemplate how to manipulate others to get what they want. It may be for power, monetary gain, sexual pleasure, or entertainment. Both inmates and staff play games, and getting caught up in them is easy. Even casual observers can get burned if they are not careful.

I often heard the terms "pitcher" and "catcher"—self-explanatory designations identifying one's preferred sexual role. Inmate Washington at Riverside was bragging about his prison carnal triumphs one day, so I asked him, "Are you a pitcher or a catcher?"

Washington shot me a dirty look and said, "I ain't no faggot! I always be pitchin.'"

"Are catchers *homosexuals*?" I asked, emphasizing the word to correct his bigoted language gently.

Washington replied, "Hell, yes! They just little fuck-boys."

CMA Burns, a Green Tag female officer I went through the Corrections Academy with, was caught exchanging love notes in

11-1-West with inmate Washington, apparently a switch hitter. As a result, CMA Burns was terminated for overfamiliarization. She may have saved her job if she had reported Washington's advances and turned his notes in to the inspector.

Sexual exploits on the job have long been a problem within the prison system. At Riverside, I knew three married couples who worked as CMAs. The usual arrangement for families was that the husbands were on one shift and the wives on another, allowing them to take turns with childcare. All three couples seemed happy and appeared to be good officers, but the wives were all having affairs with inmates and were eventually fired for overfamiliarization. These liaisons took place in 10 Building. I can only assume that the issue was as prevalent in 9, 11, and GP, as well as other prisons throughout the state and nationwide.

Deborah and Sam, one of the couples, were asked to report separately to the deputy warden's office. The inspector (the principal investigator who inquired into alleged staff wrongdoings) said to Deborah, "We have phone records showing that an inmate has called your home phone on numerous occasions, so unless you let us know exactly what's going on, both you and your husband will be terminated."

Deborah blurted out, "Don't fire Sam! He didn't know about my affair. I'm in love with inmate Gonzalez." When the husband heard about this he was bowled over, and so was everybody who knew him and his wife. In my opinion, Deborah was the best-looking female employee at Riverside. Deborah and Sam had two children in elementary school, played together on a softball team, and were active in their community. Their storybook life fell apart because inmate Gonzalez gave Deborah extra attention and had plenty of time to polish every smooth line he laid on her; his game must have been good, because she fell for it.

A third-shift sergeant caught the other two married female CMAs participating in sexual acts with convicts. These offenders probably thought they were safe on third shift because the administration was not around and supervision was minimal. But in prison, there is always someone watching. A jealous inmate snitched out the officers' indiscretions. This sort of thing happens all the time.

To catch an employee in his trap, an inmate starts by making small talk, using compliments to win the employee's approval. Eventually, he persuades the employee to bring in a joint or a pint of whiskey. Once the employee smuggles in the contraband, the inmate wants more, and the subsequent request is often for sexual favors. The inmate will say, "How much do you like your paycheck? If you don't have sex with me, I'll show the sergeant all the love notes you gave me. Plus, my bunkie witnessed you bringing me the drugs and booze."

If the employee complies the inmate is happy, but if the employee refuses the inmate makes good on his threats, so the employee is screwed either way. Employees do not want to lose their jobs, benefits, and retirement packages, so they often submit to the inmates' demands.

Once an employee caves in, the intrigue keeps snowballing. The next thing the employee knows, another inmate or two may try to get in on the drugs-and-sex scene. A convict may say, "Since you were screwing my bunkie, I think it's my turn—unless you want me to tell the captain about you and my homeboy."

To an inmate, sex is a game in which he tries to catch as many other inmates and staff in his web as possible. Each conquest is another notch in their belt, but the employees may lose their jobs and families. In time, the employee-prisoner affairs will be exposed, causing the employees' lives, inside and outside prison, to crumble quickly. I observed break-ups between employees, between employees and inmates, and between inmates and inmates. These disputes arose unexpectedly in the yard and the units. They were usually due to jealousy—it seemed as if everyone was cheating on someone. For example, a female officer was cheating on her husband with a married inmate, who was nailing anything that moved, be it inmate or staff, male or female.

An experienced con can easily manipulate staff, giving the inmate a distorted view of the employee's situation. The inmate believes he is the nucleus of the employee's world, an assumption that is not true.

Sometimes, the roles are reversed, and the employee wants sex with an inmate for pleasure, profit, or both. The profit-seekers charge money and function as prostitutes. This has proved to be a very lucrative business in prison because there is an endless supply of customers.

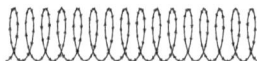

Early in my career, the prison store did not sell packs of cigarettes but carried loose tobacco in a can and rolling papers. Many psych inmates could not afford the tobacco, so they traded sexual favors, coffee, or honey buns for it. The inmates bummed "shorts" off anyone they could to get a couple of puffs at a time. Some collected cigarette butts that officers and other employees tossed out, removing the tobacco and re-rolling it in papers.

Once, at count time at Riverside, I was walking up the hallway on 11-1-East when, from a distance, I saw a brand-name cigarette lying on the floor about 15 feet in front of the office. I thought, *An inmate did not drop that smoke. When the unit opens after count clears, there will be a mad dash toward the dayroom. Soon as they see that mass-manufactured, additive-laden, store-bought and heaven-sent Marlboro Red, there will be bedlam.*

As I continued walking, I looked into the office and saw Officer Belmont, a broad-shouldered, wide-jawed weightlifting CMA. He had a granite face that made him look like the kind of guy who, if you punched him in the nose as hard as you could, would take it without flinching and say with a chuckle, "Is that all you got, punk?" right before he grabbed you by the throat and squeezed the life out of you. Belmont had a macho, arrogant attitude that could tick off anyone. I heard him boast countless times in front of officers and inmates, "There isn't a convict or officer in this joint that could kick my ass!"

He would say this to taunt any takers, and I thought it was foolish. To an inmate doing life, butchering one more victim would not mean all that much.

I had to believe that, in Riverside—a Level IV facility with about 1,400 prisoners—there were stronger inmates who were better fighters or had weapons that could take Belmont out before he knew what hit him. In general population, he probably would not get away with the kind of games he was playing in the psych unit. Some psych inmates were easy targets because they were not intelligent, highly medicated, and not all there.

Belmont was a Prick, and that capital P is not a typo. When the other badass CMAs in 11 Building were by his side to protect him, there probably was not any lone inmate who could kick his ass. Still, if he was on his own, going one-on-one with some kickboxing, street-fighting, body-building brute of an inmate, CMA Belmont would have been beaten down and tossed away like a used Kleenex.

Back to the Marlboro, which was still on the floor in front of the office. When Belmont stepped up to the office door and yelled, "Unit's open!" I heard the familiar sound of feet in plastic slippers scuffling up the hallway. As the first three patients spotted the smoke, they all broke into a slippery, slapstick run. One of them dove for the cigarette like it was a million-dollar bill, sliding across the polished linoleum. Just as it was almost in his grasp, it appeared to take on life and leap away from him magically. Another inmate laughed and dove to grab it, but it jumped again. After a few seconds, I saw Officer Belmont had taped a string to the cigarette and was pulling it toward the office door. The three inmates lunged at the Marlboro, clunking their heads on the door simultaneously. Belmont reeled up the smoke-on-a-string, laughed hysterically with the other two CMAs, then swung the cigarette back and forth like a pendulum as if hypnotizing the trio. I have to admit it was a hilarious scene, but it was also exceptionally cruel.

On another occasion, when the unit was closed after chow, I stepped out to the airing porch to enjoy the view and saw Officer Belmont had been up to his cigarette tricks again. A Marlboro on a string was hanging two feet from the porch ceiling. I could not figure out how Belmont taped the string to the 13-foot ceiling. But, as a new Green Tag in the Admissions Unit, I was only observing and was not about to question the behavior of seasoned officers.

Just then, I saw Belmont step out of the office and yell, "Unit's open!" He walked to the airing porch followed by officers CMA Geyer and Pittman, an eager audience waiting for the entertainment to commence. No one shorter than a professional basketball player could snag that 11-foot-high dangling smoke.

At first, the inmates did not see the cigarette, so Belmont stood underneath it and looked up to draw their attention. When the patients spotted it, they all began excitedly hopping up and down, trying to reach the prize. When that proved a miserable failure, they took turns running and jumping with outstretched hands as the officers chuckled.

Soon, things started to get dangerous, with inmates sliding a rickety card table from the dayroom underneath the smoke. They saw that the cigarette would still be out of reach, so they put a flimsy plastic chair on the table, thinking they could stand on it and snag it. Officer Geyer put the kibosh on that idea, telling them, "The table and chair are off limits."

The ever-resourceful inmates removed their shoes and started throwing them at the cigarette, which only made it swing on its string as the flying footwear pelted other inmates. The patients' frustration mounted as the officers watched, smugly smoking their cigarettes. It all felt like the referee at a basketball game kept raising the rim, and there was no way the players could make a basket.

I wanted to backhand Belmont, but I realized I was still green and would have to work with these officers for years, so I did nothing.

When the emergency siren blew, interrupting the officers' inhumane entertainment, I felt relieved but a little guilty.

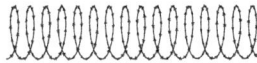

Making effective split-second decisions is crucial in or outside of prison. I learned to go with my instincts. One day on 11-2-East, I was shooting a game of pool with inmate Cisco, a muscular, long-haired man in his late 20s. As he took his shots, I stood on the other side of the pool table, checking out the angles—and trying a *little* bit to throw him off his game. After three shots, he snarled, "I know what you're doing! You're trying to fuck with me. Quit trying to psych me out!" He flipped the pool stick around and, holding it like a club, began to circle the table toward me.

I left the poolroom, crossed the dayroom, and locked myself into the unit office. Back in the poolroom, I saw Cisco glaring at me as he tossed his stick on the table and stomped out of the room. I decided that there was no talking with this man. Arming myself with my pool stick was not a good idea, either. Finding a safe place away from Cisco was my best option.

After locating his file, I plopped down in a chair to look it over. I learned that he was an antisocial paranoid schizophrenic who had done time in jail for being drunk and disorderly, malicious destruction of property, and assault and battery. As I suspected, Cisco was a very dangerous man. It did not take much to trip his trigger, and, over time, his crimes had become more serious. He ended up in our high-level psychiatric ward after catching two attempted murder cases. One involved a survival knife, and the other a baseball bat. In both cases, the victims were hospitalized in critical condition for a long time.

I had to keep reminding myself who I was dealing with and consider why they were in prison. I never asked Cisco to play another game of pool, and refrained from playing psychological games with any other inmates. The way Cisco looked at me before he came after me was the most frightening moment in my prison history. I had broken up fights and tackled convicts, but that did not feel the same way. I believe if Cisco caught me, he would have ended me. I avoided him the rest of the shift, but I still had to do my hall checks, count, take the unit to chow, and come to work every day with him there.

CHAPTER 8

Mayhem and Mischief

The Misadventures of
Dempsey, Brown, and Kowalski

"O mischief, thou art swift to enter
in the thoughts of desperate men!"
—William Shakespeare

ne day, I was escorting the unit to chow; I was at the front of the line as usual, with inmate Dempsey about halfway down behind me. The kitchen phone by Dempsey rang, and he snagged the receiver—a distinct no-no because prisoners were not allowed to use the staff phones—and said, "Officer Dempsey, 11 Building Kitchen. How may I direct your call?" He paused to hear the caller's response, then said, "Sure." Then, taking the handset away from his mouth he yelled to me, "Officer Myette, telly!"

Every classroom, playground, and prison block has its pain-in-the-ass or class clown—often the same individual—who is behind the practical jokes, misunderstandings, and things that go amok. In 11-2-East, that person was Dempsey. He was constantly in the middle of the madness, creating anarchy for amusement and enjoying how others reacted.

Standard equipment for COs or CMAs includes keys, handcuffs, CPR kits, and mobile radios. The radios allowed communication between employees, especially calls for backup. Looking back, I foolishly rarely called for backup, usually jumping into the situation alone.

On one occasion, I walked into the dayroom and saw inmate Dempsey, with whom I regularly played Scrabble. Dempsey strolled up next to me, reached down to my side and appeared to push the talk button on the radio on my belt, shouting in alarm, "Fight on 11-2-East!"

I said, "Dempsey, you didn't key my radio, did you?"

"I'm just checking the officer's response time, sir," he said. "You know, you should maintain better security on your radio!" He laughed.

I wondered if Dempsey had keyed my radio until CMAs Geyer, Pittman, and Chadwick from 11-1-East suddenly burst through the airing porch door and ran into the dayroom.

"Did you just call a fight on 11-2-East?" Geyer asked, trying to catch his breath.

"No," I answered truthfully. But I did not mention that Dempsey had.

The CMAs looked around 11-2-East, checked on 11-2-West, and stomped downstairs to 11-1-East. Regarding the officers' response time, Dempsey said, "Forty-five seconds! Not bad. Not bad at all!"

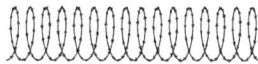

〰〰〰〰〰〰〰〰〰〰〰〰

Nurse Maybelle was known as the "Queen of Overtime" because she would work overtime on any unit, shift, or day. She would work double and triple shifts if it were possible to get away with it. Maybelle was raking in cash, getting paid time-and-a-half and double time, which allowed her to buy a new Cadillac Fleetwood. The Caddy was roomy enough to serve as her mobile home; she would sleep in the parking lot, which allowed her to be immediately available to pick up extra shifts.

Maybelle was also the "Queen of Falsies," and she earned the title from top to bottom.

Because she slept in the Caddy, she was often in disarray when she reported to work. Her long, straight, shiny jet-black wig was usually crooked. Her false eyelashes sometimes fell off. The tissue paper she stuffed in her bra often peeked out from her blouse. Maybelle was extraordinarily animated and highly entertaining, but also a harebrained, goofball RN.

One day, Maybelle was on 11-2-East, playing pinochle with the inmates, and I was sitting in the office when the phone rang, the caller asking to speak with her. I hollered out the med window at the closest inmate, "Mr. Williams, please tell Maybelle she has a phone call." She came into the office, and then inmate Dempsey walked up and stood at the med window. When she hung up the phone, Dempsey reached through the window, opening his hand to reveal the false teeth Maybelle had been comfortable enough to take out and leave sitting on the card table, and said with a smile, "Maybelle, are you trying to tell us something?"

Either unaware of Dempsey's crude attempt at humor or not caring, Maybelle grabbed her choppers and popped them into her mouth. I wondered what the boys at the table, especially Dempsey, might have done to them before returning them to her.

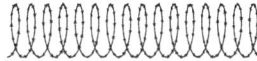

~~~~~~~~~~~~~~~~~~~~~~

Once, I observed Ms. Parker, the occupational therapist, scurrying around and secretly asking questions of some inmates. She appeared quite flustered; there was obviously something wrong. The last person I saw her talking with was inmate Smitty, so I approached the young man and asked, "What did Ms. Parker want?"

"Oh, she wanted to know what happened to her keys," Smitty replied.

This was much more serious than Maybelle misplacing her dentures. Ms. Parker constantly set down her keys and walked away rather than keeping them tethered to her side. Employees are not supposed to separate from their keys. I kept mine clipped to a cord attached to my belt and tucked in my pocket.

"What did you tell her?" I asked.

"I told her I picked them up off the table and threw them off the airing porch!" he said, starting to snicker.

"What *really* happened to them?"

"Hell if I know!" snapped Smitty.

"Where were you with Ms. Parker, and why?"

"We were having a group meeting in the Occupational Therapy Room."

"Who was in the group?"

"Boyton, Caveman, Tinsley, Dempsey, and me," he said. I could have predicted that Dempsey's name would be on the list: This caper already smelled of 11-2-East's resident trickster.

Dempsey was currently locking in the dorm room, which housed four inmates on good behavior. How he was selected to lock there was a mystery; I figured he must have buffaloed the psych.

When I walked in, Dempsey was the only inmate in the dorm room; because of his crime (1st Degree Murder), I did not like that we were alone, separated from the rest of the staff. I asked him what he had done with Ms. Parker's keys.

"Well!" Dempsey exhaled, shaking his head. "Why would you think that lil' ol' me would do something with her keys, boss?" He tilted his head and gave me a big, toothy smile.

Attempting to keep it light, I said, "Just a wild guess—and because it sounds like your modus operandi!"

"Why, I never!" Dempsey said in a mock feminine manner, batting his lashes. "I'm appalled that you would have such a low opinion of moi!"

In a more serious tone, I said to Dempsey, "Listen. Key control is crucial in the prison system. Control Center will blow the emergency siren if those keys don't reappear very soon. They'll lock down the entire joint, and there will be no movement anywhere—no weight pit, yard, phone privileges, medical callouts, or chow hall. All inmates' meals will be served in their cells, which means a lot of angry people. The administration will have to call in a locksmith to redo all the locks, which'll cost the prison tens of thousands of dollars. Every employee and inmate in this facility will want to string up whoever is responsible for the keys disappearing. So, I'm asking you again, Dempsey: If you were Ms. Parker's keys, where would you be?"

Dempsey looked at me and replied, "Oh! If I were Ms. Parker's keys...I think I would be hiding in the Occupational Therapy Room, on a ceramic half-wall, inside a blue vase."

"Finally!" I said. "Thanks."

I saw no reason to snitch Dempsey out because, as a psychiatric prisoner, he would neither receive a ticket nor suffer any other consequences. If a GP inmate took control of prison keys, he would catch tickets for theft and attempted escape, be transferred to a maximum security prison, and have years added to his bit.

A CMA sergeant was shaking down the Occupational Therapy Room as I entered. I found the keys right where Dempsey said they would be and tossed them to the sergeant, who curiously looked at me. I did not want him to turn a satisfactory encounter with Dempsey into something ugly, so I said nothing to the sergeant. I was satisfied: The keys had been located and returned to their owner, and I did not betray Dempsey's trust. Dempsey was the king of game players.

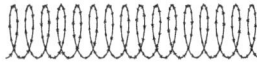

On a rainy fall evening, inmate Brown asked me to play a game of Scrabble. He was a 5' 9" diesel mechanic from Detroit with a personality as big as his muscles. Besides his short fuse, Brown seemed more stable than our other patients, so I was curious why he was in the psych unit. About halfway through the game I asked him how he got to prison, specifically Riverside's psych unit.

"I was making good money as a mechanic at Detroit Diesel," he said, "but I got greedy and robbed a drug house I'd been casing out. I tried to hit the place when the drugs and money were piled high. During the robbery, some unexpected things—like guns—popped up, and I shot some people."

Inmate Brown was the best Scrabble player I have ever come up against, but he had a smoking hot temper. During this game, he told me, "Myette, when I first saw you on the unit I wanted to beat your ass. But when I saw how you dealt with the inmates and officers, I decided you were all right. You aren't from the same mold as the other officers, and you sure aren't from the same hood."

"Mr. Brown," I replied matter-of-factly, "let me lay it all out for you. Since you arrived on the unit I've been observing you, and have determined you are a stubborn hothead who'll be getting into more than your share of altercations. And—I'll probably be the first one to jump on you. Don't fight back when I grab you, because I'm just doing my job."

Brown said, "All right. I guess you are just doing your job, so I don't have a problem with that arrangement."

I thought, *Wow! I didn't expect him to go along with it—but only time will tell if he keeps his word.*

One of the problems with psychiatric patients being exempt from tickets is that it invites malingerers, those who fake mental illnesses to avoid the consequences of their actions. Brown was the archetypal malingerer. He told me that, before locking at Riverside, he was at I-Max (Ionia maximum security prison), where he did everything he could to demonstrate that he was insane. His last act before being shipped to 11 Building was to flood his cell. He said he plugged his sink and toilet and then turned the water on while continuously flushing the toilet.

When the Goon Squad rushed Brown's cell, they slid around and fell on the water-covered floor. This aggravated them, and they released their frustration by beating the crap out of Brown, but he said that he got his licks in, too. Brown got precisely what he wanted: a free trip to a Riverside psychiatric unit, where he could kick ass at will without receiving any tickets, going to the Hole, or catching a new bit. A psychopath's paradise.

The psych units were a splendid vacation for anyone who had come from being locked down all day at I-Max. In 11 Building, Brown was out and about, hustling whoever and whatever he could. Like Jack Nicholson's character in *One Flew Over the Cuckoo's Nest*, Randle Patrick McMurphy, Brown was in charge of whatever was happening around him. He was not only the master of Scrabble but also a top-notch card player and a pool shark, and he blew everyone away at ping-pong and foosball. Like inmate Dempsey and Officer Belmont, he loved to rile up the bugs for his entertainment. After handily winning a pool game, he would have the losing patient polish his shoes, roll him smokes, or drop and do 50 pushups. But the thing that seemed to give Brown the most pleasure was opening up a big ol' can of whoop-ass.

An inmate in 11 Building could assault staff in the morning and walk around whistling Dixie by the afternoon if the psychiatrist deemed it so. I should not admit this, but there were times when being able to punch some obnoxious, arrogant, condescending blockhead with no consequences sounded like it might work for me, too.

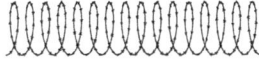

I was shooting a game of pool with inmate Boyton on a hot August night. As I dropped a bank shot, I heard a bizarre and unsettling sound I had only heard once before—after hitting a deer at about 3:00 a.m.

Back then, I stopped the car and got out. As I looked back at the deer lying on the side of the road, I heard a sound like someone screaming, crying, and wheezing at the same time—a kind of breathy, whiny squeal. Not being a hunter, I did not know that deer even made a noise other than a stag when it is in rut.

Now, that incident played in my head at high speed as I heard the telltale injured deer sound emanating from the smoking room across the hallway. I saw inmate Haggard—a longhaired kid in his early 20s—on the floor, crying out for mercy. Inmate Brown was sitting on Haggard's back and pounding the back of his head with both of his diesel-mechanic sledgehammer fists. Inmates Strauss and Cook were kicking Haggard's ribs and face as if they were going for 60-yard field goals. The three assailants seemed to be enjoying themselves immensely—but Haggard, not so much.

I tossed the pool stick on the table and ran across the hall to the smoking room, where Haggard's assailants continued to pulverize him. Diving on Brown, I knocked him off Haggard, then attempted to pull Brown's hands behind his back to handcuff him. Cook and Strauss were still kicking Haggard's torso and face; I jumped up and shoved Strauss out of the room just as he kicked Haggard's nose. Suddenly, several officers from 11-2-West arrived and grabbed Strauss and Cook. Turning around, I saw Brown was back on top of Haggard, pounding on him again. The victim's face bounced off the linoleum like a bloody basketball, and I saw pieces of his teeth shoot out across the room. I leaped back on Brown and handcuffed him, which was not easy.

After this fiasco, it dawned on me that Brown kept his word not to fight back when I was doing my job: He had not struck me or even tried to throw me off during the scuffle.

Later that night, I was waiting outside the office when Nurse Chandler returned from her chow break. The unit was locked down; Cook, Strauss, and Brown were cuffed and locked in their cells. Haggard was sitting alone on a bench in front of the office, looking as if he had just been ejected through the windshield of a car into a tree.

Nurse Chandler exclaimed, "Oh my God! Who is that?"

"Haggard," I replied.

"No way! It isn't!" she protested.

"Yes, it is, and I've never seen a worse beating in my life!" I said.

As I looked at Haggard, I felt sick to my stomach. In seconds, the three convicts broke his ribs, jaw, and nose, kicked his teeth out, and busted his ocular bone, causing his eye to drop out of its socket and into his cheek—and who knows what other damage he sustained. Haggard looked up at me with one eye, shaking, as if he wanted to say something, but he was too damaged to mumble a single syllable. The EMTs loaded him onto a gurney and took him to the hospital, and I never saw him again.

Haggard's attackers gave him the drubbing of his life after he indiscreetly claimed that he had a shank and would stick them when he had the chance. The three seasoned prisoners resolved not to allow him the opportunity. Haggard was a fish who quickly discovered that making idle threats is not a wise idea in prison, especially in 11 Building, where the absence of tickets gave inmates carte blanche to kick ass.

It is not prudent for an inmate to say, "I'm going to put this pool ball through your head!" unless he is ready for a pool stick to be swung at his, and one should not say, "I got a shank with your name on it!" unless he wants the tar beat out of him.

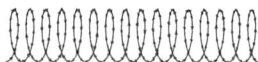

〜〜〜〜〜〜〜〜〜〜〜〜〜

As I sat in the office one evening, recording my hall rounds in the logbook, I saw two inmates arguing in the smoking room. I could see that one was a mouthy new patient named Wagner, and the other was—no surprise—my Scrabble partner, inmate Brown. Brown ripped off his denim jacket and threw it on the ground as if to say, "Okay, bring it on, motherfucker!"

Wagner steamed out of the smoking room and headed toward the front of the office where I sat; if the window had not been there, I could have reached out and touched him. Hot on his heels, Brown grabbed Wagner's arm, spinning him around. I felt like I was in the front row of an IMAX theater watching a film made especially for me. Brown leaned forward, stuck out his jaw, pointed at it, and waited like Bluto tempting Popeye to take a free shot. As I rose to exit the office, Wagner hit Brown right on the jaw, so I immediately took Wagner to the ground. I held his arms behind his back to handcuff him when Brown started beating the brakes off him. I caught Brown's eye, and he smirked at me as he continued to initiate the new kid on the cellblock.

Suddenly, CMAs Geyer and Bard appeared; each grabbed one of Brown's arms and tossed him into an empty cell. I finished handcuffing Wagner and escorted him down to his cell. Sgt. Gibson shouted through the locked door at inmate Brown, "Take off your boots and place them by the door, then go to the back of the cell!"

Brown shouted, "Fuck you, bitch! You come in here and take 'em off!"

Sgt. Gibson again ordered Brown to remove his boots, and Brown shouted back, "Fuck you, you fuckin' inbred hillbilly! Come in and get 'em, you chicken piece o' shit!"

After locking up Wagner, I walked up the hallway and told the sergeant, "I can get Brown to take off his boots." But the sergeant was mad as hell and said, "Fuck that! We're going to room-rush this prick and throw his ass into seclusion!" Then he ordered the unit to be locked down and left to round up the Goon Squad. (This was before the sergeant had placed me on the squad.)

The unit was locked down; no officers were in sight, and the unit nurse was not to be found. I was upset: I felt Brown had used me like a tool.

I cracked his door and asked, "What the hell was that?"

Brown said, "Hey, we make a damn good team!" He chuckled and added, "I knew if you saw us beefing, and Wagner threw the first punch, you'd take him down, and then I could beat him like the bitch he is. I've seen you in action before, Myette. You jump into whatever's going down without calling for backup. You're not too smart, but you're consistent."

I then realized that the film Brown was starring in had been produced for my benefit.

Ticked off, I said, "Listen up, dipstick: I'm *not* your partner. I need you to take your boots and belt off and walk across the hall to the seclusion room before the Goon Squad comes in and crunches your ass. The sarge will be furious with me when he sees that I cracked the door without backup, and he'd love to see you take a beating, so get moving!"

Brown kicked off his boots and pulled off his belt, dropping it to the floor as he walked to the seclusion room, saying, "Okay, but I still say we make a great team."

I thought about how inmate Brown set me up. He had studied my behavior enough to know I would jump into the altercation without calling for backup. Brown probably pictured me holding inmate Wagner's arms behind his back while he made a punching bag out of his face well before he egged him on. I needed to analyze inmate Brown's moves, as he was clearly a master manipulator and a dangerous dude.

As predicted, when Sgt. Gibson returned with the squad he was upset with me for moving Brown to seclusion on my own. But he must have gained some trust in my de-escalation techniques because he placed me on the 11 Building Goon Squad shortly after the incident.

If a psych patient had a weapon or was a danger to himself or others, the head nurse would contact the psychiatrists, often calling for a room rush, and the Special Operations Response Team, aka the Goon Squad, would spring into action. Most room rushes at Riverside occurred in 11 Building, primarily in the Admissions Unit.

The equipment the four of us wore made us look like *Star Wars* stormtroopers. We were decked out in riot gear: helmets with face shields, military-style boots, chest protectors, forearm pads, and shin guards over our regular uniforms.

Each cell in 9, 10, and 11 was about six feet by nine feet, with a single bed, steel sink, toilet, and footlocker bolted to the walls—a design that did not leave much space for a convict and 800 pounds of officers to wrestle around.

Before we rushed a room, the CMA sergeant would ask the inmate to stop his dangerous and destructive behavior, put his weapon down if he had one, and come out peacefully. Whether or not the inmate complied with the sergeant's request, he was restrained with handcuffs and leg irons, then escorted to a seclusion room if he cooperated—or carried horizontally face down if he did not. Compliance usually disappointed my fellow squad members, who were suited up and psyched up for a takedown.

When my squad rushed a room, the first CMA through the door would be Geyer, a 6' 225-pound scrapper with a Fu Manchu mustache and a receding hairline. He would jump on the inmate and use his powerful limbs to restrain the prisoner, arms around the head and legs around the waist—a move Officer Geyer called the "basket hold."

The second man through the cell door was Chadwick, a stocky, 5' 8" 180-pound bruiser with a flattop haircut. Chadwick would hit the inmate below the knees, and, with Geyer on his upper torso, the convict would quickly buckle. Chadwick was the CMA who hit me from behind in the incident with inmate Grant and Sgt. Nicholes, so I experienced a taste of the squad's room-rush prowess.

The third squad member through the door was Pittman, a 6' 1" 200-pound black belt in karate, with short, jet-black hair and a mustache. Pittman would ensure the inmate was lying on his stomach and handcuffed behind his back.

Being the squad's newest member, I was the last one in the cell. At the time, I was 6' 2" and 190 pounds, with a mustache and short-cropped silver hair—and the oldest member of the squad. I was in charge of placing the inmates in leg irons.

An inmate who was put into a seclusion room in general population was left with his cuffs and leg irons on, but with the mentally ill, we were required to switch the metal restraints to leathers after we had them under control, presumably to avoid a lawsuit claiming cruel and unusual punishment. I have been in hundreds of room rushes with various squad members, but this team was the most efficient and effective. I would not have wanted to be on the receiving end of our squad's handiwork.

〰〰〰〰〰〰〰〰〰〰〰〰〰

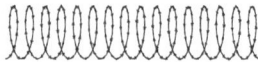

One day, after the nurse instructed the squad to rush inmate Kowalski, we discovered Sgt. Gibson was absent, and that a new man, Sgt. Walters, had been assigned to our unit. As we walked toward the inmate's cell, Walters handed CMA Geyer a large Plexiglas shield. We had never used the shield before. It was clear, curved, three feet high by two feet wide, and had two handles on the back for the officer to grip. CMA Geyer explained to Sgt. Walters that we had our procedure down pat, but he insisted Geyer go in first with the shield.

Geyer protested, but the sergeant gave him a direct order—if he disobeyed it, he would be sanctioned. This venue change concerned the entire squad. We all knew we were dealing with Kowalski, a 6' 6" country boy who had previously put serious whuppin's on both inmates and staff. He was the last person who should be the subject of an experiment when the squad had an established procedure.

Sgt. Walters keyed the cell door, and Geyer entered first, but because he was holding the shield he could not put the inmate in the basket hold. The sergeant instructed him to pin Kowalski to the wall with the shield, but the inmate grabbed it, twisted it out of Geyer's grip, and started swinging it at us. When I entered the cell, Kowalski hit me in the head so hard that it knocked my helmet off, even though it was strapped on. The squad was furious, and the inmate was laughing. Geyer grabbed the shield from Kowalski and threw it out the door, almost striking Sgt. Walters. We regrouped and eventually subdued the prisoner, but we never used the shield again. We also lost what little respect we had for the inept sergeant. He did not know our squad's methods or the inmate's demeanor, and introducing a new tool at the last minute, without giving us time to practice with it, was not a wise move.

Officers were often injured in room rushes, not always by the inmate. Sometimes, after a chaotic brawl, the inmate would accidentally be shackled to an officer. At other times, when an inexperienced officer's face shield would steam up, the inmate would punch, kick, and thrash around, causing the new squad member to grab a fellow officer's arm or leg and twist it the wrong way. Dealing with 10 limbs flailing around in a room the size of a walk-in closet can be baffling, so each squad member needed to know the game plan, be aware of their surroundings, and be familiar with the inmate's history. Geyer, Chadwick, Pittman, and I did pretty well—almost every time.

CHAPTER 9

My Introduction to 10 Building

Kitchen and Regular Unit Officer

*"The only way to make sense out of change
is to plunge into it, and join the dance."*
—Alan Watts

After two and a half years in 11 Building, nursing supervisor Karen Hanson asked me if I would like a break from the acute care patients by moving to 10 Building. I said, "Sure," but I was not moved. After I worked in 11 Building four years, Karen asked me again if I would like to move to 10 Building. Thinking back to the last time she asked, I used reverse psychology and said, "I like 11 Building and would prefer to remain." The next pay period, I was transferred to 10 Building and became the new kitchen supervisor and 10-2-East officer. I oversaw the general population inmates who transported the food carts to and from the main kitchen, and also served the food to the patients, called each unit to the chow hall, and tried to control theft.

The kitchen officer in 11 Building sometimes allowed inmates to take some food back to the unit. The nurse and officers on our unit overlooked the leniency because they wanted to watch the inmates feed the critters.

It is not unusual for inmates to behave like animals in prison—but, ironically, wild animals often bring out the prisoners' most human impulses. Inmates desperately long for companionship and entertainment;

one solution is to adopt and care for a mouse, bird, or ground squirrel—if they can conceal it from the authorities.

In late spring, when I worked on the Admissions Unit on 11-1-East, the inmates would smuggle dinner food from the chow hall and then hurry to the unit's airing porch. Like clockwork, a family of raccoons would climb over two fences topped with concertina wire to receive their nightly meal. Staff and inmates alike loved to watch the raccoons display their daring dexterity on their hazardous trek. The patients tossed out pieces of bread, cheese, fruit, or whatever they had scavenged for Mama, Daddy, and four baby raccoons.

Watching the inmates' behavior as the raccoons enjoyed their treats was intriguing. The violent, twisted souls who had been incarcerated for terrible crimes were now as gentle as the furry creatures they were feeding. This therapeutic experience could not have happened if the kitchen officer strictly enforced the chow hall rules; had he, the raccoon family and 11 Building inmates would never experience those magical moments in the springtime.

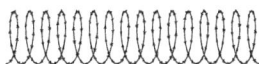

〰〰〰〰〰〰〰〰〰〰〰

As kitchen supervisor for 10 Building, I would report to the chow hall in the basement an hour before chow, where I would meet three GP inmates. Then, we would walk through the tunnels to the main kitchen to pick up two large food carts laden with the evening's fare. When we returned to 10 Building, the workers would place the food from the carts on the food line, and I would call the units to chow one at a time over my mobile radio. There were no kitchens in 9, 10, or 11 Buildings, only chow halls with food lines.

After dinner, the workers washed and loaded the empty serving containers back into the carts, and I escorted them as they pushed the carts back to the main kitchen. Once my food-service responsibilities were completed, I spent the remainder of my shift on 10-2-East, interacting with the patients and monitoring the unit.

I dealt with 10 Building's chronically ill patients, whom I was told would be less dangerous than the acute care patients in 11 Building, but there were plenty of exceptions. In 11, the inmates did not have keys to their cells, but in 9 and 10 they had door keys and could let themselves in and out of their cells.

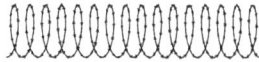

{{{{{{{{{{{{{{{{{{{{

One afternoon, during chow in 10 Building, I overheard a prisoner comment that the iced tea tasted "funny." So, out of curiosity, I walked over to the large plastic beverage cooler, took the top off, and peered inside. *Oh my God*, I thought, *it's a big ol' turd!*

Yes, that is right. A big, Baby Ruth-looking piece of human excrement was floating on top of the iced tea. With my stomach turning a somersault, I immediately removed the container from the chow line. Someone in the main kitchen wanted to surprise the 10 Building staff and inmates with a tasty treat. From that day on, whenever I wanted a beverage with my lunch at work, I bought a Mountain Dew from a vending machine and never again drank the iced tea or lemonade made in any prison.

After the spiked tea incident, I looked into the history of inmate food preparation in Michigan prisons. I learned that on March 27, 1893, George Haight, the deputy gatekeeper of Jackson Prison, and several officers were poisoned by inmate Robert Irving Latimer. This was achieved by him placing a mixture of opium and cyanide in their food as part of an elaborate escape plan.

After eating their meals, several officers fell unconscious or became immobilized. When Haight passed out, he knocked over several plates, and the noise alerted a guard who had not eaten the toxic food. Inmate Latimer told the guard that Haight was dying and needed help. When the guard left to get assistance, Latimer took a set of prison keys and two revolvers from the unconscious guards and strolled out of prison. He was later arrested but never charged for the murder of George Haight, who ultimately died from the poisoning. In 1935, after serving 45 years of a life sentence, he was pardoned by the governor. This was a posthumous insult to George Haight, who became the first Michigan Department of Corrections prison employee killed in the line of duty.

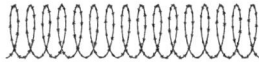

Some officers charge into danger, and others run away. It is not good to work alongside either kind because they are both dangerous. In 9, 10, and 11 Buildings, four CMAs and one RN were assigned to each unit on each shift. When I first started in the prison system, I was assigned to work in all three buildings. I would immediately size up the other three officers for their mental and physical capabilities. I was not being judgmental; I needed to know what kind of backup I had if I got into a difficult situation. I felt confident with CMAs Bower and Millett, the regular officers on 10-2-East. All officers had rotating days off, so we had a core group that overlapped, and occasionally we would be joined by CMA Mavis or someone else who was not assigned to a specific unit.

In those days, Mavis was our weak link. He was an unreliable, unprofessional, sluggish and sloppy coward who made the unit unsafe whenever he worked. He came in late, unshowered, in a wrinkled uniform, with his pants haphazardly stapled at the bottom instead of hemmed and his shoes looking like he had just strolled through a pigpen.

While Bower and I were off the unit one evening, Mavis and Goslin, a Red Tag assigned to him, were left behind on 10-2-East to watch the fort. The assumption was that the block would be safe since all but one inmate of the unit was in the chow hall. CMA Mavis and Goslin were sitting in the office when a 6' 6" inmate named Gordy walked up the hallway to use the drinking fountain outside the office door. Goslin, a 5' 8" 20-year-old redhead, jumped out of his chair, opened the door, and hollered at inmate Gordy, "Clear the hallway! The unit is closed!"

As the words left Goslin's mouth, inmate Gordy turned, grabbed the office door, and stepped inside. He immediately began to pummel Goslin, punching him in the face numerous times before tossing him like a ragdoll into the med cart. CMA Mavis took off in the other direction, toward 10-2-West; Gordy exited the office and returned to his cell as if nothing had happened.

Minutes later, I returned to the unit and saw that Goslin was a bloody mess. His nose and mouth were bleeding, his shirt was ripped, and the room was in disarray. Goslin was distressed and understandably in shock.

Looking into the connected 10-2-West office, I spotted CMA Mavis standing there. He looked like his usual unkempt self, and it appeared that he had not participated in the altercation. I was right—he had run away. When Mavis came wandering back to our unit office, I asked him, "What happened here?"

Mavis said, "I froze. Haven't you ever froze?"

I said, "No, not when a convict is beating a fellow officer next to me. Why do you think we're called guards? Our job is to protect others, especially when a Red or Green Tag is involved. The sergeant assigned the Red Tag to you to protect and train him. He is always supposed to be at arm's length. Instead, you ran to another unit while he was being pounded. You'll have some explaining to do on your Critical Incident Report."

Mavis allowed the Red Tag to make a handful of mistakes that resulted in him getting his face redecorated. CMA Goslin agitated a huge inmate he knew nothing about, then opened the door when the convict was close enough to grab it. He did not consider that the unit was half-staffed—the other two officers (Bower and I) were down in the basement in the chow hall.

If I had seen Gordy out, I would have wondered why he was not down at chow with the rest of the inmates and why he was walking up the hallway for a drink when he knew the unit was closed. There were a lot of red flags flying.

Perhaps inmate Gordy figured the cocksure Red Tag would check him (as he did) and be foolish enough to open the door. Unfortunately, Goslin must not have known that Officer Mavis was an inept chicken who would not be backing him up. These patients were insane but not necessarily stupid. I wonder if Gordy's assault was premeditated, a reaction to something Goslin said or did earlier in the shift. The psychiatrist ordered that Gordy be shipped back to 11 Building, where he was closely monitored, and his medications were increased.

I'm curious if Mavis still works for the department; in any case, his name and reputation were kaput. The incident with inmate Gordy was not the first time Mavis ran in the opposite direction when his assistance was needed. He was known to leave behind a trail of calamities wherever he was assigned. It was usually not what he did, but what he did not do that caused problems. Mavis could have been written up for inattention to duty and behavior unbecoming an officer. The sergeant who assigned the Red Tag to an officer as inept as Mavis should also have been questioned about the incident.

Officers on the unit need to be aware of which inmates are not going down to chow with the rest of the unit. They must consider who is assigned a Red Tag and whether they are competent. Just because most inmates are not on the unit does not mean it is secure.

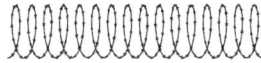

In prison, kitchens are dangerous places for multiple reasons. They are the laboratories where inmates concoct homemade libations, use tools that could be employed as weapons, and have access to open fires and scalding water. The chow halls also present potential hazards. Almost the entire prison population passes through the main chow hall doors three times a day, giving them plenty of chances to pass drugs and weapons and start confrontations. Even in 9, 10, and 11 Buildings' smaller chow halls, it was not unusual for fights to break out.

If an inmate wants to get drunk, he makes a batch of spud juice, the favored prison beverage. Convicts obtain the ingredients to make this potent potable from the prison's kitchens and gardens. The name of this blend derives from the original main ingredient—potatoes—but inmates more commonly use apples, oranges, raisins, bananas, and fruit juices. If you combine one or more of these with sugar and water and wait long enough, you will have spud juice, also known simply as spud.

Heat, along with the sugar, speeds up the fermentation process. An inmate will cut off an electrical cord from a lamp or small appliance, strip the wires, drop the exposed wires into the juice, and plug the other end into an outlet to heat the liquid. This type of altered electrical cord is known as a "stinger." The same device allows inmates to light cigarettes without matches by touching the wires together.

Fruits and juices are readily available to kitchen workers; they sometimes sell individual ingredients or finished products to other inmates.

Those who do not work in the kitchen try to hoard the juice, fruit, and sugar they smuggle out of the chow hall to concoct a batch.

When shaking down inmates' cells or cubes, I sometimes found spud in plastic bags at the bottom of an inmate's wastebasket, concealed by trash. Because no one wants to dig through someone else's garbage, one could pick up the wastebasket and judge if there was spud inside by its weight. However, that does not eliminate the presence of drugs or weapons. Once, I found spud in an inmate's dirty laundry bag—and the idea of sifting through smelly socks and soiled underwear was not appealing. In both cases, the procedure in general population prisons is to dump garbage or dirty laundry, remove prohibited items, fill out a contraband-removal slip, and write the appropriate tickets.

Inmates also hide spud in the kitchen, where they have the ingredients, containers, and equipment to heat the juice. When officers find spud in the kitchen but do not know who it belongs to, they remove it.

On one Independence Day weekend, an inmate at Pugsley Correctional Facility was visibly and audibly drunk. The sergeant told him, "Go press your bunk [lie down] and sleep it off." After that, the inmate foolishly punched him in the face. The captain arrived soon after, and the inmate spat in his face. As a result, the prisoner had tickets for substance abuse, possession of contraband, and two assaults on staff. He was placed in segregation for this litany of offenses and sentenced to serve more time for his assaults. Of course, he could have just slept it off, as the sergeant suggested. Instead, because of his inability to follow directions and his opposition to authority, he will probably max out—serve the entire term of his sentence.

As in the real world, getting intoxicated is very popular around the holidays. So, on Christmas, New Year's Eve, Memorial Day, and Independence Day, inmates may be stumbling around, throwing up, or acting foolishly.

On Memorial Day weekend in 1979, three Jackson inmates found what they thought was two gallons of alcohol in the special activities director's office. They stole the liquid, mixed it with Hi-C, and sold the concoction in the yard. The fluid turned out to be an alcohol-based toxic cleaner for the office printer. Forty-two inmates were hospitalized, including a handful who suffered neurological damage, and one died.

Although the container was marked with a skull and crossbones, the inmates proceeded with their spud-making. The three mixologists had to be segregated and transferred to another prison to prevent them from being butchered in the yard.

Inmate Redburn, where I was working, wanted to catch a buzz. He purchased a gallon and a half of spud juice. To expedite the fermentation process, the chemist who brewed the batch should have informed Redburn that he had added excessive sugar before selling him the juice. Rather than just tasting the juice, waiting for a special occasion, or sharing the spud with friends, Redburn immediately drank the entire jug and went to bed.

I hypothesize that, during the night, Redburn's body heat sped up the fermentation process because when he awoke, he could not walk or talk coherently. A unit officer called Healthcare to report Redburn's inability to function. Healthcare examined and shipped him to the Traverse City hospital, thinking he may have suffered a stroke. Redburn did not inform prison or hospital staff that he chugged a massive amount of spud because he did not want to catch a substance abuse ticket. I do not know what treatment he received in the hospital. In my class, I observed him experiencing a loss of reading comprehension and demonstrating recall problems. He may have died of alcohol poisoning if not treated, but he was willing to take that chance for a massive buzz.

Confrontations in the chow hall jump off for a variety of reasons. Just as in the real world outside the walls, when people are hungry, they become ornery. The victim can get nasty if another inmate tries to steal or mess with someone else's food. Also, when a prisoner tries to take extra food from the chow line and an officer catches him and removes it, the prisoner gets upset.

After they announced the Riverside psych units were going to close, I got an interview at Ionia Maximum Security Prison for a CO position. I was given a hypothetical scenario: "In the chow hall, an inmate takes two milks rather than the one allotted. The other inmates notice. As the kitchen officer, what would you do?"

I do not believe there was a cut-and-dried answer to this question. I replied that it is essential to consider variables, like the size and personality of the inmate taking the extra milk. Another factor is the relationship between the inmate and the kitchen officer and what other inmates are in the chow hall. If an officer says, "One per inmate," the inmate might return the milk. On the other hand, he might scream, "Fuck you, bitch! What are you going to do about it?" Now, there is a problem.

The interviewer claimed there was indeed a correct answer. He said that if the officer waits until the inmate is through with chow and leaves the chow hall, he can call the inmate aside and remind him of the one-milk rule. This way, both parties can save face—the officer has not ignored the infraction, and the inmate has been warned.

The chow halls at older facilities like Riverside had tables and chairs that could be flipped over and broken up, and the legs could be used as weapons. The newer facilities have round stainless-steel tables bolted to the floor, with four stools welded to each table. This design is much safer because the table and chairs are not going anywhere; also, there cannot be more than four prisoners seated at each table.

Timing is essential when calling each unit to chow because there must be as many seats as inmates. If a rookie kitchen officer calls the next unit too soon, there will be a need for more available seating. The officer may need to rush the seated inmates out before they are finished eating. Now, the kitchen officer has upset both the incoming and out-going prisoners. Another potential problem with a shortage of seats is that inmates may be forced to sit next to someone of another race or religion or affiliated with a rival gang; all are a recipe for trouble.

Like school cafeterias, prison chow halls are often hothouses for teasing and bullying. The problems become even more acute and complex with mentally and emotionally disturbed prisoners. It does not take much to push an unstable inmate over the edge: just a word, glance, gesture, or gang sign can do the trick.

Most officers eat in chow halls along with the inmates; when we hear a tray hit the floor, it might mean that a fight is breaking out. I grew so accustomed to jumping to my feet when I heard a loud noise in prison that, when I dined in a restaurant in the real world and heard a server drop a dish or a busser set down a bus tub too hard, I would embarrass myself by hopping to my feet.

This was not the only situation where I had trouble separating how I responded in prison from how I reacted in the real world. When two people got in each other's faces in a bar, I would jump between them and push them apart. The bouncer would arrive and say, "Hey, I got this!" I would return to reality and think, *Yeah, what am I doing? I'm not getting paid for this; it's none of my business.* Before I started working in prison, breaking up a bar fight would never have occurred to me.

The ones who get loud are saying, *Help! Send over somebody because we're both scared and don't want to fight!* But when an inmate truly wants to hurt someone, he will. He does not yell or draw attention to himself before he sticks his victim with a shank or hits them with a lock-in-a-sock. He does the deed, moves on quickly, and ditches the weapon. His goals are to inflict pain and avoid catching another bit or going to the Hole. Silence is not always a good thing.

Working as the 10 Building kitchen officer was a great experience for me. It allowed me to get to know the officers from the four 10 Building units and supervise inmates from the general population. I had worked in at least a half-dozen restaurants, but until I started my position as 10 Building kitchen officer, I had never set foot in a prison's main kitchen. There, I saw how the kitchen workers, inmates, and staff cranked out meals for about 1,500 thrice daily.

CHAPTER 10

A Couple of Heavy Hitters

Wilson and Womack

"It's not whether you get knocked down,
it's whether you get up."
—Vince Lombardi

It was always disappointing when you came to work and were assigned to sit on a one-on-one. This meant four hours of sitting in a chair in front of an irritated inmate's cell, with the door open and the inmate unrestrained, and neither of you wanted to be in that position. I had a horrible feeling about a certain one-on-one I was assigned to for several reasons. First, because it was with inmate Wilson. I knew him because he was previously locked in 11 when I worked there. The psychiatrist thought he could handle more freedom and placed him in 10-2-East. Every day, Wilson walked 20 miles in his cell. He did abdominal crunches (50 to a set) and pumped off hundreds of upside-down pushups with his hands on the ground and his feet on the wall. When he was in 11, he jumped over the picnic table and trash barrels in the small yard as part of his personal conditioning program. At 5' 6" and 160 pounds, he was one compact muscle mass, a powder keg ready to detonate.

There were some other reasons for my disappointment in this assignment. Wilson was not four-pointed or restrained in any way, and his cell was at the far end of the hallway. If an inmate is on suicide watch or is presumed to be a danger to others, he should be in underwear only, in a seclusion room close to the office, not at the far end of the hall, especially if he has a violent record like Wilson's. Ignoring this protocol was the psychiatrist's wrong decision.

I was upset, nervous, and not thinking straight, because when sitting in a chair outside Wilson's door, I started by asking, "What are you in for?"

Wilson unfolded his tale. "I found out my girlfriend cheated on me, and I had a plan for the little bitch. So, I take her for a ride in the country and tell her we'll have a romantic picnic. I parked on a two-track in a field near some woods in the middle of nowhere."

Wilson told me the rest of his story with lip-smacking relish. When he got out of his car and opened the passenger door for his girlfriend, she placed her hand over the top of the open door. He kicked the door shut and watched the woman's face as her fingers were crushed between the roof and the door frame. Then he decided to snap her fingers backward one at a time as she sat there, helpless. He watched her eyes roll back in her head, and her eyelids flutter. Then he walked around to the trunk, where he had stowed his weapons of choice: a claw hammer, a barbeque fork, and a crowbar.

Wilson enjoyed my discomfort as I listened to his detailed account of the attack. I said, "Wilson, I don't want to hear anymore." But that did not stop him.

With an unnerving smile, he continued giving me the gory details and said, "She asked for it like you asked to hear my story."

I had heard more than enough, but I could not leave without a replacement, so I waved to the officer at the far end of the hall and shouted, "I need a bathroom break!" CMA Bard came down the hall to relieve me, and my "bathroom break" lasted for the rest of the shift. I was distressed by Wilson's tale and disturbed by how much he liked telling it. I wanted to confirm the veracity of his story by checking his file, which proved to be the most terrifying I had ever encountered.

Wilson was a thrill-seeker, someone who got immense satisfaction from the suffering of his victims. He enjoyed making people tremble with fear, seeing them cringe, and hurting them until they cried out in pain. Inmate Wilson was trying to terrify me as I sat in the chair in front of his cell—and it was working. I thought, *Another murder would not affect his life sentence without parole, and I'm sure he'd enjoy the experience.* Bailing out when I did may have saved my life, because Wilson seemed to be getting more excited as his ugly story progressed.

My heart was still pounding as I sat in the office and read through Wilson's file. I thought about what a colossal mistake I had made. I knew I was vulnerable at the far end of the hall with this dangerously strong inmate. If I was interested in his offense, why not pull his file rather than risk my life by asking a stupid question?

⦚⦚⦚⦚⦚⦚⦚⦚⦚⦚⦚⦚⦚⦚⦚⦚⦚⦚

CMA Karlsson was an enormous, blond, Viking-looking man who stood 6′ 8″ and weighed 350 pounds; he was one of the largest officers I have ever seen. I have met some who were taller but did not have such an immense frame. Yet, despite his intimidating appearance, he was a gentle giant who treated inmates and staff respectfully.

One day, as Karlsson was doing hall checks in 10-2-East, inmate Wilson stood behind his cell door, waiting. When Karlsson peered into Wilson's cell, the inmate shot out like a cannonball, sucker-punching him in the temple and knocking him out cold. CMA Karlsson fell like a sequoia, and Wilson hopped on top of him and beat him savagely.

Fortunately, inmate Holmes, a large, muscle-bound man who locked next door, saw the attack. He jumped on Wilson, knocking him off of Karlsson, and held him until several CMAs cuffed Wilson and stuffed him in the seclusion room.

Officer Karlsson was still unconscious when the EMTs arrived. They needed assistance loading his mighty mass onto the gurney. When Karlsson returned to work a month later, he told us, "The doctor said that if my skull weren't four times as thick as a normal human's, I'd be dead." I thought, *That could have been me before I bailed on the one-on-one.*

I was not surprised by the power of Wilson's punch; I had seen him work out for hours on end. I talked to several inmates at different facilities who chiseled their physiques, and they said the key to carving their bodies was not the weight but the number of repetitions.

Previously, as we shot a game of pool, Wilson told me his father had been a Marine drill sergeant who had been unable to give up his military mindset after he left the service. He used to force his sons to suffer through brutal workouts and box each other daily. Because his brother was older, larger, and stronger, Wilson would suffer severe beatings from him. This may explain Wilson's obsession with working out and his wanting to attack those who were larger.

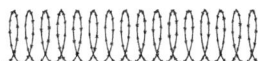

Shift change is a window that allows inmates to get away with something. It is when the officers are busy exchanging equipment with their successors; it is also when the outgoing shift is supposed to inform the next shift about any unusual incidents. I would get frustrated when something crazy happened on my shift without the staff on the previous one letting me know there had been indicators of trouble brewing.

One afternoon, I received my equipment from a first shift officer and began to conduct my first hall check. All inmates must be in their cells at shift change and count time. As I walked down the hall, I thought about the convict from I-Max smashing CMA Dintz's nose, inmate Edwards snapping Officer Pittman's neck with his first punch, and inmate Wilson knocking out Officer Karlsson. Officer Dintz and Pittman had a severe lack of judgment before being assaulted, but Karlsson was just making his rounds.

I missed the cell doors in 11 Building, which automatically locked when they were shut; here in 10, the patients could let themselves in and out, which made for more freedom for them but potentially more problems for us. I also thought about Karlsson's skull being four times thicker than mine. I was thinking about all these things because I was approaching inmate Wilson's door halfway down the hall on the right.

When I arrived at his cell, the door was closed, and a towel covered his window. This was a bad sign because inmates were not allowed to cover their windows. Officers need to be able to look inside to verify that the prisoner is present and alive.

I heard a huge fart and chuckled, thinking, *He's alive.* But as I reached the end of the hall, I contemplated the towel. *Prisoners might cover their*

windows for various reasons: Maybe Wilson is sitting on the toilet, mas-
turbating, smoking, mutilating his body, or…hanging himself! Hanging?
Hanging could make him lose control of his bodily functions.

I walked swiftly back toward Wilson's cell, banged on the door, and
said, "Wilson! Don't play games." There was nothing—not a sound.

I shouted, "Wilson, take that towel off your window!" Still nothing.
My heart raced, and I felt nauseous.

I had no choice. I keyed the door, stepped inside, and saw him swinging like inmate Hogan. I looked up at Wilson's pale, blue-gray face, then
exited his cell. Starting up the hall, I hollered, "I got one swinging! I
need help!"

CMAs Bower and Millett came running, and we cut him down and
laid him on the floor in the hallway. I opened the first-aid kit on my belt,
donned my latex gloves, and placed the plastic CPR mask over Wilson's
nose and mouth. I started blowing breaths into the mask, and Millett
began the compressions. I thought, *Wilson is a goner. Judging by his pallor,*
he is not coming back to this world. Healthcare soon relieved us, and the
paramedics continued CPR as they took Wilson away.

Walking up the hall, I told Bower, "It seems silly to do CPR when
you know they're gone."

Bower shot me a glance of disbelief and said, "You never know. We
always do CPR. I don't care if the prisoner is decapitated. Sometimes,
they might need a jump-start; the first few minutes are critical. Our
inmates never die on state property—maybe in the ambulance on
Riverside Drive or at the hospital, but not on our unit, on our shift,
in our hands. The powers that be will ask if you attempted CPR, and
your answer *better* be yes."

About a week after Wilson hung himself, I sat in the office with
CMA Bower. We saw a huge male nurse pushing an inmate slumped
over in a wheelchair. Next to them was our unit nurse, Peggy Garvey.

I asked Bower, "Who's in the wheelchair? It can't be Wilson!"

Bower replied, "You never know. I guess it got a little hot down there.
Maybe Wilson and Louis Cyphre didn't hit it off so well; they're too
much alike."

Bower surprised me with his reference to the 1987 movie *Angel*
Heart, where private detective Harry Angel, played by Mickey Rourke,

is hired by Louis Cyphre (a sound-alike moniker for Lucifer), played by Robert De Niro. *Angel Heart* was packed with symbolism and twists. I had yet to talk to anyone who had seen it, which was not a big surprise because it did not quite break even at the box office.

I looked at the nurse and asked, "How did he survive that one?"

"He wouldn't have if he didn't work out daily," she said. She told me that as the paramedics loaded Wilson into the ambulance, he took a big breath of air when they shifted his head. She thought that he may have lost too much oxygen because he was very subdued, but she, like me, never thought we would see him again.

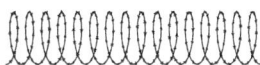

CMA Bower came from a long line of well-respected corrections officers. I still see him walking down the hall, twirling his keys in circles. He reminded me of the '60s "Keep on Truckin'" comics character, leaning back with a big ol' smile and size-12 boots kicking out before him. He was a ginger hard-body with a pockmarked face and a Fu Manchu mustache.

Bower was the alpha male of 10 Building and was respected by everyone at Riverside. He possessed a Buddha-like air of infinite wisdom. He made snap decisions prudently; prison is not where an officer can leisurely ponder the options. Bower, like many of the officers from Ionia, started working in the prison system at age 18. When I met him, he already had 12 years in. In contrast, I started with the department at 33 and was beginning my fourth year.

Bower had heard stories from his grandfathers, father, uncles, aunts, cousins, and school chums, who all worked in the system. Ionia, like Jackson, is a longtime prison town, so there was over a century's worth of tales to be told. In addition to being highly intelligent, Bower grew up so immersed in the culture that, at 30, he was completely comfortable and highly efficient behind the walls.

CMA Millett was small but strong. With his coke-bottle glasses, he resembled an out-of-place computer programmer. He was usually in Bower's shadow, chuckling at his jokes like a mini-Ed McMahon to his colleague Johnny Carson. Millett's reaction to Bower's humor led

Bower to more outrageous words and actions. Bower knew which staff members were the most avid gossips. For his entertainment, he would feed them fabricated scandalous rumors about inmates and staff because he wanted to see how far his ridiculous inventions would fly—and how much they would mutate.

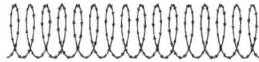

〰〰〰〰〰〰〰〰〰

Working on 10-2-East at Riverside, I watched a particular inmate's intensive workout for a few minutes almost daily. On my way down to the chow hall for my kitchen officer assignment, I would stop on the second-floor landing and look out the window. From there, I could see the handball court—close to my vantage point, at the south end of the oval asphalt track—and the softball field in the middle.

From this viewpoint, I saw a chiseled general population inmate athlete jogging around the track, throwing jabs, ducking, bobbing, and weaving as he ran forward and backward. He would drop to the ground every 25 yards to do sets of 25 push-ups. Next, he did a couple of hundred crunches on the handball court, where he set up an obstacle course of plastic pop bottles. He zigged and zagged his way through the bottles, punching the air, twisting and turning—all without knocking over a single pop bottle, as graceful as a ballerina. Although I never saw him fight, I imagined that he would have been an outstanding boxer.

One day, I was checking out his routine when Officer Bower walked onto the landing. I asked, "Have you ever watched this guy's workout?"

"Yeah," he said, "back in the day, he was on track to be the next world heavyweight champion."

Thinking he was kidding, I said, "Yeah, right."

Bower said, "I'm serious. That's Ricky Womack, out of Detroit. He trained at the Kronk Gym, and as an amateur beat the world champion, Evander Holyfield, twice, right before Holyfield turned pro in '84. Howard Cosell called him 'Wonderful Womack' and predicted he would be competing in the '84 Olympics."

"That's amazing," I said.

Bower added, "He caught a 12- to 25-year bit for armed robbery.

Before he messed up, he fought at the Trump Hotel in Atlantic City, the Tropicana and Caesars Palace in Vegas, and Madison Square Garden. Even after Holyfield took the world heavyweight championship, he said Womack was the real deal. He knew that the title could have easily gone to him.

"Kronk set him up with a rent-free condo. He signed a two-year training contract with the gym for $150,000. Womack didn't want for anything. But in December '85, he walked into a video store in Redford Township, pulled out a 9mm, grabbed some videotapes, took a couple of hundred bucks from the till, pistol-whipped the female clerk for no reason, and walked out. Maybe the jerk should've been the champ, but he didn't deserve it."

"What an idiot," I said. "Is that why he's here?"

"Partially. I think he got away with that one, because he was still on the streets in January when he went to rob another video store in the same neighborhood. This time a customer walked in during the act, and Womack freaked out. He shot the customer and ran out, leaving his car keys on the counter, so he escaped on foot instead of driving away. The police found his wallet on the seat of his car, parked in front of the store. He must have taken too many punches to the head."

"Sounds like he deserves to be here, not sitting on top of the world with the heavyweight title," I said.

Ricky Womack's home life was filled with violence. His father beat his mother and, according to rumor, also murdered his two-year-old son. Later, during an armed robbery, his father was murdered, and Ricky was placed in a foster home. One of these traumatic events could have been enough to cause serious repercussions; together, they may have pushed him over to the dark side.

Womack was released from prison in 2000, six years after Bower told me about him. His tenacious training paid off once he hit the streets—he won his next four fights.

One of the closest people to Ricky was his twin brother, Mickey, who said that, after prison, Ricky could not adjust back into society. Rick Griffin, Womack's trainer, agreed: "Those 16 years [in prison] made it hard for him to come home."

At his final fight in Auburn Hills, Ricky was upset with his performance and the poor turnout. He told his doctor that he was contemplating suicide. Less than two months later, he borrowed a gun from his nephew and allegedly threatened his wife. On January 19, 2002, Ricky Womack sat down on the couch in his basement apartment, put the gun to his head, and pulled the trigger to end his life. If Womack had received counseling and been placed on proper medication to keep his act together, the history of boxing could have been forever changed.

Inmates Wilson and Womack came from families with extremely violent fathers. After taking out their pent-up aggression on others, they became so depressed they both tried to end their own lives. This phenomenon has become common in our society today. However, some take it to another level. Individuals who have been the target of bullies let their frustration build, become obsessed with revenge, and unleash their wrath upon innocent people.

II:
CORRECTIONS OFFICER AT MID MICHIGAN CORRECTIONAL FACILITY

CHAPTER 11

New Prison, New Position

Middle of the Mitten

*"You're always one decision away from
a totally different life."*
—Mark Batterson

After working at Riverside for about five years, those of us working as CMAs were informed that we needed to seek employment at another facility. The state was moving the Riverside psych patients to the Forensic Center in Ypsilanti, so we could move there or apply as COs at other prisons with openings. Unfortunately, most available jobs then were either in the densely populated Detroit area or in Michigan's desolate Upper Peninsula, and neither choice appealed to me.

One day, we were informed that the deputy warden (DW) and assistant deputy warden (ADW) from a Level I prison in St. Louis were coming to our facility to interview officers onsite. All we needed to do was sign up for an interview and walk over to the Administration Building when it was our turn.

The interview was a cakewalk, and 21 Riverside officers were selected to work at the Mid-Michigan Correctional Facility. Most of the officers already working at Mid-Michigan had about five years in the system, and I was shy of that. I could work second or third shift, but a first shift job was not an option.

My assignments at Mid-Michigan, a general population Level I prison, were quite different from my routine as a CMA at Riverside. There would be no more shooting pool or playing Scrabble. I could now write tickets so that inmates would see consequences for negative actions. In GP, writing tickets was the primary means of control over inmates. I had developed my communications skills at Riverside to the point that I realized I rarely needed to write a ticket at Mid-Michigan.

My move from the psychiatric wards was not only a change for me. Twenty-one new officers coming aboard had to alter the dynamics of the entire facility. The inmates were affected by new authority figures telling them what to do and how to do it, and staff had to adjust to working with all the new officers.

During my first week, it sunk in how dangerous the environment at Riverside had been. I asked a CO if they had many critical incidents, and he replied, "An old man in Echo Unit had a heart attack just last week." I did not tell him that I was thinking more along the lines of an inmate being shanked for selling an eight-ball of cocaine and then not delivering it.

It was not long before I learned that Riverside was the ultimate training ground for the rest of my prison career. I would probably not be exposed to such extremely violent individuals or situations. Even the notorious I-Max, with its highly volatile Level VI inmates, was no match for Riverside because I-Max inmates were locked up almost all the time. In contrast, Riverside had criminally insane Level IV, V, and VI inmates freely roaming around 11 Building, and with their liberty came many more opportunities for trouble.

At Riverside, I learned a lot about the criminally insane, but I still had much to learn about the various CO assignments in general population. As a CMA, I reported to a specific unit and worked there for eight hours, five days a week.

At first, I worked on numerous assignments around the prison complex in St. Louis. When a facility receives new hires, the brass places them in different positions and shuffles them around to find where they will fit best.

At Mid-Michigan, I was sometimes assigned to drive the area reconnaissance vehicle (ARV) around the prison's perimeter for four hours.

The drivers were instructed to look for anything unusual around the prison grounds, such as any vehicle or people who looked suspicious or were not authorized to be on prison property. The ARV was equipped with a shotgun, and the officer was armed with a .38 revolver.

Most of the time, the position is mundane, but a driver never knows what might happen. For example, on July 15, 2010, three convicted murderers in Kinross Correctional Facility in the U.P. (Upper Peninsula) jumped into a semitruck inside the prison for delivery and floored it toward the fence. The actual truck driver arrived on the scene just as they crashed through. The officer ordered them to stop, and he shot and killed one of them when they did not. The other two inmates stopped the vehicle, got out, and laid on the ground.

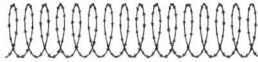

The St. Louis prison facilities are in Gratiot County, smack dab in the middle of the Michigan mitten. Glaciers flattened the area by scraping the land away from the Saginaw Valley. This allowed the winter winds to whip across the region without mercy. Today, the county's farmers have allowed the electric company to place giant windmills on their properties in exchange for large sums of money.

The next town west of St. Louis is Alma, Michigan. I once talked to an Alma College professor who claimed that Gratiot County is one of the flattest and most fertile places on earth, which is why it is up to its ears in corn, not to mention its bounty of soybeans, navy beans, and sugar beets. Gratiot County is also known among hunters for its large, crop-munching deer, which the local farmers love to shoot to get even with the scoundrels for destroying their crops. I am told that these deer yield tastier venison than the gamey ones dwelling in the woods and swamplands. Many of the officers in St. Louis grew up on the farms in the surrounding area.

When I first came to Mid-Michigan, I occasionally worked the prison yard. One blustery winter night, I walked across the yard with the wind chill registering 50 below. Even with my Elmer Fudd-style hat flaps down, turtleneck sweater on, coat collar up, and scarf over my nose and mouth, I still developed an ice-cream headache, and I sought refuge in the yard's guard shack to defrost for a while.

When assigned to the yard, two officers would check the sensors on the perimeter fence, one from the inside and the other from the outside. I would sometimes have to trudge through crotch-high snowdrifts while pounding the fence with a steel bar, the Control Center officer confirming that the sensors were activated each time the fence was hit. We were also required to check all the buildings' windows and doors. It was necessary to wear insulated gloves, socks, and boots to prevent the loss of fingers and toes to frostbite. I kept thermal underwear and snow pants in a locker in case the sergeant unexpectedly placed me on yard duty in the winter.

Yard officers also performed various other duties. At count time, we picked up the count slips from each unit and the kitchen and delivered them to the Control Center. The C.C. officer would tally the count sheets to ensure they matched the current number of convicts. We also helped unit officers pass out store orders, assisted kitchen officers with running the chow lines, and supervised the inmates who cut grass or shoveled snow.

A yard officer must respond to problems anywhere on the prison grounds. If yard officers hear "Fight on Charlie Unit," they best beat feet in that direction because the regular unit officers in other buildings cannot abandon their posts to assist. Yard officers are usually the outdoor type, in good physical shape because they may have to run several hundred yards, tackle convicts, and de-escalate volatile situations. I believe that yard officers are the backbone of every correctional facility.

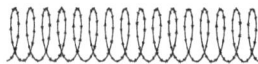

◊◊◊◊◊◊◊◊◊◊◊◊◊◊◊◊◊

After I had been bounced around between the Control Center, the area reconnaissance vehicle, the yard, and various units, the brass finally made me a regular unit officer on Charlie Unit—a position I had been hoping for. I liked knowing where I was going and what I would be doing.

One warm midsummer night, while working my regular assignment on third shift in Charlie Unit, I looked down the hallway and noticed a short, tanned inmate with shoulder-length hair who I did not recognize. I did not know where he locked, so I strolled down the block to see which cube and bunk he had been placed in. The unit rules stated that a convict was not to venture beyond his "area of control," in this case beyond his cube down the hallway.

When I returned to the office and grabbed the unit count board, I knew that this inmate was defiantly venturing beyond the area of his control—i.e., where his bunk was located—thus qualifying for a major out of place ticket.

I saw that he had an older, lower prisoner number, which meant he had been incarcerated for some years or had returned to prison. In either case, he would know that he was committing an infraction.

I saw the prisoner's name was Hester and remembered I attended middle school in Muskegon, Michigan, with a kid of the same name. I picked up inmate Hester's institutional file and saw that he was from Muskegon and was born in 1956, which is also my birth year. He was the same Charles Hester from my seventh-grade gym class at Orchard View Middle School. Back then, Hester was a screwup whom Coach Becker punished severely and regularly. When Hester would not keep up with the calisthenics or be late for gym class, Coach Becker would give him a choice of the canoe paddle or the Zot gun. The Zot gun was a towel reinforced with duct tape on the end and snapped at the subject's butt or legs after his shower. Chuck was still breaking the rules and getting into trouble a quarter century later.

I waved over an inmate coming out of the bathroom and said, "Williams, could you please send your new cubie [roommate in an open-bay setting in Level I or II facilities], Hester, up here to talk to me?"

A few minutes later, Hester stood in my office doorway and asked, "Did you want to see me, officer?"

"Yes, Mr. Hester," I replied. "Give me your ID and take a seat. You have an older number, so you should know the rules around here."

"What did I do wrong, officer?"

"I'm sure you know. You were going beyond the area of your control, which you should realize is against the department's rules."

"But I..."

"But nothing," I interrupted. "You broke the unit rules and should be punished. I'm going to give you a choice."

"What kind of choice, sir?"

"Hester, would you like the canoe paddle or the Zot gun?"

Chuck Hester's jaw hit the floor, and he swallowed hard. Finally, he said, "Wha…wha…what did you say?"

"Do you want the canoe paddle or the Zot gun?" I repeated. "You know, just like the choice Becker gave you all the time back at Orchard View Middle School."

"How…how…how do you know about that?"

I picked up his file and said, "Mr. Hester, it's all here in your file—every time you were sent to the principal's office. Every time you whacked off thinking about Coach Becker hitting your ass with the canoe paddle or the Zot gun. We're watching you. Now, get out of here! And don't go beyond your area of control!" I wanted Hester to know I was watching him and knew that he had broken the rules, but I would not do anything just then.

Hester sat there stunned, so I said, "Go on, git!"

Chuck stood up and left the office. That night, he walked by twice on his way to the unit bathroom. Both times he looked at me as if he were thinking, *Are you serious? How the hell could you know about Becker? And the canoe paddle and the Zot gun?*

The next time he passed, I motioned for him to come into the office and said, "Hester, do you have a small bladder? This is your third trip up here in a half-hour. And besides that, you need to stop trying to stare me down."

Hester said, "I just got to know: What's up? Why are you messin' with my head?"

"Hester, I checked you on going beyond your area of control because you broke the rules, and that's my job. So, what's the problem?"

"That's not what I'm talking about. How did you know about Becker hitting me with the canoe paddle and the Zot gun?"

"Oh, that. I was in your gym class at Orchard View. Now, go press your bunk, and don't be so paranoid. Here's your ID back."

A part of me wondered, *Why did I tell him? I should have let him believe his whole life was recorded and we had it in our files.* But I refrained from playing any psychological games. Sometimes, I am just Officer Friendly.

CHAPTER 12

Learning From the Past

Changes

*"Every murder strikes at the heart of civilization;
it is an attack on all mankind."*
—Elinore Denniston

The horrendous stories the instructors shared with us at the Corrections Academy needed to be told so employees would think about what could happen. One of our classes was called The Anatomy of a Setup. In the class, we learned to recognize when an inmate was trying to set up staff. We were also informed that we needed to be cautious any time there was a change that would affect the inmates. This is especially true when staff are new to a position.

Inmates detest change, so staff must carefully implement new or modified rules and procedures. The authority figure should explain to inmates why the changes are being made to ensure a smooth transition. An explanation of the changes can soften the blow for all involved.

Abrupt changes have proven to be deadly throughout the history of prisons. In 1921, T.B. Catlin was the new warden at the Marquette Branch Prison in Michigan's Upper Peninsula. When he took the helm, he removed some liberties the previous warden had granted to an inmate. This loss of privileges was the convict's motive for stabbing Warden Catlin on December 12 during a Sunday afternoon movie show in the auditorium. Deputy Warden Menhennett tried interceding and was mortally wounded in the altercation.

Thinking back, Officer Earl Demarse was stabbed to death in Marquette Prison's auditorium in 1975, just like Warden Catlin and DW Menhennett in 1921. In addition, Josephine McCallum met her demise in Jackson State Prison's auditorium in 1987. Marquette and Jackson are 100-plus years old, and the auditoriums in these prisons should be approached with caution.

After I terminated a tutor in my class at the St. Louis Level IV prison, he passed me in the yard and said, "You'll be sorry," casually but threateningly. Statements like these cannot be taken lightly in prison. I relayed the inmate's warning to the lieutenant on my shift, the officers on the inmate's unit, and the school officer. I do not know if they shook down his cell to look for a shank, restricted his movement, or transferred him to another prison, but I never saw him again.

The possibility of prison employees being murdered by inmates is a constant concern. In 1960, Bernard Fancher was the assistant athletic director at Jackson. On April 28, an inmate porter (janitor) whom Fancher employed in the gym was being loud and abusive toward other inmates, so Fancher warned him to keep his voice down and watch what he said. When the obnoxious porter did not change his behavior, Fancher terminated him.

Fancher was sitting at his desk a few days later when the ex-porter barged in, swearing and swinging a baseball bat. Fancher scrambled from behind his desk, tore out of his office, and ran from the building with the inmate hot on his heels. In his haste, Fancher eventually tripped over a wheelbarrow, giving the inmate an opening to pounce on him and plunge a shank into him 13 times. Bernard Fancher was pronounced dead on the scene.

In another tragic incident, Tammy Sperle was hired to operate the prison store at Huron Valley Men's Facility in Ypsilanti. Wanting to start fresh, she let the previous storekeeper's inmate helper go and hired somebody new. On February 5, 1996, she was found in the store, strangled to death by the terminated convict, who was in prison for armed robbery and attempted murder. Sperle left behind a husband and two sons.

Doris Taylor was a food service supervisor at the Thumb Correctional Facility. In 1998, she announced her plans to retire at the end of the year; she had worked for the department for 11 years. On May 17, a Level II inmate, who worked with her for four years and had no previous record of assaultive behavior or misconduct, stabbed her to death. He then slashed his throat. Authorities speculated that the inmate attempted suicide because he had difficulty accepting Taylor's retirement decision. He survived, was tried, and was sentenced to life.

Because of such tragic incidents involving employees, I considered how inmates might react to any changes I would initiate. I thought about Bernard Fancher and Tammy Sperle whenever I kicked a student out of class or terminated a tutor. I thought of Doris Taylor when I moved to a new prison or when I was about to retire. These good people were only trying to do their jobs when their lives were snuffed out years before their time.

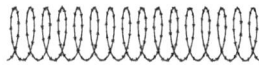

When I first came to Pugsley Correctional Facility, it seemed like a typical Level I prison. There were the usual power struggles among the ranks and petty snitching, but the prison took a significant downturn when there was a *change* in command. In addition, the governor decided to tax our state pensions, close some prisons, privatize the food service area, and generally make things worse for the prison system and its employees.

The state opened 20 new prisons when Michigan's incarceration rate shot up in the 1980s, some of which were built as temporary units. A pole barn-like design was used because it was less expensive, and the population was expected to return to its previous level. When this reduction failed to occur, the temporary structures remained in use.

The design of these units left the inmates exposed and at risk. In the hallways, the cubes had chest-high half-walls without doors, just openings that anyone could walk through. The cubes' back walls, running down the middle of the units, did not go all the way to the ceiling, allowing intruders to enter over the center wall from the other side.

The bigwigs decided to implement another *change* and wave the higher-level inmates down to lower-level prisons. By 2013, seven years into my stint at Pugsley, the prison was out of control, with an astronomical number of inmate-on-inmate assaults, especially on those incarcerated for Criminal Sexual Conduct (CSC). If an inmate suspected that another had been convicted of that, he would have someone on the outside verify the crime on the internet; if his suspicion was confirmed, an assault often followed. Of course, there were several other reasons for the vicious attacks.

Some offenders were attacked at night with a lock in a sock or at the end of a belt. Then there's the old Vaseline in a bowl of water, which is heated to a boil in a microwave and thrown on the face of a sleeping victim. The Vaseline makes the mixture hard to wipe off because it adheres to the skin like homemade napalm.

Because of the frequency of assaults at Pugsley, Traverse City 13th Circuit Court Judge Philip Rodgers Jr., ordered an investigation of the facility. Rodgers said, "This couldn't happen if the guards were doing their rounds." He requested that the facility install security cameras to record inmates' movements.

Toward the end of my prison employment, Pugsley flooded the Grand Traverse court dockets with assaults, sexual assaults, drug smuggling, and possessing dangerous weapons. Poor leadership contributed to the prison's violence problem. Inmates were getting paroled, and higher-level inmates were moved into lower-level prisons that could not handle them.

I witnessed the results of this misguided approach almost every morning when I passed by a large group of predominantly White inmates who were bandaged up, with broken noses and black-and-blue eyes, seated on the bench and the floor across from the Control Center. They refused to return to their units, where the primarily Black gang members would be waiting. There were only two seclusion rooms at Pugsley, so the two participants in one fight would fill them up; if another fight broke out or someone was assaulted, there was no safe place to put them other than the hallway across from the Control Center.

This new, bolder breed of inmates often traveled in packs at night like wolves. Sometimes, they came in the main entrance to the cube, but other times they would drop down over the middle walls which divided the unit in half. They would lower themselves onto a top bunk located up against the wall; this allowed them to travel from the front of the unit to the back and vice versa. By moving about this way, the inmates avoided being seen in the hallways by officers or the newly installed cameras.

Inmates were eligible four times a year to obtain a Securepak (food and hygiene items), a store order worth $85, higher than the usual $50 per month. When the Level I gangsters would find out who had a Securepak, it was armed robbery time. Usually, three masked robbers entered a cube wielding shanks. They would make the victim open his locker and order him to get under his bunk as they cleaned out the victim's locker. If the victim did not comply, he would be beaten down, stuck with shanks, or both.

The thieves increased the value of their take in several ways. For example, after stealing $10 worth of ingredients, the thief could make $32 by baking a batch of fudge and selling slices for $1 apiece. With a bag of coffee costing $3.62, the thieves would sell two spoons or shots for 50 cents, seriously increasing their profit margin. Like dope or tobacco, stolen consumable goods are often divided into smaller portions to increase revenue.

There were 63 recorded inmate-on-inmate assaults at Pugsley in 2013 and 64 in 2014, toward the end of my employment there. In 2015, after the department followed Judge Rodgers's advice to upgrade the security system, there were only 34 assaults. Unfortunately, the $2.3 million spent to make Pugsley safer was all for naught because the state turned around and closed the facility in 2016.

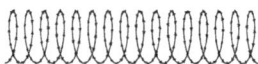

Inmate Beard was a tutor in one of my classes. I remember him saying, "Today's prison 'stickings' are different from back in the '80s and '90s. In those days, when someone got stuck, they were done. An inmate would slit someone's throat or stick him in the heart, and it was over. If an inmate knew he was in danger of being stuck, he would put layers of newspaper or magazines around his torso, under his prison blues, to protect himself."

I said, "They talked about those homemade vests in the Corrections Academy. The instructor said that Ted Bundy wore a vest made of magazines to protect himself in a Florida prison."

Beard said, "I bet he had to, since he killed about 30 girls."

I asked him to give me the lowdown on weapons in prison.

"I'm sure you know that there are shanks, and then there are shivs," Beard said. "A shank is a knife made from a piece of metal and is usually sharpened on cement. The handle might be wrapped in cloth and tied with string. When the prisons brought in metal detectors, shivs became popular because they were made of plastic or plexiglass and weren't recognized by the detectors. Tape was eventually labeled contraband because it was used to wrap the handles of shanks and shivs.

"Black gangs commonly use shanks and shivs on someone who has disrespected a member. Disrespect has to be avenged, so a group of gangbangers will swoop in on their target and stab him 20 or 30 times, though they try to avoid major arteries and organs. That way it's not life-threatening and they won't catch a murder case."

I had heard the expression "buck-50" several times but wanted to hear Beard's take on the term.

"Yeah, that's when a snitch is slashed from the mouth to the ear; it symbolizes the victim shooting off their mouth to someone's ear. When someone receives a buck-50, the scar announces to all that he's a snitch and'll be in for a rough ride. It's called a buck-50 because it takes about 150 stitches to sew it up, and there's no way to hide that."

"I don't remember hearing about the buck-50 or the Vaseline-and-water microwave concoction until recently."

Beard replied, "You're right. This place is getting out of control. If someone is being assaulted, ripped off, or threatened, he's gotta respond, or it keeps going back and forth. So, someone keeping his head down and trying to do his own time can get sucked into the madness. When a gang tries to recruit new members, and a new inmate doesn't want to join, the gang might pressure him for sex or money. If he says no—and he should—he has to be ready to defend himself."

"It'd be hard to defend yourself and not catch a fighting ticket," I said.

Beard shook his head and said, "But an inmate attacked by another has to strike back quickly and hard. There has to be closure, or you'll be attacked again. If one guy walks into another guy's cube or cell, slaps him around, destroys his property, or rips him off, he's gotta retaliate. If an inmate threatens to murder another, and they see each other daily, the threatened inmate must kill the other."

I asked Beard if there was some way to avoid being targeted.

"Some inmates pretend they're crazy," he said. "The trouble with going that route is that it's a full-time job. If an inmate pretends he's a bug, he'd better do it for his entire bit, or his enemies will be furious when they see through his game."

I said, "I learned years ago at Riverside that it's not a good idea for an inmate to let others know he has a weapon."

Beard nodded, saying, "If word gets out that someone has a weapon, other inmates will be gunning for him. If you have a shank or a shiv, you have to be ready to use it. And if you do, you might catch a new bit for murder. So, you're gonna need lookouts, diversions, and perfect timing. You may need to be friendly to your target so he lets down his guard before you stick him in a kill spot at the right time. Then you gotta get rid of the weapon."

Beard spoke from years of experience, many of them spent in Jackson, Marquette, and other high-level facilities, so his insights were authoritative and informative.

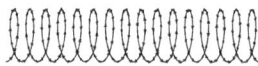

$$\text{\textit{QQQQQQQQQQQQQ}}$$

I asked a tutor who had 20 years of experience in the department, "How does an inmate fly under the radar and stay safe?"

Inmate Mabin said, "It's best if prisoners just do their own time, but that isn't always easy. Especially, with changes in management and the disposition of new convicts, it's good to live by the seven unwritten prison rules."

The seven rules Mabin recited to me:

1. Don't talk about religion.
2. Don't talk about politics.
3. Don't talk about race.
4. Stay away from young boys.

5. Don't gamble.
6. Don't get involved with drugs.
7. Do your own time. If you meddle in others' business, trouble will follow.

This list of rules will help those in prison but may also help folks in the "real world."

The same holds for implementing change. People do not like change and become upset when it is thrust upon them without an adequate explanation. Citizens want to feel they have a say in how things are run, whether in or out of prison.

CHAPTER 13

About Drugs

Coke in a Condom

"You don't have to look for drugs or violence in prison.
They follow each other, and one or the other
will eventually find you."
—Jack Myette

When I started working in the prisons in 1990, I heard inmates talking about an inmate named "White Boy Rick," a native of Detroit's east side. I learned they were referring to Richard Wershe Jr., who, at 14, was an informant for the FBI, responsible for the arrest of several drug lords. When the FBI was through with him, Wershe became a Detroit drug kingpin and was arrested in 1987 at 17. Authorities said that he was in the top echelon of local drug traffickers, which is why I heard his name come up often when prisoners were discussing the drug trade.

In 1988, Wershe was sentenced to life under the then-current law that mandated that penalty for anyone convicted of possessing 650 or more grams of cocaine. White Boy Rick was caught with over eight kilograms (8,000 grams or 17.6 pounds) of coke and thousands in cash. In 2002, changes in the 650-lifer law made Wershe eligible for parole the following year.

Wershe's childhood friend Robert James Ritchie, aka the musician

Kid Rock, testified on his behalf in 2003 before the Michigan Parole Board. The Kid did not have much juice with the state because White Boy Rick remained in the Oaks Correctional Facility in Manistee for another 14 years. He was paroled and out of the state's grip after 30 years in April 2017, making him the state's longest-serving nonviolent youth offender. After Wershe enjoyed a few short months of freedom, he was delivered to U.S. Marshals on another case and booked into the Florida prison system in September 2017. He was released in July 2020.

White Boy Rick was making a killing on the outside, and plenty of inmates and officers were supplementing their income inside. Prisons have a flourishing trade in tobacco, alcohol, and drugs (the most common being marijuana, cocaine, and heroin). Because visitors were shaken down, they and their inmate cohorts had to find creative ways to get the drugs inside the walls.

Some visitors smuggled the drugs into the facility in balloons or condoms. For example, a woman packs a condom with heroin and inserts it into her vagina. She enters the prison to see her boyfriend. The officer in the bubble gives the woman a thorough shakedown but is not required to strip-search her. She has a visit with her boyfriend, during which she squeezes the condom out of her vagina and into her panties. Toward the end of the visit, when the officer is not looking, she makes sure her hands are not in view of a security camera, retrieves the condom, and slips it into her mouth. She leans over to kiss her boyfriend goodbye, transferring the condom from her mouth to his. He swallows it and leaves the visiting room. He is strip-searched and subjected to a cavity check, but nothing is detected. The next day, he passes the condom and begins to deal the drug.

The officers on the prisoner's unit notice how popular he is becoming and that his locker is overflowing with new items from the store. The unit is frenzied with activity, and confrontations have sharply increased. Officers start pressing the unit snitches for information. The drug dealing prisoner and his customers observe the snitches being called up to Control Center, and they begin to plan their retaliation.

The prison's siren is blown, and the State Police bring in the drug-sniffing German Shepherds. Some drugs may be found, but not all, because there has been plenty of time for staff to tip the inmates off purposefully or inadvertently. Some inmates scramble to consume their drugs; others throw theirs over the fence, flush them down a toilet, or, more likely, conceal them in a place where they may not be detected. Once the shakedowns are over, the dogs depart, the game of hide-and-seek begins again, and the drug dealers take care of the snitches.

At a Level I facility, if an inmate is gate pass-eligible, he is permitted to be escorted outside the fence for public works projects. This provides the opportunity for someone on the outside to drop off drugs in a cemetery or park where the inmates are cleaning up. The accomplice may slit open a marked tennis ball and shove in an ounce or two of weed, then drop it by the tennis courts for the inmate to pick up and bring back to the facility. Before the inmate is brought inside and strip-searched, the convict tosses the ball over the fence, and his homeboy picks it up.

Visitors are sometimes busted and prosecuted for attempting to bring in drugs, but many are never caught. If gate-pass inmates or visitors smuggle drugs in, the inmates can make big money. Dirty officers have incentives to stop prisoners and visitors from smuggling; by doing so, they reduce the supply, increase demand, and can corner the market and capture the profits themselves.

At Pugsley, a female CO was conducting her unit shakedown when she found a suspicious substance belonging to a prisoner. She took the packet from the inmate, exited the housing unit, and headed across the yard toward the Control Center. The irate inmate ran outside, tackled her in the yard, and retrieved the packet. Then, two yard officers tackled him as the inmate started running back to his unit. The inmate fought fiercely with the officers before they could pry the packet from his grasp.

Testing revealed the substance to be heroin. The inmate's overreaction ensured that he would not be released anytime soon. If he had remained in his unit, he would have still caught tickets for substance abuse and possession of heroin, but not for the three assaults on staff. The offender had confirmed his use of hard drugs and the extent to which he would go to obtain them. He was the type of man who would max out of prison.

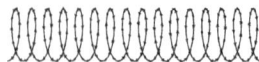

One day, the prison sent three inmates to the hospital because they overdosed on an unknown substance. One of them was freaking out so badly that, when he was triaged, he had to be four-pointed and sent to an acute-care psychiatric facility. The culprit was the mind-altering jimsonweed, a plant in the nightshade family known as loco weed, moon-flower, devil's trumpet, and devil's weed. Overconsumption of this plant can be fatal. The weed had been growing on the prison grounds, possibly naturally. The inmates were chewing the seeds and boiling the leaves to brew a hallucinogenic tea. After employees discovered jimsonweed was responsible, the plants were removed from the property.

Inmate Smallwood, a student in my class, was one of the nightshade experimentalists. After returning from the hospital, he said, "I'm having trouble reading. I can't see straight, and the words don't make sense."

When another inmate heard how the weed scrambled Smallwood's brain, he said, "I'd like to try some of that!"

I replied in disbelief, "Didn't you hear the man? The drug fried his brain; he can't even comprehend a book."

The inmate responded, "Well, then it must be good shit."

Wanting to see a new student's writing skills, I asked inmate Antoine to write an essay about a skill he did not learn in school. I was happy when I looked over and saw he was writing away. But, I was not so delighted when he turned in an essay about selling crack cocaine.

Unfortunately, I neglected to tell Antoine what topics were off-limits. The best writers write about what they know, and Antoine was no exception. Despite some rough spots, his work exemplified an excellent GED essay. I warned Antoine that his future essays could not be about drugs, sex, or gangs.

I have to admit I was curious and wanted to see his writing ability, so I looked the essay over. Antoine did an excellent job of telling me how to prepare and sell crack cocaine. He said first, you have to have the proper mix. Next, you have to cook it up. Then, you have to know how, when, and where to sell the product.

Antoine's mix was 28 grams of cocaine and 14 grams of baking soda. If it is too strong, there will not be enough profit; if it is too weak, there won't be any return customers, so you will lose money.

He advised to mix powder cocaine and baking soda and put it into a baby food jar or empty mayonnaise jar, depending on the amount. Put the mixture in the jar and pour in enough water to cover the mix. Fill a small pot half-full of water and bring it to a boil. Set the jar in the boiling pot of water until it looks foggy and the substance comes together in a more solid form. Swirl the mixture around so it blends, and then add ice or cold water into the jar, which will seal it together to a solid form.

Some folks use scales, but Antoine preferred to break them into rocks, hit the streets, and start making money. The rocks are a little softer than chalk. Antoine said some folks sell a gram for $50 and a half for $25, but he eyes out $20 pieces.

He said he buys an ounce of coke for between $700 to $1,000 and sells it in rocks for about $3,600, so he clears about $2,500 an ounce. He said he could buy more significant amounts of cocaine cheaper; from a pound of coke he could make at least 40k and twice that for a kilo. He said you can sell it on the corner or out of a crack house, but you have to be careful in both spots because of the police and the "stickup kid." They both want your money and drugs.

You also don't want to step on someone else's turf. You want to sell in your hood where people know you. If someone from outside your hood comes in, they will be run out or get hurt. Antoine said he sold dope from the time he was 14 until he got caught at 27.

He said his brothers and cousins taught him the ropes, and they were all quite successful, but crack cocaine sales can be a dangerous game if you don't play by the rules.

Antoine will do very well in writing and math regarding measurements and conversions.

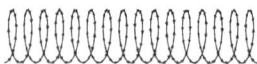

Drugs are smuggled into prisons in numerous ways. In 2015, the mother of an inmate called her son, unaware that their conversation was being recorded. She told him that she was going to send drugs to him via the mail. Mailroom employees discovered that the mother had concealed suboxone behind the postage stamps on an incoming letter. Suboxone is a prescription opioid in a film taken orally, commonly to treat opioid dependence. Its popularity has been growing in the prison system. The prisoner's mother faced felony charges for delivering a controlled substance.

Resourceful prisoners and their accomplices on the outside have found all sorts of ways to conceal drugs in thin strips. So, in 2017, the department banned inmates from receiving mail with stickers (including address labels), perfume, or lipstick kisses on the envelope. The policy also forbids writing with anything but black or blue ink or lead pencil.

Toward the end of class one day, I heard one of my students, Siler White, mention to someone that he had been granted parole and feared reentering the real world. This was a natural feeling for anyone imprisoned for over 20 years. White was in his late 60s, and his apprehension reminded me of Brooks Hatlen, the librarian in the 1994 film *The Shawshank Redemption*. After years of incarceration, he could not adjust to the real world and decided to hang himself rather than try to adapt. I pulled White aside and said, "Although some things have changed in the world, things work out if you have a good attitude and stay strong."

I expressed my concern about White to my principal before we were off for the weekend. He said, "I don't have time for this nonsense." I went to the psychologist and voiced my trepidation, but he shrugged me off. I then spoke to a custody supervisor, who also did not care to listen. The "Inmates ain't got nothin' comin'" message was loud and clear. No one cared about an old Black convict concerned about facing the world after many years of incarceration.

When I returned from my weekend, I took a roll in my last-hour class. After I repeated his name three times, a couple of students said, "Siler White is dead."

I was so upset I could not think straight. I had no way to vent my feelings. I had already talked to anyone that was supposed to intervene. I called his unit to ask what had happened to him. An officer said he swallowed a balloon full of heroin his girlfriend smuggled in when she visited him the previous day. Apparently, the balloon burst before he could pass it, and he overdosed.

I wondered why someone would fool around with drug smuggling when he was ready to walk out the door. He probably had someone waiting for him on the outside: his girlfriend, a child, a friend. I thought, *He could have had a serious heroin addiction, but I doubt it. He could have been hoping to catch a new case so he could stay in prison, but there are easier ways of doing that. His girlfriend could have tampered with the balloon in a misbegotten attempt at assisted suicide, but that would be an expensive way of sending him out. White could have bitten the balloon on purpose before swallowing it…or maybe the balloon burst on its own.* I will never know precisely what happened to Siler White or if someone could have made a difference.

CHAPTER 14

Escapes: Successful and Otherwise

Toilet Paper Heads

"How did I escape? With difficulty.
How did I plan the moment? With pleasure."
—Alexandre Dumas

ount time is taken very seriously in prison and is conducted numerous times daily. We had to account for the whereabouts of every inmate at all times. When I looked in a cell, I did not automatically count a lump under a blanket; I needed to watch for movement—the rise and fall of the chest, for instance—and a healthy skin tone. I did not want to count bodies that were dead or gone, although that mistake had been made.

When making rounds at count time, if I did not see any movement, I would kick the door to try to get a response. If there was none, it was time to open the door and shine a flashlight on the inmate's face. I would have rather upset a prisoner than have the warden ask questions after an inmate escaped or died.

On August 27, 1931, four inmates tried to shoot their way out of Marquette with guns and ammunition smuggled into the prison. Dr. A.W. Hornbogen was temporarily filling in for the regular doctor on vacation. He and a trusty were shot and killed during the escape. When armed officers surrounded the inmates, they shot and killed themselves.

Most inmates planning an escape solicit help from people on the outside. On November 5, 1939, several prisoners scaled the 34-foot wall of the State Prison of Southern Michigan (Jackson) with the help of a rope and a bent metal pipe. Once outside, they hopped into a waiting getaway car. Chief Inspector Fred Boucher ran after the automobile wielding a revolver, shouting for the prisoners to surrender. One of them stuck a shotgun out of the window and shot him dead in his tracks. The convicts were eventually apprehended, tried, and sentenced to life for the inspector's murder.

In 1963, four inmates escaped from 8-Block at Jackson, leaving dummies in their places. The bodies of these makeshift doubles consisted of thermal underwear stuffed with rags and clothing; the heads were rolls of toilet paper wrapped in clothing. The inmates even pilfered hair from the barbershop in an attempt to make the dummies look more realistic.

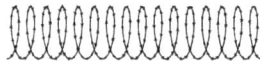

〰〰〰〰〰〰〰〰〰〰〰〰〰

I remember hearing about an elaborate escape from Jackson on June 6, 1975. Inmate Dale Remling had a friend hire a helicopter pilot to fly the friend from Plymouth, Michigan, to Lansing. Shortly after they were in the air, the friend pulled a knife on the pilot and ordered him to head to Jackson Prison instead. The pilot landed in the prison yard, picked up Remling, and flew six miles to where two getaway cars were waiting. Remling got away, but the police apprehended his friend.

Police arrested Remling the next day in a bar in Leslie, Michigan, just 20 minutes from Jackson. After such a bold, high-profile escape, one might think that Remling would have traveled farther from the prison rather than sitting down and ordering a cold one at a local bar, likely a hangout for prison employees. Escapees sometimes value their bragging rights more than their freedom.

After inmates escape, it is not unusual for them to do things that draw attention to themselves and cause someone to contact the police. It makes one wonder if they are trying to get caught; some even get so paranoid that they surrender to the authorities, believing that another few years in prison are preferable to living on the outside in constant fear of capture. An escape is a public-relations nightmare for the governor, the director of prisons, the prison's warden, and others down the line. If the policies and procedures were not followed, anyone associated with the incident would be raked over the coals. Did the staff do what they were supposed to, and did they document it?

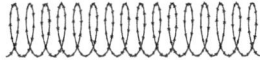

The escapees usually leave town on the rare occasion when there is an escape. After they steal a car, they typically return to their old stomping grounds in southeastern Michigan, where they have family and friends. In the event of an escape, prison officials first check the escapees' call lists, phone records, and the addresses of their visitors. Often, escapees are apprehended at the home of a girlfriend or relative. This was the scenario when two inmates escaped from Riverside one night.

An inmate somehow obtained a hacksaw from Maintenance and cut through the bars of his cell window. After the third shift officer made his rounds, the duo fashioned dummies from pillows and clothing and placed them under their blankets. In the dark, they slipped out the window, dropped onto the roof of the Administration Building, and jumped to the ground. Earlier that day, crows had been setting off the security sensors on the flat rooftop, so when the alarm went off as each inmate dropped to the roof, the Control Center and staff just assumed birds were the cause.

The escapees stole a car from a nearby home and drove it to Meijer, a large grocery store on the edge of town, where they ran out of gas. They hotwired a second vehicle there and drove it to Flint, where the girlfriend of one of the inmates lived. After the Absconder Unit checked the prisoner's phone and mail records, they went to the girlfriend's home, where they found and apprehended one of the fugitives. When they asked him where the other inmate was, he said, "Upstairs, under the bed," and that is where they found him. Before one of these masterminds escaped, he had less than a year left on his bit, but now both convicts picked up another five years for escape.

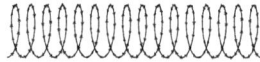

In 2009, a CO from Carson City Correctional Facility took his Level I public work crew out to clean up debris, clear brush from drainage ditches, and cut down trees with chainsaws. At the end of their shift, the officer loaded four of the five-member crew into the van. The fifth prisoner, a 22-year-old, crept up behind the officer, stabbed him in the back of his head with a pitchfork, left him for dead, stole his van, and drove off with the other four convicts.

When the officer came to, he stumbled across a field and through a forest, falling numerous times before reaching a home, where, distressed by the sight of the bloody man, a woman called 911. The officer was transported to Carson City Hospital but was so severely injured that he had to be airlifted to a Grand Rapids hospital, where he remained unconscious and in critical condition for quite some time. When he finally came to, a fellow officer asked him how he was, and he gave him the thumbs-up and said, "Thank God they used the pitchfork instead of the chainsaw."

All five of the Carson City inmates were apprehended, but it appeared that four had not been part of the escape plan; they had been kidnapped by the convict who stabbed the officer. The perpetrator received 30-to-75 years for attempted murder—a serious sentence for a serious crime. Whether an inmate is Level I or V, there is no way to tell if he can be trusted and to what degree. Inmates eligible for work release have not been involved in violent or sex crimes and have earned a degree of trust, but one never knows. The young culprit who committed this heinous crime would probably have been up for parole very soon, but after he tried to kill an officer and escape, he would not see the parole board for decades.

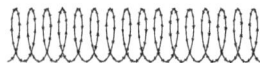

While working in the MDOC, I often thought about prisoners doing a lot of time. During my teaching years, my tutor McIntosh, who went by Mac, had such an old prisoner number that I had to ask, "With all the years you have in, did you ever think about trying to escape?"

Mac looked at me with a proud smirk and said, "I did more than think about it. I was 19 when I started a two-to-five at MTU [Michigan Training Unit, also known as Richard A. Handlon Correctional Facility, in Ionia]."

"You tried to escape when you were only doing a two-to-five?"

"I was young and dumb. I'd observed the closest guard tower to my cell and our third shift unit officer. We called him Officer One-Round because, after the 11:00 p.m. count, he never made another round on his shift. I also noticed that the officer in the tower went to lunch at 1:00 a.m. every night. I knew this because he was a chain smoker, and I didn't see a cherry glowing on his cigarette from 1:00 to 2:00 a.m."

"Did you try to escape by yourself?"

"I talked to three other cons about it, and Larry, Curly, and Moe were all on board. One night, after One-Round passed by, we all met in my cell, wearing street clothes under our prison blues. We went over our plan and wrapped cloth around our hands to protect them from the barbed wire. We had two metal rods to help us over the chain-link fence, one bent into a Z shape and the other like an S. The Z could be used as a step and the S as a hook to pull ourselves up."

Mac sat in front of my desk, got comfortable, and continued.

"One-Round wouldn't be back again that night, and the chain smoker was out to lunch, so we slipped out of the unit through the window I'd prepped earlier to pop it out when the time came. We headed for the section of the fence under the empty tower. I'd brought a blanket to protect us from the barbed wire, with a pair of shoes attached to give it weight so I could throw it over the fence. I was the smallest, so the Stooges let me go first.

"They hoisted me up and practically tossed me over the fence. Then Larry and Curly boosted Moe up, and he joined me on the other side. Larry climbed on Curly's shoulders, and Curly gave him a lift. Curly made it up and over with the help of the Z step, S hook, and brute strength."

"So, where'd you go?"

"We removed our blues and stuffed them in a culvert by the road. It was a warm night in August, and I could see the clouds starting to roll. We'd been running through cornfields and soybeans all night, and when we got to a five-acre stand of trees, we decided to lie down and rest. It kept getting cloudier until we couldn't see the moon. The wind made the trees creak, and I heard heavy breathing and snoring from the Stooges. I fell asleep with a big smile, knowing that I'd planned and pulled off a quadruple prison escape.

"We were rudely awakened by a thunderstorm and got dumped on, so we ran to the nearest farmhouse. We cased the place out, and nobody was home. I elbowed the window on the back door, reached inside, twisted the lock, and we were in. We tossed some wood in the potbelly stove, lit a fire, took off our wet clothes, and hung them over chairs to dry. We raided the cupboards and fridge in our skivvies and stuffed our faces with lunchmeat, apples, and cookies—whatever we could find."

I said, "Lucky break, huh?"

"For a minute. At 5:00 a.m., we heard a crunching sound; a truck was coming up the gravel driveway. It pulled around the back of the house, and I wondered, *Who's up this early?* I peeked out the window and saw an old couple in a green Ford pickup. The Stooges grabbed knives from the butcher block, and I picked up a meat-tenderizing mallet, thinking I could knock out the old coot if he came into the house."

"Did he?"

"They got out of the truck, and the old man walked toward the back door and noticed the window was broken, so he shouted something to the old lady. He crept up and peeked in the side window, so we flattened against the wall. The old woman hollered, 'Get away from the house! Let's call the police!' They got back in the truck and sped off."

"Close call."

"So, we got dressed, grabbed some food and drinks for the road, and got out of there. We reached a little town in about a half-hour and walked down the main street. This drunk saw us coming his way, so he stood up and yelled, 'Hey, whatchoo guys doin'? You gots any spare change? You gots a smoke?' A cop car was slowly driving up the street. Since it was still early in the morning, we stood out like a neon sign, and the drunk didn't help. The cop pulls up and rolls down his window: 'What are you doing in my town at this hour?'"

"I said, 'Our car broke down, and we're trying to get a ride to a friend's house. After that, we're going to get my car fixed.'"

"Did he buy it?"

"He said, 'Climb in. Let me give you guys a lift.' This guy was a real Barney Fife. Doesn't it sound like Barney to pick up four escaped convicts and chauffeur them around? We weren't sure about climbing into a cop car, but we got in and asked him to drive us to Larry's mom's house. On the way, he told us how he was the backbone of Mayberry's police department, and, if there was a case to be solved, he was the man—like he was taking on the Cornfield Crips and the Barley Bloods. When we got to Larry's mom's, we hopped out and thanked him. Barney waved goodbye and drove away."

"Did Larry's mom treat you right?"

"Not really. She and her boyfriend came out of the farmhouse, and she said, 'What the hell are you doing here? Who are these guys? Why aren't you in prison? I think you need to go away.'"

"Larry said, 'What about, Hello, how are you? Good to see you, kid!'"

I said, "This does not sound good."

"No. The vibes were definitely bad. I thought, *We shouldn't have come here*. I was eyeing the boyfriend's Chevy crew cab truck, and he reached down, picked up an axe leaning against the woodpile, and said, 'Y'all need to leave—or else.'"

"I go, 'Or else what? Or else you're going to chop some firewood?'"

"Larry's mom says, 'Or else I'm calling the cops.'"

"Did she?"

"She didn't need to. A cop car pulled into the drive just then, and we all looked at each other like, 'Now what?' When Barney II got out of the car, he goes, 'My deputy said you boys had car problems and needed some help. How about I give you a ride back into town, and we can sort this thing out?' The boyfriend put the axe down and said, 'That sounds like a good idea, officer.' I sat in the front, and the Stooges went in the back. I said, 'We sure do appreciate your help.' The Stooges agreed.

"The officer said, 'Where exactly did your car break down?'"

"I said, 'I don't know because we walked into town and then got a ride to Larry's mom's, and now we're going back to town. It was dark, and I'm confused because I'm not from around here.'"

"Did he buy that one?"

"Don't know. We were too tired to think straight. When we got to the cop shop, we sat on a bench. The cop went to his desk, kicked his feet up, and crossed them. He pulled out his .38, flipped it open, started spinning the cylinder, flipped it shut, and then did it again a few times. He was trying to intimidate us."

"What was his plan, or didn't he have one?"

"I'm not sure. We just hung out, wondering what his next move would be. He told us how he had been the star of his high school football team and was a black belt in karate, and then the phone rang. He answered, and his attitude went from macho man to wimpy wuss. 'Yes sir, yes sir. I think you need to send someone right now.' Then he hung up; he was shaking like a leaf. His feet came off the desk, he snapped the cylinder into the gun, pointed it at us, and said, 'Okay, boys. When I open this cell, I want you all to step inside.' I assumed the call came from a higher-up at MTU [Michigan Training Unit], who told him that he had four dangerous escapees on his hands."

It blew my mind to think about how long Mac had been down. We were peers, but when I was a junior in high school in 1974, Mac was 19 and headed to prison at MTU. We both grew up listening to vinyl, then 8-track tapes, then cassettes. There were only landline phones back then, so most folks kept a couple rolls of dimes and quarters in the car to make calls from phone booths when on the road. Mac missed out on CDs, cell phones, and 40 years of life in the real world, which might have included marriage, a family, and a career in a field he enjoyed.

Mac had a chaotic childhood. He was removed from his biological parents' home because they abused him. He was placed in one foster home after another, but acted up and could not be controlled, so each set of foster parents returned him to the state like he was damaged goods.

The last couple of foster parents Mac lived with before he ran away were religious fanatics who tried to beat the devil out of him. Mac said that in the past, because of his upbringing he was always in escape mode, longing to move on, and would do whatever was needed to be free.

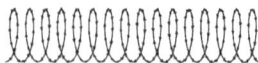

In higher-level prisons, officers were assigned to the gun towers, but because of budget cuts these sometimes went unmanned. The tower shifts were usually four hours long. In the towers, officers are on constant watch, continually scanning the yard and surrounding area. These COs prevent serious injury or death if a yard disturbance occurs. If an inmate tries to climb the fence, the tower officer may fire a warning shot. If the inmate does not stop, the next shot should be to stave off an escape.

An officer at the Carson City Level IV facility told me he was in one of the towers when he saw an inmate hit the fence. He recalled, "I touched off my warning shot, then Control Center called to ask what was happening. I told them I had a convict climbing the fence, and my warning shot didn't stop him. I had him in my sights, and Control gave me the go-ahead to shoot, so I pulled the trigger, and he dropped dead. I followed the correct procedure, so my ass was covered."

I wondered if the inmate planned to commit suicide by an officer. I am sure that looking through crosshairs, pulling the trigger, and seeing someone drop dead weighs heavily on a person's heart and soul. In this case, about five years later, the officer who pulled the trigger died of a heart attack many decades before his time.

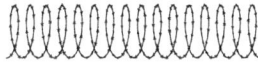

〰〰〰〰〰〰〰〰〰〰〰〰〰

I would not want a prison in my backyard. Every state prison in Michigan blows its emergency siren at least once a month on each shift for practice mobilizations. The community residents have no way of knowing if it is a drill or if there is an actual emergency, such as a riot or an escape.

When prisons are built near each other, the sirens are so loud that it is hard to tell which facility is sounding the alarm. I often asked officers in Ionia and St. Louis, "Is that our siren or next door's?" The same problem occurs in other prison towns like Jackson. I can imagine mothers telling their children, "Time to come inside and lock the doors, kids. Chop chop! We don't know if a murderer or rapist has escaped or if the prison is just practicing."

III:
ADULT BASIC EDUCATION TEACHER AT ST. LOUIS CORRECTIONAL FACILITY

CHAPTER 15

Early Teaching Days

The ABCs and ABE

"Celebrate endings—for they precede new beginnings."
—Jonathan Lockwood Huie

While working as a CO on third shift at Mid-Michigan Correctional Facility, I returned to Central Michigan University to renew my teaching certificate. At the time, Michigan teaching certificates expired after 10 years of non-use. Mine expired in 1990, and I began working on adding a Reading Specialist endorsement (similar to a college minor). I chose Reading because illiteracy is a massive problem in prison. One of the main reasons for renewing my certificate and seeking a teaching position was that education is the best deterrent for inmates returning to prison. According to the U.S. Department of Education and the National Institute of Literacy, 32 million adults in the United States—14% of the adult population—cannot read. This is a lamentable situation, but the illiteracy problem in U.S. prisons is even worse. Seventy percent of the inmates cannot read above the fourth-grade level, and some cannot read at all. I planned on teaching the lower-end inmates to read and write in an Adult Basic Education (ABE) class.

I was excited to hear that a new prison was being built in St. Louis and hoped to be one of the first teachers hired there in late 1999. As part of my college Reading program, I volunteered to tutor inmates at the

Mid-Michigan facility. My tutoring would allow me to get acquainted with the school's principal, who would also be the principal at the new prison. In addition to my prison tutoring, I tutored a high school student on probation for a previous crime.

After renewing my certificate, I began to work on my master's. As one of my class projects, I decided to produce an orientation video for the new inmates arriving in Mid-Michigan. I needed approval from the regional director and the warden to bring a digital still camera and a video camera into a state prison. Throughout the production process, I had to communicate with practically all departments at the facility, including administration, custody, and housing employees.

The video was designed to inform the inmates about available services and where they were located. This information helped everyone: the classification director, athletic director, special activities director, Healthcare staff, assistant resident unit supervisors, resident unit managers, sergeants, lieutenants, captains, corrections officers, and all the other employees who dealt with the prison population.

When I interviewed for the St. Louis teaching position, the interview panelists were familiar with me from my tutoring work and video production. The administration liked that I had a decade of experience as an officer working with prisoners at high and low levels. I was offered a teaching position, and I was ecstatic. Now, I could make a difference in some lives.

Following my divorce, I had been living with my parents and son, Max. With my new teaching job, I would be working regular hours, relieving my parents of the responsibility of watching Max and allowing them to live elsewhere and enjoy their retirement. I purchased their house so Max and I could live there and found a condominium for my folks. Finally, after 10 years of working on second and third shifts as an officer, I would work from 7:00 a.m. to 3:00 p.m., with weekends and holidays off. This was the first time in my life that I would enjoy a regular schedule in a full-time job where I could use my degree, and it felt fantastic. This change meant a new life for Max, my parents, and me—freedom for all. Max and I would no longer depend on my folks; they could focus on being grandparents rather than parents. I took Mom, Dad, and Max out to dinner to celebrate.

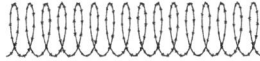

I need to add some more history behind the prison educational system. In 1982, the Federal Bureau of Prisons established its first mandatory literacy program, and its influence was soon felt around the country. In 1990, when I was hired into the MDOC, a survey revealed that 13 states, including Michigan, enforced a mandatory literacy program.

Research by Emory University in 2021 showed that the recidivism rate among prisoners who have completed some high school courses is around 55 percent. Even basic education significantly reduces the recidivism rate; the higher the education level, the less likely prisoners are to return.

Michigan spends roughly $48,000 per inmate annually. The state has about 32,000 inmates as of 2024. Based on budget considerations alone, the reduction in recidivism that prison education programs produce justifies their existence. Further participation in the education program would benefit the men and the prison budget.

Vocational training also cuts recidivism, so lower-level prisons offer classes in Culinary Arts, Horticulture, and Building Trades. Because of security concerns related to the equipment these classes require, some classes are not permitted at higher-level prisons. Vocational training is particularly valuable to inmates with little formal education, as it helps them obtain gainful employment.

Warren Burger, ex-Chief Justice of the U.S. Supreme Court, said, "We must accept the reality that to confine offenders behind walls without trying to change them is an expensive folly with short-term benefits—a 'winning of battles while losing the war.'"

Education is a gift that keeps on giving. Reading expands our view of the world and can change our thoughts and ideas, allowing us to see new opportunities and understand that we have choices. If we want inmates to change their thinking, we must provide the tools to help them learn.

Inmates may get involved in various community projects in prisons that offer Building Trades classes. For example, the prisoners have built picnic tables, benches, trash receptacles, and gazebos for city and county parks; trophy cases, desks, and podiums for local schools; and wooden bridges over waterways and swampy areas for hikers. They have also removed old railroad tracks that were later transformed into bike paths for the "Rails to Trails" program, constructed churches in various communities, and built houses in all 83 Michigan counties. In the Detroit area, the participants in one prison's Building Trades program built a neighborhood of 17 homes and a playscape for the children. Such projects give inmates a sense of pride—when they are released, they can take their friends and family to see the fruits of their labor—and provide new, low-income housing for needy families.

In 2017, Michigan prisons had a big push to expand skilled trades programs; many tradespeople in the outside world left the state during the 2008 recession. To help fill this gap, the first prison "Vocational Village" opened at Richard A. Handlon Correctional Facility in Ionia and the second at Parnell Prison in Jackson. The inmates in these vocational programs were certified in various fields, from construction to computer numerical control, automotive, welding, and more. Those who complete such programs leave prison with certification, and some receive job offers before they walk out the gate.

Some prisons offer custodial maintenance programs that train inmates to keep the facilities clean. There is a dire need on the outside for people to fill service and manual labor jobs; our towns and cities require them to function. The COVID-19 pandemic taught us how important these "non-essential" workers are. Paroled inmates who have received vocational training are good candidates for such positions.

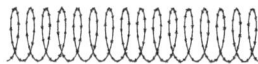

〰〰〰〰〰〰〰〰〰〰〰〰〰

I was eager to start a new career teaching in the prison system. Five other teachers were hired soon after I signed on at St. Louis, and the six of us ordered the books and classroom supplies needed to open the prison school.

The principal, Ron Joliffe, asked me if I wanted to work with the inmates locked up in segregation. I told him that I would prefer to work as an Adult Basic Education teacher with students on the low end of the educational spectrum so that I could apply the techniques I learned in my Reading program.

The entire unit was locked down in segregation, and the inmates were housed in one-man cells. Instructing these prisoners is highly restricted because the inmates cannot come out of their cells to attend class, so the teachers must pass papers back and forth by sliding them under the solid metal doors or through the food slots. Any conversation between teacher and student had to be held through a closed door and would be heard by the other inmates up and down the hallway. Between visiting the segregation students twice daily, the teacher would sit in a broom closet converted into an office. I would feel as if I were the one in segregation. There was barely room for a little desk, chair, filing cabinet, a stack of books, and wastebasket. I would have taken the job if I had to, but when given a choice opted for the classroom, where I could interact with the students and make a difference in their lives. I was happy to start my teaching career in an Adult Basic Education classroom.

Principal Joliffe had his hands full: In addition to the St. Louis Level IV facility where I was now working, he oversaw the schools in a minimum-security camp in Grayling, a Level I prison in St. Louis, a Level V in Manistee, and a Level VI in Ionia. He supervised these five prisons' academic and vocational teachers, stopping in all the classrooms to talk with the instructors. I enjoyed working for Ron because he was a good man who supported his staff and assisted them in reaching their goals.

Every year at Christmastime, my mother would prepare small gift bags of peanut brittle for me to give to my fellow teachers, the school secretary, and the principal. Ron was the biggest fan of the peanut brittle. One year, he and his wife, Debbie, threw a Christmas party at their house in Lansing. At the party, I told him, "I'm going to ask Debbie how she liked my mom's peanut brittle."

Ron pulled me aside, pushed me against the wall, and sternly said, "You will do no such thing. I've got a long commute from St. Louis to Lansing, and that stuff's addictive." His face had a guilty look on it as he spoke. "She's never tasted a crumb of your mom's peanut brittle."

"Not in the five years I've been bringing it?"

Ron looked at me pleadingly and barked, "Not a word!"

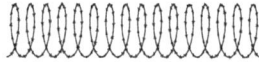

The St. Louis Level IV school was up and running by early 2000. Initially, my classroom had bare white cement-block walls, but after my decoration, it looked much like a typical high school classroom. There were five tables, two dozen blue plastic chairs, seven study carrels with computers, several file cabinets, my desk, and my chair that rocked, rolled, and swiveled. I covered my walls with various items: inspirational posters with nature scenes, a U.S. history timeline, a banner displaying the lineage of U.S. presidents, and maps of the U.S. and the world. In this once sterile but now lively environment, I enjoyed teaching adult basic education classes at St. Louis for six years.

The computers ran educational programs in the five areas of the GED: Science, Social Studies, Reading, Writing, and Mathematics. I preferred that the students work out of their books and use computers only as a supplement.

There were numerous problems with the software the state purchased. The software representatives would visit my classroom and ask if the programs had bugs. At first, I typed out a list of the mistakes and even wrote down exactly where I found them, but unfortunately, the reps never did anything to correct them. After a while, when they asked if there were any problems, I said, "Yes, but you aren't going to fix them." They just agreed and went on their way.

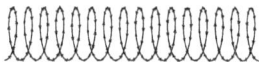

The Level I inmates I had been watching as an officer for the last five years at Mid-Michigan were usually within three years of going home. The students at the St. Louis Level IV facility were 10 years or more away from being released into society, if they ever would be.

My experiences before I joined the department helped me, but the most valuable lessons I learned in prison came from working with the criminally insane inmates at Riverside. The psychiatric units were an environment that heightened my senses to the maximum. Handling those intense situations gave me the confidence I needed in the general population housing units, the chow halls, and the prison classrooms.

CHAPTER 16

Low-Level Students in a High-Level Prison

Walking Dictionaries and Reading Kites

"We may have all come on different ships,
but we're all in the same boat."
—Martin Luther King Jr.

t St. Louis Level IV, one of the first things I noticed about the students was their sticky fingers. I could not set a pen down on my desk without it growing legs, and if I placed a pile of lined paper there, the entire stack disappeared almost immediately. I learned to keep my pens in my pocket and to hand out paper one sheet at a time. The only way I would give a student a pencil was if he would give me his prison ID in exchange; I returned it when he returned the pencil. Although the principal provided me with pocket dictionaries for the students, I did not leave them sitting around the room because they, too, would walk. I kept close tabs on my supplies so I would not have to shake down every student before they left class, each hour, every day.

I included one six-inch-thick unabridged dictionary when I ordered my classroom books and supplies. As the class ended one wintry day, I noticed a student exiting the classroom who looked seven months pregnant. I asked him to approach my desk and said, "I need you to unzip your coat." When he did, I laughed and said, "No wonder you're in prison. Please put the dictionary on my desk and get out of here." The colossal tome was so obvious that I would not have felt right about writing him a theft ticket. If I, an ex-corrections officer, did not notice someone swiping an unabridged dictionary, *I* would be the one with the problem. As usual, I was being tested by students to find out what they could get away with.

Through my previous jobs as a camp counselor, park director, and student teacher, I learned that it is best to start being strict with the students. You are on stage when you are in charge, and everyone looks and listens. Students will be ready to pounce and feast on the fresh meat. One can lighten up eventually, but starting easy and trying to play the heavy later does not work.

My ABE students at St. Louis were the lowest on the school's educational spectrum. I would move them to the Pre-GED class if they progressed to a fifth-grade reading level and started working on fractions.

I was exceedingly proud of one of my adult basic education students, the only one at St. Louis who started at a second-grade reading level and completed all the steps necessary to receive his GED while he was there. When the young man entered my room, I could tell he was different. He was not trying to be a thug—he was just a happy, friendly guy. He looked at me with a big smile, and I saw that he was missing his front tooth, but he did not care.

"Good mornin', sir," he said. This pleasant and respectful greeting surprised me, and turned the other students' heads.

I asked, "Where're you from?"

"Detroit, sir," he replied.

"No, you're not," I said. "Inmates from Detroit do not come in here smiling, nodding, and acknowledging the teacher and other students. They don't say polite things like 'Good morning, sir.' They come in snarling and acting like they'll punch someone out. Now, where are you *originally* from?"

"Tupelo, Mississippi, sir," he said, still with that grin that compelled me to smile back.

I asked him what had happened to his front tooth.

His smile widened, and he proclaimed, "Bumper jack, sir."

Everybody in the room laughed. This guy was a stitch. I said, "From now on, you'll be Mississippi Bumper Jack." He smiled and nodded as if to say, *That'll be just fine.*

When Bumper Jack made it to the fifth-grade reading level and started learning fractions, I placed him in the Pre-GED class taught by Nathan Colthorpe. He worked hard, and eventually, Nathan moved him up to Joe McGuire's GED class, where he obtained his diploma. It was phenomenal that a student starting at a second-grade reading level and elementary math could receive his GED in a few short years. This had never happened at our school. Students who started at that level often studied there for years on end or were transferred to another facility before they were anywhere near graduating. Some students moved from ABE to Pre-GED, but Bumper Jack was the only student who accomplished this feat in my six years of teaching at St. Louis.

When I was a CMA at Riverside in Ionia and, later, a CO at the Mid-Michigan Facility in St. Louis, I had access to the inmates' institutional files. As an officer, I could look up information about their backgrounds and crimes, but as a teacher, I could only review their educational files. So, I did not know Bumper Jack's criminal history, but he did not seem the type to be dealing drugs or harming anyone unless he was defending himself or someone else. I could easily see him moving into town and innocently getting caught up in something shady.

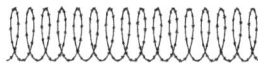

〰〰〰〰〰〰〰〰〰〰〰

The principal at St. Louis hired some excellent teachers. Nathan Colthorpe, the Pre-GED teacher, was a "yooper" (person from Michigan's Upper Peninsula) who moved to St. Louis for a teaching job; he later moved back to his old stomping grounds and worked in two U.P. prisons. He was president of the Michigan Beekeepers' Association and very involved in his town's high school sports programs. He kept time for the school's basketball games and cross-country meets and was the announcer for the football games. He made and sold the most beautiful wooden kayaks and Adirondack chairs I have ever seen. Although pleasant in appearance, they are the most uncomfortable chairs I have ever sat in—and almost impossible to get up from without looking like a klutz.

Once students were working at the ninth- or tenth-grade level, they were promoted to a GED class taught by Joe McGuire. He designed the documents (plotters) we used to keep track of the five GED subject areas and devised innovative ideas for the curriculum. McGuire should have been promoted to principal long before, but failed to fawn over the correct people adequately.

If a student needed additional help in mathematics, he would be placed in Dave De Vries's class. Dave had played football for Western Michigan University and later taught high school history for 30 years before working in prison. Coincidentally, his father had taught mathematics at my high school for 30 years. Anyone who had Mr. De Vries at Eastern High or Dave in the St. Louis prison said they were phenomenal teachers.

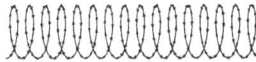

〰〰〰〰〰〰〰〰〰〰〰〰〰

To be motivated in the classroom, lifers must recognize the advantages of education. For students to understand the importance of literacy, the teacher must present a convincing case. In most prisons, an inmate cannot obtain a paying job until he has received a GED. This rule provides an incentive. In the real world, the higher the educational level, the higher the pay. It is hard enough for an ex-con to feel comfortable applying for a job, but this is only possible if he can read the application.

Sitting in my classroom on my first day of teaching, I noticed that Cannon, a 22-year-old student from Flint, had not done a lick of work, so I said, "Mr. Cannon, it's time to get busy."

"Why should I?" he replied petulantly. "I'm doin' double life. I got all the time in the world."

"Do you want your bunkie to read all your kites [intra-prison correspondence] and personal letters to you? Do you want to pay your homeboy to write your kites? Or do you want to be your own man?"

My words inspired Cannon. I did not know it then, but he was trying to appeal his case. His mother was sending money to pay a "legal beagle," an inmate who supposedly knew something about the law, to work on his appeal. But Cannon could not read his paperwork and suspected the paralegal was ripping him off, which was a pretty safe bet.

Later, when I became better acquainted with Cannon, I asked him, "How did you end up catching a double-life bit?"

He replied, "I was ridin' with a couple of my homeboys who talked me into doin' a home invasion. They said an old couple they knew was out of town, so it would be easy pickin's. So, we bust out the back-door window of the garage, reach in, and open the door. We try the door from the garage to the house, and it's unlocked. I followed my rappies [co-conspirators], who had tactical flashlights.

"Suddenly, the old man walks out of the bedroom, flips on the light, and yells, 'What the hell are you doin' in my house?' My homeys started beatin' him down with their flashlights, and his wife comes out screamin'. One of my dawgs went after her, so I left because I didn't want any part of that. I ran all the way home and never saw those two again. A couple of weeks later, the cops come to my place and take me down to the station. They said they had picked up my dawgs, who told them I was there when it all went down."

"But you left the scene?" I said.

"I did, but my rappies killed the old man and lady."

"Did the cops know you left?"

"The law says it don't matter. My paralegal told me that if anyone's killed during a felony and you were in any way involved, everyone gets life. Two got killed, so I got double-life. The law sucks. If I'm the driver when my partner robs a 7-Eleven and he kills the cashier, I'd get life, too. If the driver knows what's goin' down, he's part of the crime."

Cannon knew he was committing a felony when he entered the old couple's home. Now, he is doing a double-life bit, and I do not believe his appeal will make any difference unless the law is changed.

I was glad I talked with Cannon early on about being able to read and write. He realized it would be easier for him to do his time and work on his case. He had a long way to go and plenty of time to get there.

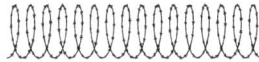

When an inmate enters the system, he takes the Total Adult Basic Education (TABE) test at the Reception and Guidance Center. At the St. Louis Level IV, kindergarten through fourth-grade inmates were placed in my ABE class. The principal also placed English as a Second Language (ESL) students in my classroom, so I had not only low-testing U.S. students but also students from Mexico, Central America, Cuba, Puerto Rico, Iraq, Iran, and other places where English is not the native tongue.

It is frustrating to attempt to teach students how to read and write if they do not want to learn. Most of the students in my class dropped out or were expelled from the public school system and were struggling with multiple issues. Some students at high-level prisons attend school only so they can get out of their cells and socialize—understandably, as the cells are cramped and cold in the winter, muggy in the summer.

My ESL students were more interested in learning than most born and raised in the U.S. Foreigners want to speak, read, and write English, so I particularly liked teaching them. In addition, they tended to be more knowledgeable about U.S. history, politics, and geography than many U.S. citizens. ESL students were eager to know about the United States, wanted to explore it from coast to coast, and had the most questions about my travels because they hoped to go there themselves.

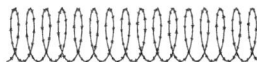

Carlos, one of my St. Louis ESL students, initially hailed from Puerto Rico. He spoke English reasonably well but needed to improve his reading and writing. He was motivated and sincere, completed the kindergarten and first-grade books, and was working on basic second-grade reading lessons.

One day, Carlos raised his hand and asked, "Mr. Myette: What is this word?" I walked over to him and saw that he was pointing to the word "if."

I said, "The word is 'if.' It has a short *I*, as in 'is,' 'it,' and 'bit,' followed by an f, as in 'Felipe,' 'fat,' and 'fart.'"

Carlos laughed and said, "Okay, it is pronounced if. But what does it mean?"

"It's a conditional thing. If you do this, I'll do that."

"What is a conditional thing? What is this? What is that?"

"Okay, Carlos, how did you make money in Puerto Rico?"

"I sold crack," he confessed, and the students around him laughed.

"All right," I said. "*If* you give me $20, I'll give you a rock of crack."

His eyes lit up, and he said, "Oh—if! 'If you give me 20 bucks, I'll give you a rock of crack.' If…a conditional thing. This for that!"

"Yes, very good," I said. "Quid pro quo. This for that. Do you understand now?"

"Si! Gracias!"

"De nada," I replied.

CHAPTER 17

My First Three Inmate Tutors

Flint, the Conductor; Miami, the Enforcer; and Pablo, the Interpreter

"I think I have learned the best way to lift one's self up
is to help someone else."
—Booker T. Washington

After my first day teaching, I was carrying a stack of papers while walking out of prison with Principal Joliffe, who asked, "Jack, what do you have there?"

"I have a ton of papers to grade," I said, "so I thought I'd take them home and work on them tonight."

"You're not grading those papers tonight," Ron said firmly. "The state is *not* going to pay you overtime. When you leave the prison, you must leave it all behind. You can talk to the classification director tomorrow; he'll supply you with a list of inmates in the academic tutor pool. You can pull their files to examine their TABE scores [reading, language, and math grade levels] and educational backgrounds. After interviewing about a half-dozen, you'll hire three and have them grade the students' papers, so you won't need to take work home. If you want to work for free after regular hours, get a job with the public schools."

Per Ron's advice, I visited the classification director and said, "I'm here to pick up a tutor list and find out if you have any inside information on the candidates."

He gave me the list I requested, which was very helpful. When I needed to hire a tutor, I could look at the educational files of those in the pool. I wanted to see if the candidate completed college studies or obtained a degree. I selected tutors who scored at, or close to, the twelfth-grade level in all three areas of the Total Adult Basic Education test. I wanted to hire people who knew how to write essays and do the math. I also wanted them to have pleasant personalities because they would be in the classroom with me, other tutors, and students all day.

To inmates, the academic tutor position was attractive for several reasons: the pay, the opportunity to be out of their cell or cubicle all day long, the satisfaction of helping others, and the chance to be in control.

I asked the classification director if there was anyone he interviewed who he thought might make a good tutor.

"There's an inmate who has bachelor's and master's in education and has taught in public schools for 30 years. I'd recommend that you take a close look at him. But you can't just take my word; you'll also need to interview him and several other candidates at the top of the list." After conducting these interviews, I hired the teacher that he endorsed and two others.

My adult basic education class was structured differently than a public school classroom. In St. Louis, I taught students studying five subject areas at remedial levels. I used peer tutoring, which allows the students to receive one-on-one attention and enables the teacher to focus on the special needs of the students, work on progress reports, and attend to test paperwork. Peer tutoring combines behavior modification and individualized instruction. It has been a worldwide success. Oxford University in England operates a tutoring/mentoring program for its Rhodes scholars (with one tutor for each student vs. my three for a class of 20).

In the real world, most inmates had negative experiences with their peers. They socialized with the wrong people, struggled with their families, and experienced failed relationships. However, students in my classroom enjoyed positive, give-and-take collaborations with the tutors.

I saw academic improvement and social/emotional benefits in both the tutors and tutees. More than once, I selected a shy, soft-spoken inmate who talked in a monotone but who I thought had the potential to be a good tutor. After he worked for a short while, I observed that his eye contact, volume, inflection, and interaction all improved.

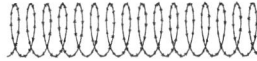

The three tutors I hired were Flint and Miami, both Black, and Pablo, a Hispanic. The ethnic makeup of my tutors reflected the racial makeup of my students. Flint, the ex-music teacher whom the classification director recommended, suggested that I introduce classical background music to the classroom. He explained: "Different genres of music instill desires in the students. There is sound in every classroom, from the gentle whirl of the air conditioner to mumbled conversation, so playing music allows the teacher to control the primary sound base in the classroom."

Flint explained that when music is being played and half the class is talking while the others try to listen, those who respect their fellow students and want to hear the music will press the others to quiet down. This saves the teacher from being the sole disciplinarian in the classroom.

The music teacher said the classical period music, from 1750 to 1820, helps students work at maximum capacity and creates discipline. This phenomenon is known as "the Mozart Effect." The music helps students feel at ease and forget that they are working. When their stress level is reduced, they tend to be less noisy and more willing to work for long periods.

Flint compared this to the feeling one gets when driving on the open road: the cruise control is on, the air conditioner is blowing, and the passengers feel comfortable enough to fall asleep. The environment is constant, so the nervous system is at ease. When this constancy is disturbed—when the driver turns off the cruise control or enters stop-and-go city traffic, or when the air conditioner is no longer cooling the car—the passenger will usually wake up.

I liked the idea of using background music to relax the classroom atmosphere, so I approached Ron for permission, and he gave me the okay. I purchased a CD player with built-in speakers and brought in a variety of classical CDs. I introduced Flint's recommended styles, including baroque, classical, romantic, and contemporary. All these had soothing effects on the students, but baroque was the most calming.

The students referred to classical music as "cartoon music" because they had heard the pieces while watching Bugs Bunny, Daffy Duck, and friends on *Looney Tunes*, the animated series of short comedies produced by Warner Brothers. My three tutors all enjoyed adding music to the classroom; I was expecting similar appreciation and even excitement from the students, but they did not seem to care one way or the other. Then I remembered that I was in a Level IV prison, where good manners and expressions of gratitude are a sign of weakness, and rude comments are encouraged.

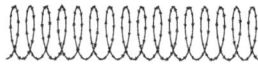

◊◊◊◊◊◊◊◊◊◊◊◊◊◊◊◊◊

Although Flint's idea to add music to the classroom was good, I set the classical music aside when my students said they were interested in hearing different music. I introduced jazz, which was a massive hit with most students. It was almost *too* big of a hit because the tutors from other classrooms started coming to our room under the pretense of borrowing supplies to get a taste of my expanding jazz repertoire.

If some students were not working and started to disturb those who were, I would fade the music out. This would upset most students, and, as Flint predicted, they began to enforce noise control themselves.

I learned that for a classroom music program to work, the teacher must know both his individual students and the group's overall dynamic. Without the correct pairing of students and music, there is little point in playing anything over the chaos.

I experimented with playing different genres of music so I could see what worked best. When I played The Temptations, Marvin Gaye, or other Motown artists, the students would begin to sing along, snap their fingers, tap on the table, and even dance around the room. Motown is great for a party but does not work in an academic setting. Most people love it, but these fellows were especially appreciative because, like the artists, the majority were Black and from the Motor City, where the music was born. I would only play Motown as a special treat on a Friday at the end of class, or I might slip in a few tunes before a holiday weekend. I found that I could calm down or excite a classroom simply by changing the genre.

My students began discussing the music, and many said their parents turned them on to jazz. The music enticed them to attend class, and their academic work showed improvement. My students and tutors began to suggest a variety of jazz artists whose music I could bring to the classroom. I observed how different jazz styles affected the students. Jazz fusion was too chaotic, and the big bands were too upbeat. Smooth instrumental jazz turned out to be the answer; there were no words the students could sing along with, or that would take their minds away from the subject. It is hard for a student to write down his thoughts or concentrate on reading when other words from another source occupy their mind. I played Boney James, Bob James, Herbie Hancock, Cornell Dupree, Dave Koz, and others, and the students loved it.

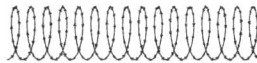

The second tutor I hired, Miami, resembled Wesley Snipes and had the jokey demeanor of Eddie Murphy. He was my head of security, my enforcer, making the students laugh while keeping them in line. Miami, whose nickname reflected his hometown, caught his bit when he ventured north to Detroit, and his drug deal went south.

Miami's friend Raul owned a grocery store in the South Beach neighborhood of Miami Beach. One evening, Miami and Raul were sitting around talking, and the latter said, "I'm tired of calling tow trucks to have cars hauled out of my lot while the owners spend the day at the beach. The towing services and storage lots are making big bucks, and I'm spending my time monitoring the parking lot and not making a dime."

Miami contemplated Raul's situation and said, "I've got an idea on how to solve your parking problem and make money for both of us."

Raul said, "I'm all ears."

Miami soon implemented his plan, purchasing car boots (wheel clamps preventing the vehicle from moving) to control the parking situation. He patiently sat under an umbrella in a chair in Raul's lot, reading a book. When someone parked in the lot and headed to the beach rather than the store, he would slap a boot on the vehicle, making sure the violator saw him do so.

Miami related how his conversation with the car owner would typically go:

Miami: "Look—I'm putting a boot on this vehicle."

Violator: "Hey! What're you doing to my car?"

Miami: "Putting a boot on it."

Violator: "Why?"

Miami: "This parking lot is reserved for store customers. [He points at a sign.] 'Customers only. All others will be towed.'"

Violator: "I'm going into the store."

Miami: "Oh, okay, you're going in the store—with your towel, cooler, and beach chair? I'm putting this boot on your car."

Violator: "Wait—I'll move it."

Miami: "Not with this boot on, you won't."

Violator: "I'll pay you 20 bucks to take it off."

Miami: "Twenty bucks. Ha! I don't think so. It costs $200 to remove it, but I will have your car towed. That'll cost another $200, and your car will be impounded, which will cost another $200 to get it out. So, in the end, you'll be paying $600."

Violator: [now in panic mode] "Look, you just put the boot on. I'll give you a hundred bucks to take it off."

Miami: "It'll cost you $600 in the end, and you want to give me $100? [Scoff.] I'm calling the tow truck."

Violator: "Okay—I'll give you $200."

Miami: "Make it $300, and I want cash. No tow truck, no impound, no hassle. There's an ATM right over there."

Violator's wife: [screaming] "I told you not to park there!"

Violator's kids: [crying] "We want to go to the beach!"

"By now," Miami continued, "the schmuck is willing to fork over $300, but I'd never take less than $200, no matter how much they carried on.

Sometimes, I'd pretend to call the tow truck to watch them beg. It was the same story all day long.

"To some, this job would be a nightmare, but for me, it was perfect because I'm kind of a prick. No offense, Mr. Myette, but rich White folks pushed me around when I was a valet, a bellhop, and a waiter at the Ritz. My new profession gave me a chance to push back. I'm just being real with you. Raul loved not having to spend his days looking out the window and chasing people out of his lot. I showed my appreciation by flipping him a couple of C-notes daily. My investment in the business was $300 for two boots, and then I was rolling. When I wanted a day off, I had a few friends who were more than happy to get paid for hassling honkies.

"South Beach is beautiful, the weather is excellent, and the parking is scarce, so it's one big, long money parade. I could knock down two or three K per day, but the best thing was that nothing was illegal about the job other than me not reporting my income to the government. My downfall was getting greedy and reinvesting my profits in the wrong place. I was up in Detroit trying to unload some 'goods' from South America when some people got hurt, and I got popped."

Miami knew how to explain math using real-life experiences, which made him an excellent tutor. And if a student tried to get out of work, Miami would not be buffaloed. You cannot con a con; he was one of the best. His anti-theft focus and strict enforcement of classroom rules were valuable qualities. Miami was my watchdog. He ensured that no one would walk out of the classroom with one of our pencils, pens, pads of paper, or pocket dictionaries—just as he did not let beachgoers park in Raul's lot. He appeared to enjoy confrontation in the prison classroom—just as he did in South Beach.

Sometimes, my other tutors would inform me of theft after the inmates were back on their units, but they would not directly confront the thief in the act. Miami, though, did not hesitate to challenge inmates on the spot. I overheard him being called an Uncle Tom, a snitch, and Miami Vice, but I never saw him back down from anyone. The students always surrendered the goods, so I stayed out of it. He was loyal to the one who signed his paychecks, and I was glad that was me.

I was impressed by the loyalty I saw in more than a few inmates. If you showed them respect, they respected you. These guys would watch your back, defend your position, and protect your life. If a new inmate entered my classroom and was disrespectful toward me, I checked him on his comments. Miami sometimes reprimanded him, and often other students chimed in.

The third tutor I hired was a bilingual inmate named Pablo, who had an intriguing pre-prison life. Having a tutor who can speak and write in Spanish is imperative in an ESL classroom. Pablo would interpret for me when the ESL students were tested for their academic abilities.

After Pablo worked for me for a couple of weeks, I told him that I had heard he had been a drug smuggler and asked him how he got started in that line of work.

"I got my pilot's license at 18 in Colombia. I eliminated the middlemen by buying the cocaine directly from the coca growers and personally flew the product into the U.S. In the middle of the night, I swooped my plane under the radar, over the Caribbean, around Cuba, and to small landing strips in the Florida panhandle or southern Alabama. I was wined and dined at high-end clubs in South, Central, and North America. I lived in the fast lane and wrapped my first Porsche around a tree at 19.

"I was making hundreds of thousands of dollars on each flight to the U.S. I had so much cash coming in that I bought a jet engine that I shipped back and forth in a crate between Colombia and the States for the sole purpose of smuggling coke. I packed the engine with the product, which upped my take to three-quarters of a million per delivery. Some people I knew who worked in the customs department at the airport helped me. I made myself and several others into multimillionaires. I did time for international drug trafficking in a U.S. federal prison, but my lawyers got me out early on a technicality. When I got released and deported to Colombia, I was so relieved to be free that I gave up moving drugs.

"Out of the blue, I started getting calls from Don, a major cocaine distributor out of Detroit. He owned a car dealership where he laundered his drug money. He had a home in the Detroit area and a beautiful summer home on Lake Michigan. In the old days, I would visit the up-north house, and Don would take me out on his yacht. He was more of a brother to me than a business partner, and we made each other very wealthy.

"Don said he was in a life-and-death situation and begged me to make one last delivery. But, after my first federal bit, I was banned from setting foot in the States. My mother and sister begged me not to go, but I wanted to save Don's life. I grabbed one of my fake IDs and hopped on a commercial flight with a load of powder hidden in my luggage.

"When I pulled into the hotel parking lot in Detroit, I thought I spotted several fed vehicles—I should have bailed out right then, but I checked in anyway. Don showed up and gave me the cash, so I gave him the goods. There was a knock at the door after he stepped out of my room, so I assumed he had forgotten something. When I opened the door, the feds rushed in. One shoved a gun in my face, and another slapped the cuffs on me and read me my rights.

"It turned out that the DEA [Drug Enforcement Administration] caught Don selling to an undercover agent, and they wanted to take down his supplier. They had a search warrant and turned his place upside-down. They found his little black book. I hadn't done business with Don in a while, but my name was still in his book, and when the feds saw it, it jumped out at them—they still had a hard-on for me because I got off on a technicality. They thought that I was the one who brought so much high-quality blow into Detroit.

"The DEA told Don they would cut him a serious break on his sentencing if he sold me out. They convinced him to talk me into making one last deal; the rest is history. So, because I have a soft heart, I'm doing hard time."

I am unsure how Pablo ended up in a state prison, having been convicted of a federal crime, but there must have been extenuating circumstances that I was not privy to. Whatever the case, it was a fascinating story that I always thought could have been made into an intriguing true-crime film.

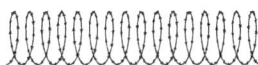

ⅩⅩⅩⅩⅩⅩⅩⅩⅩⅩⅩⅩⅩⅩ

Pablo had an endless supply of stories about his felonious exploits. One time, he told me about his travel habits. "In my younger days," he said, "I'd fly first class, but with a twist. I had a friend who worked at a morgue in Colombia, and he stole the identities of dead people. Under one of those names, I would buy $10,000 in traveler's checks that Lloyd's of London insured, fly to Europe, check into a luxury hotel, and contact Lloyd's to claim that my traveler's checks had been stolen. Lloyd's would ask if I wanted a new set of checks or if I'd prefer cash. Of course, I always took the cash but pocketed it for later. Then, I'd use the checks that I claimed were stolen, but only in small shops and restaurants that weren't tied into large databases and couldn't verify the checks. After vacationing like a king, I would come home with 10 large compliments of Lloyd's in my pocket."

Hearing about Pablo's experience as a drug runner and his travel adventures was part of what made my job so interesting. He was at a Level IV prison because of the large amount of product he was moving. I often picked his brain because I enjoyed learning about life in Colombia.

I felt good about my three tutor choices. Pablo was essential to my academic team, filling a void only a bilingual tutor could. The Hispanic students placed in my class immediately felt at home. Miami quickly set anyone thinking about stealing supplies straight, and adding music at Flint's suggestion provided a relaxed atmosphere I utilized for years. I was rollin' with an excellent tutor team and academic environment.

CHAPTER 18

Dealin' Drugs and Sellin' Guns

Baghdad, Birdman, and Hangnail

*"Drugs bring in guns.
They bring in all these Black-on-Black crimes."*
—Snoop Dogg

Sometimes, I sat in my classroom and wondered who was learning more, me or my students. One of my students in St. Louis was nicknamed Baghdad because his family and extended family migrated from Iraq. Their first stop was Malta, an island in the Mediterranean, then the U.S., where they disembarked at San Diego before settling in nearby El Cajon and, eventually, in Dearborn, a city by Detroit. Dearborn is home to about 110,000 residents and has the largest Muslim population per capita in the U.S.

Baghdad was the black sheep of his family because he did not conform to their Chaldean ways. Chaldeans are Catholics of Iraqi descent. Baghdad explained that Chaldean children generally continue to live in their parents' homes as adults, work for the family business, and donate their earnings directly to their father. When the children get married, the father starts them in their own business. As a rebel, Baghdad did not work at his father's gas stations nor live in his house, so, as they say in prison, he had nothing comin'—according to his family's customs.

One day in the classroom, I asked Baghdad, "What brings you to our fine establishment?"

He said, "My brother and I were on our way to a concert, cruising down Woodward in his Mustang convertible, with the top down. Four buzzed White boys in a black Honda Civic pulled up beside us at a light, and one hollered, 'Go back to Iraq, you fucking sand niggers!' Then another one pointed a snub-nosed .38 at us and started laughing."

Although I knew that such racist confrontations were not uncommon, hearing Baghdad relate this incident so matter-of-factly angered and saddened me and made me wonder how I would handle such a situation. "So, what'd you do?" I asked.

"I thought he was going to shoot us, so I reached under the seat, pulled out my 9mm, and fired several rounds at them. They took off, spotted a cop car in a parking lot, pulled over, and told the cops that two Arabs in a white Mustang had just shot them. It turned out that one of them was wounded, and the other was critically injured. My brother and I were arrested for carrying a concealed weapon, reckless discharge, assault with a deadly weapon, and attempted murder."

Wanting to hear more, I asked him if he had engaged in other criminal activities before getting busted for that offense. Inmates enjoy being out of their cells and, like most people, love talking about themselves, so Baghdad was more than happy to go on.

He laughed and replied, "You got a minute? I had hustles from Cali to D-Town. When my family first came to the States, we lived in El Cajon; I still got lots of family and friends there. I'd shoot down to Mexico, where I'd buy kilos of weed dirt-cheap, rent a diesel pickup with dualies, and take it to a chop shop where I had a connection. They'd pack the tires with weed. Then, I'd pick up some old furniture at a garage sale and toss it in the back of the truck to look like I was moving. I'd drive it cross country to Detroit, where I'd sell the weed for a whole lot more than I'd get in Cali. After we moved to Detroit, I had hustles there, too. If a Chaldean moved into town, I would help him get a car through my contacts and get a piece of that action. If they needed car insurance, I'd have that covered, too."

"Did you have a license to sell insurance?"

"No. It wasn't *real* insurance. I just gave them an official-looking card, and they'd give me $200 and put the card in their glove box in case the police asked them for proof of insurance. The card looked legit because it was professionally printed, but it didn't cost a couple of grand like a real policy would. If they got into an accident, they couldn't file a claim; that's the beauty of no-fault insurance. I'd renew the 'policy' for a C-note when it expired in a year. Insurance companies are such rip-offs," he said with a wink.

"Sounds quite profitable," I said. "Anything else?"

"Sure. I also sold cell phones for 200 bucks. The phone came with a number that was good for three months. They could call anywhere, even back home to Iraq."

"How'd that work?"

"I'd just buy cheap Tracfones, and I had a girl who worked for a phone company who'd give me numbers for money. When their phone would cut out in three months, the customer would return to buy another three months for $100. Sometimes, they'd renew their 'insurance' and buy a bag of weed while they were at it. Or they'd bring friends who needed the whole enchilada. I was the go-to welcome wagon guy for Chaldeans. I'd help non-Chaldeans, too, if I could trust them and they had money. It all added up and kept on coming. The more people I helped, the more people they brought my way. I didn't have to bang on any doors."

Baghdad paused momentarily, then said, "Hey, when I get out, I could use another driver to make runs from Cali to Detroit. You have the kind of look I want for the job."

"Thanks, but no thanks," I replied, thinking *I'd rather work in prison than lock in one.* "You should consider trying something legit yourself. I can tell you have some serious business skills."

Baghdad taught me how Iraqi families made their way into the United States and how they operated as a unit to build their empires in a new land. Before talking to him, I had little knowledge of the Chaldean ways. They are quite an industrious lot.

In prison, there are a myriad of entrepreneurs and hustlers who are proud of their shady business deals and criminal careers. They proudly tell stories of how they made piles of money by screwing people over. They do not look at their scams and drug deals as wrong; in their minds, they are just being smart and looking out for number one. If they can get one over on another person, a business, or the government, they are happy; they say the victims were dumb and deserved to be burned.

Before talking to Baghdad, I did not know Chaldeans were not Muslims but Catholics. Iraq has more Chaldeans than any other country. Their people existed almost a thousand years before Christ. Nebuchadnezzar II was known as the greatest king of the Chaldean dynasty of Babylon. Baghdad schooled me on these facts in my classroom.

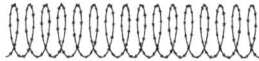

One hustler in my third-hour class was a tall, slim man nicknamed Tippy Toes because he could be in and out of places without anyone knowing he was there. Although he was into B&E for a while, he made the lion's share of his money by peddling crack and weed. I asked him where he sold his dope.

Tippy Toes replied, "Out of an abandoned house on the east side of Detroit. It was beat up and boarded up, and that's how I wanted it. I got the power and water turned on through a friend of a friend. I secured the windows and doors with two-by-fours and composite boards that I screwed into the studs. I'd sell weed and crack out of the back of the house through a small opening in a boarded-up window. No one was coming in, and I wasn't going out 'til I was good and ready."

"Did you buy rocks and sell them?" I asked.

Tippy Toes gave me a look like, *What cave did* you *crawl out of?* and said, "No. I bought powder, cut it, and cooked it up. You can make a lot more money off crack than powder."

"Did you ever smoke crack or snort some lines yourself?"

He gave me another one of those looks and said, "Mr. Myette, the number one unwritten dope dealer's rule is: Don't get high on your own supply."

I asked him, "When was your busiest time?" He shot me another glance that implied that I was an idiot.

"Enough with the looks already," I said. "I'm obviously not a drug dealer, just a curious White guy trying to understand what it is like to sell drugs in the hood. Thanks for helping me."

"Okay. The busiest time is when the welfare checks come in. That's when it gets wild. Any dope peddler will tell you to stock up before the eagle flies," he said, using a slang phrase for when government checks are received.

I said, "I think they should drug test everyone on welfare. No one should be getting high on the taxpayers' dime. I work for the state and get drug tested, so there should be mandatory drug testing for people who get food stamps, welfare, or subsidized housing from the state."

"Then no one would be getting paid. Why you wanna be messin' with everyone's paycheck? If you take the crackheads' dope away, there's gonna be a lot of ticked-off dope fiends and dealers."

I said, "I also have mixed feelings about legalizing weed. I think it's good for medicinal purposes. I know it'll bring money to the state and take it away from the drug cartels, but what has me concerned is the potency of weed these days. I can see people drinking alcohol, smoking a bowl, and being too ripped to be on the road." In 2018, years after my conversation with Tippy Toes, Michigan legalized marijuana for recreational use in some places, so my opinion on the weed topic was moot.

"How do you know about the potency?" he asked.

"I talk to people," I said. "I read." I was being truthful: I had not consumed any cannabis since I began working for the state, but I had heard many anecdotes about its increased strength.

"Yeah, right. What about crack? What's your plan on that?"

"Rehab centers. When crackheads get popped with a couple of rocks, they should be fined and have to go into a rehab center instead of jail or prison. Then they can see some of the lives they destroyed."

"Okay, that's better than being locked up."

I asked, "Why don't you get a real job?"

"I'm dealin' cause most of the legit jobs don't pay enough to live on, so a man gots to do what a man gots to do."

"There're jobs out there, and there's training available. I think there should be subsidized programs for people working for low wages. It seems like the mentality of drug dealers is, *I'll get my welfare check, food stamps, and whatever else I can scam, and I'll sell dope on the side.* Dealers are leeching off society, not helping anyone."

"I don't feel like I got any choice," Tippy Toes replied. "As long as I can get one over on the government, I'll take advantage of it, and I'm not alone."

I said, "Drugs are a real problem in our society. It's good to think and talk about the possible solutions, whether we agree or not."

"We *don't* agree. How'd you like it if I tried to take away *your* job? I don't have an education, so I have trouble making enough money to get by. You can't make ends meet by working at Micky D's or doing the Burger King thing."

"Well, at least now you're moving in the right direction. Get your GED, and go to a community college when you leave."

"I don't have the money for college," he scoffed.

"You should see a counselor and ask about getting financial aid for school. You'll qualify; the less money you make, the more they'll give you. It's good that we only pay you 59 cents a day."

"Very funny. I wouldn't know what classes to take."

"That's why you'll see a counselor, but your major or minor doesn't matter. You'll have to take certain classes, called prerequisites, no matter what direction you choose. If you start whittling, you'll reach your goal."

I was glad that I got Tippy Toes thinking. A couple of days later, he told me more. He said he would sell out of the old, boarded-up crack shack for three or four months, take some time off (presumably to spend the money he had earned), and then return to the shack for another stint. I asked him how he kept from going crazy, being confined like that for such long spells.

He smiled and said, "I had it made with my big-ass TV and tons of video games. My mans would check in on me and drop off pizzas, burgers, or Popeye's chicken whenever I asked. I was making a killing. I thought about everything I would buy when I decided to leave."

"How'd you know when that time came?"

"Depends on if my supplier could re-up me or not. I'd take a time out if there was a dry spell. I had to watch for the stickup kid and the cops—when my mans said they weren't around, I could leave the house."

"Yeah, timing is everything. Besides the money, was there anything else you especially liked about being in the house?"

Tippy Toes looked up at nothing as he pondered my question. "I liked it at five in the morning 'cause that's when the first bird sings."

That comment took me by surprise. What a juxtaposition: in a boarded-up crack house in the middle of the ghetto, a drug dealer is moved by the first bird singing in the early morning. This put Tippy Toes in a completely different light. With the risks involved in his endeavor, it was remarkable to think that he would get excited about something as commonplace as a bird. A "bird" in street language is a kilo, or 35.274 ounces, of cocaine or heroin. There is a flying, feathered, singing King of the Birds, and then there's Tippy Toes, a dope-slinging King of the Birds.

I realized that Tippy Toes and other students in my classes had more in common with me than I had previously thought. I just needed to ask the right questions to bring that information out. These young men did not readily expose their gentler side but would let down their walls if they trusted you.

It is incredible to think about what is happening at night in the inner city as most of us watch TV and check out Facebook or Twitter. I will never forget my conversations with my students, who took a walk on the wild side but still listened closely for the first bird to sing.

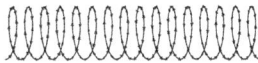

ⵔⵔⵔⵔⵔⵔⵔⵔⵔⵔⵔⵔ

A large number of my students had dabbled in the drug trade, which meant they needed protection. This provided a market for the sale of guns. In these precarious times, plain old muscle or carrying a club does not get it.

One day in my second-hour class, I asked if anyone had experience in firearm sales. Hangnail, a short man from Detroit's west side in his late 20s, gave me an affirmative nod. I invited him to sit at my desk and asked, "How'd you break into selling firearms, and where'd you get them?"

He said, "Different places. One time, I met this cat named Jasper at a party who owned a guns-and-ammo store in the city."

I asked him if anyone had ever robbed his store. He said, "I've been ripped off now and then, but no one ever broke in and cleaned me out. I wish someone would, 'cause I'd take the insurance money, get out of the city, and move to Mississippi to be with my family. Of course, I'd have to get a cut on the stolen merchandise, too.

"Anyways, after meeting Jasper, I thought, *This introduction is an invitation to opportunity.* Jasper and I stepped outside, talked it over, and worked out an agreement."

"Was that the end of your gun sales?" I asked.

As I expected, he answered, "No—that was just the beginnin'. When you got a good thing, you stick with it. I had a friend named Leon who worked for a company that shipped stuff by rail. My mans taught me how the railcars are marked on the outside so you know what they're carryin' on the inside. Leon told me where the railcars were gonna be and when. I took my crew and emptied the cars with guns, ammo, computers, leather goods, and whatever else would move on the streets. I'd pay Leon a percentage of my sales for the information. Guns move fast and can be sold in bulk, especially with gangs. They're my favorite customers; they pay cash, buy in bulk, and don't ask no questions."

"Why were your customers buying guns?"

Hangnail nodded. "If you want to off someone, the .38 Special is a great gun; they're cheap, you got six shots to do the job, and they never jam. You can pop the fool, toss the gun, and you're tight. AKs and Uzis are more for your drive-bys because you want to make a statement that won't be forgotten. Your Street Sweeper [an automatic shotgun] says, 'Hello, we're here!'"

Baghdad, Tippy Toes, Hangnail, and others were quite proud of how they made their money. However, no one expressed concern about healthcare benefits, 401(k)s, or building Social Security. The MDOC should help inmates see the big picture, making them more aware of how the world works. Of course, inmates need their GEDs, but other topics should be taught to help them help themselves.

CHAPTER 19

The Language of Prison

HOMES for the Homeys

"The downtrodden are great creators of slang."
—Anthony Burgess

nmates use a lot of slang in prison, just as they did on the street. I sometimes had trouble understanding the conversations of some of the inner-city convicts. My ability to comprehend came with time and asking questions.

For instance, I recall several prisoners coming in from the yard on a summer day, saying, "It be hot as a mug!" I thought, *Hot as a mug? A hot mug of coffee?*

About five months later, on one of the coldest days of winter, a shivering inmate walked in and said, "It be cold as a mug out there!" I thought, *He must mean a nice frosty mug of cold beer.*

So, a mug could be either a very hot or very cold mug.

I asked my class, "Okay, guys—here's a question. Hot as a mug in the summer and cold as a mug in the winter. What does mug actually mean?"

A student said, "Mr. Myette, if you *really* want to know what mug means—it means motherfucker."

There was laughter around the room. "Oh," I said, "a mug is a euphemism."

I walked over to the blackboard and wrote out the word, knowing most of my students would be unfamiliar with it. "A euphemism," I continued, "replaces an unpleasant or offensive expression. It's a more politically correct or acceptable way of saying something."

One student said, "Give us some examples."

"Okay," I said. "But you're going to have to forgive my French—or better yet, I'll forgive yours, just this one time. I'll say the euphemism, and you tell me what it *really* means—*in a quiet indoor voice.* Ready? Shoot means…? Darn means…? Fudge means…? Shucks means…? Friggin' means…? BS means…?"

Not surprisingly, the students aced my impromptu euphemism quiz.

In prison, like in many arenas of the outside world, some words and phrases require clarification if we have not been exposed to them. By talking to the inmates about different subjects, I could better understand the world they came from. On the units and in my classrooms, I heard some inmates using the term "sportscoat." I was unfamiliar with the word's meaning in this context, so I asked my student, Tippy Toes, what sportscoat meant.

He replied, "A sportscoat comes around when a man goes to prison or stops paying attention to his lady and looks elsewhere. Because the lady's lonely, she begins to look around. When another man notices that she's on the prowl, he makes his move. Someone locked up for a while might come home to see a sportscoat lying on the couch. You don't know whose it is, but odds are there's probably a butt-naked man upstairs with your old lady."

I got the impression that while Tippy Toes was in prison, his lady was cheating on him. I am always interested in different perspectives, so I asked Night Train, a tutor decades older than Tippy Toes, for his take on the term "sportscoat." Night Train was a big man: about my height, just under 6' 3", but with a larger frame. He was mild-mannered, helpful, and understanding—but then again, I did not know what brought him to prison.

Night Train said, "I definitely know what a sportscoat is because I was one. A sportscoat is a man who steps up to the plate and takes care of a woman's needs, emotionally, sexually, and financially. The sportscoat keeps her satisfied if the boyfriend, husband, or baby's daddy is absent—or running around, cheating on her. If her man isn't paying the bills, the sportscoat ensures the electricity isn't cut off, and the kids have food in their bellies. He doesn't give gifts to the kids but gives their mama money so she can provide for them herself.

"He's not trying to be the kids' dad or the woman's husband, and he doesn't want to move in with her—he just enjoys her company and wants her love and affection whenever possible. He wants a girlfriend, but unlike a sugar daddy, the sportscoat is not manipulative. He isn't trying to buy her love; he wants a relationship without the baggage of a marriage license or a mortgage. His woman is pleased and tells her friends about her new love. They are excited for her and wouldn't mind trying on a sportscoat themselves."

Sometimes, I heard terms used by prisoners and thought, *I do not know what they are talking about*, but the best way to gain understanding is to ask. Tippy Toes and Night Train saw things differently in the sportscoat scenario. One felt betrayed, and the other felt justified, so one was a scoundrel and the other a savior.

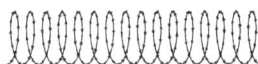

Nicknames have long existed among gangsters, boys in the hood, and prison inmates. The origin of a prisoner's nickname sometimes concerns his hometown. In Michigan, someone from Flint might be referred to as Flintstone; a Pontiac native might be called Yaktown; Muskegon, Ski-Town; Saginaw, Sag-a-Nasty. Out-of-staters might include Tex, Diego, and Philly. Alternatively, a nickname might be based on occupation: Pilot, Sarge, Schoolboy, or Doc. Or it could reflect appearance (either accurately or ironically): Shorty, Tiny, Red. This nickname game is a way for one's identity to remain somewhat private yet individual at the same time.

Nicknames for criminals are as prevalent in the headlines as they are inside the walls. Old timers remember Pretty Boy Floyd, Baby Face Nelson, and Machine Gun Kelly, but few would recognize the names Charles Arthur Floyd, Lester Joseph Gillis (aka George Nelson), and George Kelly Barnes.

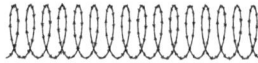

I told one of my classes, "We use slang all the time, but the terms may differ from state to state, city to city, and even within one neighborhood." I gestured toward a student and added, "I bet Bookie here could rattle off a half-dozen or more slang words and phrases."

Bookie asked, "You want some hood slang?"

"Sure. Give me some terms people in your neighborhood use."

"Okay, I went to my G-ma's, stopped at the bat cave, hit the traphouse, and ended up in the spital."

"I'm guessing you went to your gramma's and ended up in the hospital, but I don't know about in between."

"You're right on those two. G-ma be your grandma. The bat cave be your crib where you live. The hood be called the trap, and the traphouse be a crack house. The hospital is called the spital. Also, the spot be a blind pig, where you get high and drunk, gamble, and get laid. The chill spot or honeycomb hideout be the safe house where dealers or thieves keep their stash and lay low." Before I could compliment Bookie on his examples, he loudly proclaimed, "Some criminals be thinkin' they be superheroes. I know I do, 'cause I be Spookity Bookity!"

I told the class, "In here [prison], our 'slang' is mostly acronyms." I paused, wrote "acronym" on the board, and explained that acronyms are made from the initial letters of the words involved: SCUBA for Self-Contained Underwater Breathing Apparatus and LASER for Light Amplification by Stimulated Emission of Radiation. I said, "We use these acronyms but often do not even know what each letter stands for.

"You guys know most of the prison acronyms. An ARUS is an Assistant Resident Unit Supervisor. A RUM is a Resident Unit Manager. The DW is the Deputy Warden. An inmate's ERD is his Early Release Date. PV stands for Parole Violation. All of the state prisons have acronyms for their names; for example, MR is the old Michigan Reformatory. RCF stood for Riverside Correctional Facility. Michigan Training Unit is known as MTU, and all the other facilities have an abbreviation."

〰〰〰〰〰〰〰〰〰〰〰〰

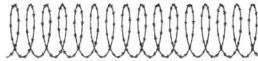

When I was new to the department, I asked an inmate, "How much time are you doing?"

"I'm doing all day."

"Does that mean you're doing a life bit?"

"Yeah. 'Doing all day' sounds better than 'doing life without parole.'"

Prisoners use language that minimizes the amount of time they are doing. If sentenced to five or 10 years, they will say, "I gotta nickel" or "I'm doin' a dime." When an inmate is out on parole for six months or a year and then catches another case or violates his parole, on returning to prison he will say, "I was out on the streets for a minute."

If a prisoner is closing in on his ERD (early release date), other prisoners or employees will say, "He's short." The term "short-timer" is used for an inmate doing a short bit, such as 12 to 24 months, or for someone approaching his release date, usually less than 12 months away.

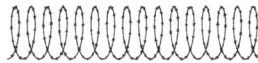

〰〰〰〰〰〰〰〰〰〰〰〰

When introducing new concepts to students, I needed to think about how easily they would grasp them. For example, I was teaching measurements and conversions, and I related the topic to the students by talking about kilos, pounds, ounces, and grams. Oddly enough, although they had great difficulty remembering something like there are 5,280 feet in a mile, they knew 28 grams in an ounce and 16 ounces in a pound. Hmm?

When I talked about U.S. cities, the inmates did not know much about them, but when I asked, "Where would I find the Cowboys, Dolphins, and Broncos?" they were instantly able to identify Dallas, Miami, and Denver, so their knowledge of sports helped them better understand the reason for each team's mascot and where these cities were geographically located.

I sometimes used devices to help the students remember facts. When discussing the Great Lakes surrounding Michigan, I would tell the students to remember HOMES. H is for Huron, O for Ontario, M Michigan, E Erie, and S is for Superior.

In a math problem, the more steps there are, the more confusing it gets. The steps in the order of math operations are P for the numbers inside the Parentheses, E for Exponents, M for Multiplication, D for Division, A for Addition, and S for Subtraction. That is a lot to absorb and retain, so we use mnemonics to aid our recall: Please Excuse My Dear Aunt Sally, or, as one of my tutors put it, Pimps Everywhere Make Diamonds And Sapphires.

CHAPTER 20

Disputes and Misunderstandings

Location, Location, Location

"You don't see any borders between countries from space.
That's man-made, and one experiences it only
when you return to Earth."
—Sunita Williams

After I transitioned from corrections officer, a custody position, to teacher, a non-custody position, I was no longer in the loop, so I did not know what was happening on the units. The inmates were my only channel to what things were like. On one occasion, CO Cappelletti called me and said, "I just wanted to let you know about a couple of inmates in your third-hour class. Miller stole Williams's store order in 3-B. There could be a confrontation; a snitch told me that, this morning, Williams told Miller that he's a dead man. So be ready for a blowout."

I was pleased that Cappelletti took the time to call and alert me; I was also shocked because that was the only time during my teaching stint when an officer gave me a heads-up. I immediately shared what he told me with the school officer. I also intercepted inmate Williams and talked to him before Miller arrived. There was no confrontation in my third-hour class that day or in the future, and that bit of good fortune might have been due to Cappelletti's prescient, thoughtful call.

All facilities in the system could use more professional officers like

Cappelletti. One CO told me that most officers thought the teachers coddled the inmates. I am unsure why—the officers did not seem to harbor the same animosity toward the nurses, psychologists, psychiatrists, and others who also worked for the inmates' best interests.

During my prison career, I taught in three prisons, and my classrooms never saw a fight or assault, although there were some close calls. Once, a couple of Hispanic inmates in my class were having a heated argument, hollering at each other in Spanish. I said, "Hey—be quiet! There will be no fighting in my classroom. You'll have to settle this on the yard." The two stopped arguing and were quiet for the rest of the period. And apparently, they took my advice to heart: Later the same day, a yard officer told me that, after walking out of my classroom and into the yard, two inmates started to throw fists immediately. I regretted suggesting the yard.

I used some tricks I had discovered over the years when I sensed trouble brewing. If a student acted up and would not pipe down, I would ask him to step out into the hall. If he kept on ranting, I would say, "Stop! Look me in the eyes. I know you can control your behavior in the classroom. I want you to apply yourself in there. Can you do that for me? Or should I call the yard officers to escort you back to your unit?"

Inmates appreciated that I asked them to step out in the hallway to keep our conversation private. They were not used to being shown respect in prison, especially by authority figures, but I learned that when I gave them some respect, I would get their attention. It would not have gone well if I had told my students to look me in the eyes and reprimanded them in the classroom. No one wants to lose face in front of their peers.

When the eye contact technique was successful, it significantly impacted the inmates' behavior. Most prisoners will not make eye contact when they are carrying on. They might say, "This is bullshit, blah blah blah." But when I said, "Look me in the eyes," and they did, their behavior magically changed; they would calm down and return to the classroom without incident.

Eye contact is a big thing in prison. Inmates use it as an intimidation tool. There is even a prison term for staring someone down: *marquetting*. I assume that it originated at the maximum-security Marquette

Branch Prison, which has sat on the shore of Lake Superior in the Upper Peninsula since 1889.

Still, there were a couple of times when my students got out of control and would not calm down. After I told them to step into the hallway, I had the school officer call the yard officers, who took away the offending student in handcuffs. Even this had a positive effect on controlling my room: The students would shake their heads, indicating that the troublemakers were out of line and deserved to be removed. They knew anyone I called out in the hall had crossed the line. They also realized that if they pushed that line, they would be removed wearing bracelets behind their backs. I gave them that choice based on what I learned in my Non-Abusive Psychological and Physical Intervention (N.A.P.P.I.) training. This made them responsible for deciding what they would do—in this case, calm down or go to the Hole. It was their choice.

After I was a seasoned employee in the department and was assigned to train new staff members, whether it was a CMA, CO, or a teacher, I would advise them, "The best way to avoid problems with prisoners or staff is to treat them with respect, be fair and consistent, and always remember the Golden Rule. If you want to have a good relationship with anybody, put yourself in their shoes and treat them as you would like to be treated because, under different circumstances, it could be you in their position. Of course, anyone who gets out of line or is just being a major pain has to be put in their place. You have to use common sense."

Before teaching, as an officer I carried a mobile radio, which we used for communication between staff, including calling for help. However, teachers did not have radios, so our go-to procedure in an emergency was to use a personal protection device (PPD). This device sends an alarm to alert the Control Center that the wearer needs help. A personal protection device is a touchy animal resembling a garage door opener. It attaches to one's belt, and, depending on where on the belt it is placed, it can be easily set off. In my years in the department, I never intentionally pressed the button on my PPD. But I did hit it accidentally several times. It was embarrassing when the yard officers ran into my room unnecessarily. Still, I was not the only one who made that happen; even this error positively affected my students. Inmates knew who would show up if they stepped out of line and just how quickly.

Whenever a new student entered my classroom in St. Louis, the other students asked, "Where you from?" If the answer was Detroit, the next question was, "East side or west?"

The dividing line between Detroit's east and west sides is Woodward Avenue, the main thoroughfare connecting Detroit with the northern suburbs and Pontiac. In 1909, Woodward (M-1) was the first street in the country to be paved with concrete, which was laid on a one-mile stretch near the city's northern limits. The avenue has been a landmark urban highway for over 100 years and is home to the Woodward Dream Cruise, the world's largest one-day automotive event.

No matter where people are from, many believe that their area of town is somehow superior to the others, so when a person is labeled by where they live, they wear the nickname proudly. In Detroit, if someone is known as Southwest or Dirty East-Side, their names refer to where they live in relation to Woodward Avenue. Inner-city gangbangers have strong opinions about each other's roots.

I tried to point out things the east- and west-siders had in common. All of them were people whose parents settled in specific neighborhoods for various reasons: to be closer to work, to be closer to family, or because the apartments or houses were more affordable.

I asked the students why they thought the people in their neighborhoods were better than those who lived elsewhere. I hoped to make them think about how silly turf wars are, locally and globally. I wanted them to question their moral code without getting them riled up.

I told them how students in our high school thought our school was the best. School pride is good, but hatred of outsiders is terrible. In reality, the schools we went to were often determined by where our grandparents or parents lived. Our religion is passed down through generations in the same way. Whatever religious sect the parents and grandparents preferred would most likely be adopted. The same is true of politics, prejudice, and pastimes. Right or wrong, we often follow suit.

CHAPTER 21

Black on Black

Choosing Colors

"Care not what they say about the color of your skin;
let the brilliant light of your soul blind them."
—Michael Dolan

While I was working on my master's degree, I read a book titled *Teaching Community: A Pedagogy of Hope* by bell hooks (like e.e. cummings, she spelled her name with lowercase letters only), the pen name of Gloria Watkins, an African American feminist educator. In her all-Black classroom, Watkins surveyed her students, asking, "If you were to die and could come back as a White male, White female, Black male, or Black female, which would you choose?"

Sitting in my St. Louis classroom, I thought about Watkins's question. I was apprehensive about asking my students but curious to hear their responses. I asked my four White male co-workers during my lunch hour. They all answered without hesitation, "White male," then asked, "Is this a joke?" These men did not have to ponder their answers; they were comfortable with both their race and gender, perhaps thinking, as I did, that women and Black people have more difficult paths in life.

To administer such a survey in a prison classroom, a teacher must have earned a high degree of trust from the students. Certainly, these questions could not be asked on the first day of class or with the wrong mix of students. I hoped that, because I had worked with my current students for some time, I could survey them with little fear of resistance or ridicule. After lunch, I presented the question to 10 Black students in my fourth-hour class, asking them to come to my desk individually.

Not one of them answered immediately as my White male colleagues had done. They all agreed this was a tough question and took it seriously, unlike my fellow teachers. When they finally responded, I was flabbergasted. Nine of the 10 said they would prefer to be White.

Tippy Toes said, "I've tried life as a Black man in the ghetto, and it ain't easy. I'd like to give the Caucasian thing a try."

Another student said, "This is a really hard question, but I think I'd come back as a White man because they have an economic advantage from the get-go."

The only student who chose to remain a Black male was Lieutenant Riggs.

The eighth man I asked replied, "The most powerful being on earth is a woman, and the most powerful race is White, so I'd like to try life as a White woman." I thought his comments would be met with laughter and ridicule, but I was wrong. Another student who had just answered "White male" said, "I'd like to change my answer to White female. Women control men and populate the earth, so I'm goin' with White woman, also."

So, two out of 10 answered that they would like to try life as a White woman. This blew my mind. I assumed the majority would say, "I'm a Black man, and I'm proud of it." I thought this way because I am old enough to remember the Black Power salute at the 1968 Olympic games and James Brown's song, "Say It Loud—I'm Black and I'm Proud," which hit number one on the R&B charts for a record-breaking six weeks in a row. The song was released in 1968, four months after Martin Luther King Jr. was assassinated.

My students' total honesty surprised me. The other inmates in the class could hear our conversations if they were listening, and they were. Considering the random manner in which I conducted my little experiment, I wondered, if the Black man who said he would like to be a White woman had been one of the first students to be questioned rather than the second to the last, would the results have been very different? I might have had several more Black men who would have followed suit with the White-female answer.

I believe that, in a classroom of White males, it would be next to impossible to find one who would admit that he wanted to change his color or gender, and if he did, he would be mocked to no end. I also do not think that there would be many who would say that women are more powerful than men unless their wives and girlfriends were standing over them, glaring threateningly.

My informal survey demonstrated the poor self-image of Black men in the United States today. Of course, these men were incarcerated, which would affect anyone's self-image, but I do not believe the answers from most Black men on the street would be significantly different.

This exercise made me aware of the importance of the female in the Black man's world. I remember my African American students talking about the mothers and grandmothers who raised them, but rarely did I hear any mention of their fathers. For the most part, fathers and alternative male role models did not play significant parts in their lives. African American father figures were largely absent from their experience, so as Black males themselves, they felt little self-worth. It is no wonder that 70 percent of the small sample I surveyed said they would try life as a White man and 20 percent would change both color and gender.

I have since posed Gloria Watkins's question to several White male friends outside of prison. When I said, "I want to ask you a personal question, and I would like you to give me an honest answer," they all became somewhat hesitant, not knowing what area of their private lives I was about to probe.

When I asked the question, the majority laughed with relief and said, "You're joking, right?"

I would reply, "No, I'm for real. I'm taking a survey, so give me an honest answer."

Every one of them said they would stick with White male.

I am glad I decided to survey the students in my prison classroom because I know I will never have another chance to poll such a brutally candid group of men. The White men may have been honest, but their quick answers showed they wanted to maintain the status quo. In contrast, the Black men considered the question seriously and gave answers demonstrating that they were not as content with their lives as my colleagues and friends—and I—were.

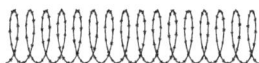

〰〰〰〰〰〰〰〰〰〰〰〰〰〰〰〰〰

Looking back at my classroom survey, I thought about Lt. Riggs being the only student who wanted to remain a Black male—I assumed it was because he was the lightest-skinned of those I interviewed.

Providing some context for her provocative question, Gloria Watkins pointed to a deep-seated but generally unspoken belief in our culture that darker-skinned Blacks are inferior and are here to serve Whites. She added that, for much of our country's history, most African Americans did not have access to formal education, except in all-Black communities. In such locales, the teachers were primarily lighter-skinned Blacks who were shown favoritism because they were considered upwardly mobile.

The racial dynamics I observed in prison were much the same as in the real world: White and Black inmates and staff treated lighter-skinned Blacks better than darker-skinned Blacks.

Watkins's assertions about skin tone prompted me to ask the Black students in one of my classes, "Do you think light-skinned Blacks receive preferential treatment over dark-skinned Blacks?" They all agreed that light-skinned Blacks are shown favoritism, in and out of prison.

When I asked for examples, one student said, "I worked at Value City and Meijer [retail stores], and only light-skinned Blacks were promoted to supervisor jobs. Dark-skinned Blacks got the grunt jobs, stocking the shelves at night and unloading trucks. It's like they don't want the 'darkies' to be seen or heard."

Another student nodded in agreement and replied, "My supervisors at Meijer, Burger King, and the Ford plant treated light-skinned Blacks better. The good jobs were always given to the Whites and lighter-skinned Blacks."

I asked one of my tutors, who appeared to be a light-skinned Black, "Zohar, what's your heritage?"

"My father's mother was a blend of Black, Native American, and

White," he replied. "I know my lighter skin tone has opened doors for me. I believe the more White you have in you, the smarter you are."

I asked him why lighter-skinned Blacks are treated better in our society.

He replied, "People think they're more intelligent."

I asked a very dark-skinned Black student, "Do you ever feel discriminated against by other Blacks?"

The classroom conversation had provoked him. He said, "I don't like the special treatment given to those baby shits," his affectionate term for some light-skinned Blacks.

I asked the class, "Do Blacks use a lot of different terms for Black skin tones?" This question brought the entire room to life, and the students shouted, "Cornbread…high yellow…caramel…redbone… brown sugar…chocolate!" and some things that I could not hear due to the ruckus I created.

"Okay, I'll take that as a yes," I said. I was unfamiliar with some of these terms that were part of the vocabulary of a scorching hot topic in the Black community, where it was discussed in detail.

While I had my students' attention, I asked, "What skin tone do you gentlemen prefer in a woman?"

"Light-skinned!" they all chanted. I asked if they could be more specific. The majority said redbone. Several men pointed at a Hispanic student when I asked how redbone looked.

Like so many others, that classroom conversation was very enlightening. In tandem with the responses to my original Gloria Watkins survey, and given my limitations as a White male, I gained at least some comprehension of how African American males look at themselves, other Black males, and females. I realized I did not have an outside control group to compare the inmate responses, but I felt more sympathetic to the Black males' struggle. All students need encouragement and recognition for their efforts, but those things were severely lacking in the Black population.

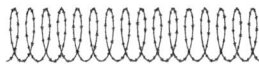

I thought about how I could increase the students' knowledge of African American history in my classroom. Coincidentally, during Black History Month, I was talking with a student from Chicago whose nickname was Chi-Raq (from one of the city's many epithets; it conflates Chicago with Iraq because both are hotbeds of violence).

I asked him, "What side of the Windy City are you from?"

He replied, "South Side. State Street to the west and Lake Michigan to the east. From State to the Lake, we say. I lived in the Ida B. Wells Housing Project. Ida was a sister who went through the struggle."

"What kind of struggle did she go through?"

Chi-Raq looked at me with one eyebrow raised as if disappointed and said, "I'm going to tell you what you tell us, Mr. Myette. Look up Ida B. Wells in the encyclopedia—or in your case, go online."

That night, I got on it. The following day, I told the class, "Chi-Raq used to live in the Ida B. Wells projects on the South Side of Chicago. This is February, Black History Month. Can anyone tell me who Ida B. Wells was or why she's an important figure in Black history?"

No one spoke up or raised their hand.

Chi-Raq asked me, "Did you do your homework?"

I told him that I had, and I shared what I had learned with the class. Wells was heavily involved in the civil rights and women's suffrage movements. She was born in 1862 to enslaved people from Mississippi who, along with one of her brothers, died of yellow fever. Ida was the oldest of her family at 16. She moved her brothers and sisters to Memphis, where she somehow managed to raise them while teaching school. One day, as she rode the train from the rural school back to the city, the Chesapeake & Ohio Railroad employees ordered her to move from a first-class car to the smoking car. Wells had a first-class ticket and knew her rights had been violated, so she sued the railroad.

She challenged the Jim Crow laws in her writings for a Black newspaper, campaigned against lynching, and helped found the National Association for the Advancement of Colored People (NAACP). The housing project bearing her name was built from 1939 to 1941 and was demolished over several years, ending in 2011.

Chi-Raq listened closely as I shared what I had learned. When I finished, he smiled, applauded, and said, "Mr. Myette, you *really* did your homework!"

"And I learned a lot," I said. "Ida B. Wells is one of the most important Black women in American history, and I'm embarrassed to say that I didn't know her story until you brought her name up. Thank you for suggesting that I research her life."

IV:
LEARNING ABOUT A
DIFFERENT WORLD

CHAPTER 22

Southern Time

"Shoveling horseshit and getting chased by bloodhounds"

*"Knowing it can always get worse,
I try to be grateful for whatever good I have."*
—Elizabeth Smart

My entire career with the department fascinated me. When I heard the inmates' backstories and talked to them about their feelings and values, I was learning about a different world. I could talk more candidly with the inmates once I transitioned from a corrections officer to a teacher. I asked about their pasts and tried to instill hope for their futures. Building confidence is a part of assisting students in achieving their GED.

After interviewing inmate Rodriguez, I saw some qualities in him that made me think he would be a good tutor, so I hired him. He was born and raised in Texas and spent time in prison there, too. He was a handsome, short, muscular man with medium-length black hair sprinkled with a bit of white and gray at the temples and a handlebar mustache.

One day, Rodriguez overheard the students complaining about being forced to work toward their GEDs. He said, "I can't believe these young punks are complaining about going to school. They should count their blessings and be glad they aren't doing time in Texas. Here, the classroom is warm in the winter and cool in the summer, and the state pays them to go to school. It's a lot different where I come from."

"They don't pay inmates to go to school there?" I asked.

"No. You will go to school if you don't have your GED or high school diploma, but you don't get paid. If you're not in school, you're working but don't get paid for that either. It's usually crazy hot: 100-plus degrees from sunup to sundown, and you're outside cutting Johnson grass with a sickle. They call that being on the 'hoe squad.'"

"Were the COs on horseback like in the movies?"

"Yup. They sit up there with their rifles and handguns, watching you and making you keep pace with the other inmates. They make you four-step it: 'one and two and three and four.' If you don't keep up, they'll two-step you, and that's twice as fast. 'One and two, and one and two.' It's hot and sticky, and dust is kicking up into your eyes and nose, but if you slow down, the guards will make you go into 'garden mode,' which is where you grab the sickle close to the bottom and cut the grass with a dull blade."

I groaned and said, "My back couldn't handle that."

"Believe me, garden mode is a real backbreaker, but if you stop, they'll lock you in a wooden box, and you cook in the sun. If you don't get with the program, the next time you'll get 30 days in the Hole, and six months for the third time. As I said, these punks should be glad they're at the Pugsley Country Club."

Rodriguez went on. "If the Johnson grass is cut and there's no gardening to be done, the guards would order us to dig ditches where there didn't need to be ditches, then make us fill them in just to be assholes. If it's planting season, you'll be hoeing and growing, weeding around the tomatoes, squash, onions, peppers, and whatever else. They'd give the extra food to the Salvation Army and soup kitchens in the area."

"That's cool," I said. "More prisons should be self-sufficient and help others. Did you do any other work?"

"Yeah. If you locked in a low-level unit, did well on the hoe squad, and followed the rules, they'd make you a trusty. Every Texas prison has stables for the horses and kennels for the bloodhounds, and the trusties may work with the animals. You'd brush the horses down and learn how to shoe them. You had to shovel a lot of horseshit, too, but the rest wasn't so bad."

"Well, it sounds better than working on the hoe squad, anyway."

"Oh, it was. Another fun job you might be asked to do is work with the bloodhounds to keep them sharp. The officers would dress you in a padded suit and make you run through the swamp and woods while the dogs chased you; it was a hell of a workout. Running in those padded suits is hard, especially if you're a little runt like me. But shoveling horseshit and getting chased by bloodhounds is still a step up from the hoe squad.

"In Texas," Rodriguez continued, "they don't allow you to choose your hairstyle—no ponytails, mohawks, or dreadlocks. Everyone has a butch cut and is clean-shaven—no beards, goatees, or mustaches."

"Seems like it would be hard to tell the inmates apart," I mused. "I remember when I attended my son's graduation from Army boot camp, all the soldiers looked the same with their butch haircuts. It was hard to pick him out of a group."

"That's a *good* thing in a Texas prison," Rodriguez said. "You don't want to stand out."

I could see Rodriguez getting lost in his memories of the harsh Texas system. "If you don't follow the rules," he said, "you get a ticket and most likely lose the chance to make the one phone call you're entitled to every six months."

"Only two calls a year?" I said. In Michigan Level I prisons, inmates can call whoever is on their phone list whenever the phones are available.

"If you get in a fight *here*," Rodriguez continued, "you might find yourself in the Hole for 30 days, but it usually isn't that long. If you get in a fight in Texas, it'll land you in the Hole for *200* days."

"Geez, that's a long time to be in the Hole," I said. I wondered what it was like in Texas for prison staff. I asked Rodriguez if the COs there made decent money.

"I don't know," he replied. "But I think some of them take the job because they heard they can make big money on the side. Some female officers would bring in rubbers and give inmates BJs for 50 bucks a pop, or they'd take it up the butt for $100."

"Are you serious?"

"Yup. Now *they* were on the 'ho' squad," the inmate grinned. "A female officer would go from cell to cell making cash calls. If they took in $400 daily, five days a week, for 50 weeks, that would be a six-figure side job. The money depends on their looks, personality, abilities, and how motivated they are."

"I think there might be people having sex here, but I'm sure it's not that organized or open," I said.

Rodriguez said, "A mixed-race couple worked at one of the prisons where I locked. The husband was a huge, mean Black lieutenant in his 30s with a little patch of a mustache in the middle, so everyone called him Black Hitler. His wife was a blonde, blue-eyed hottie in her mid-20s. She had an hourglass figure, and her uniform fit her like a glove. This little chick was making a killing on the side, giving BJs. She eventually got busted and was put on probation. Inmates would holler at her husband, 'Black Hitler, your wife loves to suck my dick.' That made him even nastier. Then his wife got popped one too many times giving head; they fired her while she was still a Green Tag."

"So, Texas uses the Red, Green, and Black Tag system, too?"

"Yeah, they did when I was there; I don't know if they still do."

"What were you in for?"

"Drugs. I got busted bringing weed across the border a couple of times. Did four years on my first bit and another two for assault on a second bit."

"Did you do time in more than one prison down there?"

"Yeah. In Texas, they called the prisons units. I was in Garza West, then Robinson, both units in Beeville. Next, I was in Dolph Briscoe in Dilley, then Darrington in Rosharon. Now, Darrington Unit, *that* place was tripped out."

"What do you mean?"

"The officers were mostly Black women, and they were selling sex all the time. It was out of control. One of the girls would walk down the block and motion to another officer in the bubble to pull the switch to open the doors. The officer walking the block would sell rubbers to the inmates, and the inmates had their choice of what they wanted to do with them and paid accordingly."

"Damn. Was the whole Texas prison system one big bordello?"

"All the units were corrupt, but Darrington's big thing was sex, mainly because of the number of female COs. Officers in Texas would bring in anything else you wanted for a price: weed, liquor, knives, you name it."

I asked Rodriguez if he had any hustles going on in Texas.

"It was hard to pass up since I wasn't getting paid to work," he answered. "I'd get officers to bring a pound of weed for $400. I'd pay $200 for the pound, and the other $200 would go to the officer. He'd bring the weed in three or four ounces at a time. It'd be packaged in Saran wrap or Ziploc bags, along with peanuts to cover the smell. I didn't care how he got it in as long as I eventually got my pound. If I sold the pound in ounces for $80 each, I'd get $880 in profit, or I'd sell skinny joints for 10 bucks apiece and make a killing. This was back in '94 in Texas, but joints here in Michigan are going for $10 now [in 2015]. Of course, the weed is more expensive up here than down by the border."

"Could you listen to music or watch TV?"

"Hell, no. These guys here complain that they have to pay too much for the MP3s for their players, and they whine about what hours they can watch TV. In Texas, there are no MP3s or TVs. And the inmates don't play basketball, tennis, or softball. They have softball diamonds, but I never saw anyone using them."

"Man—no sports, music, or TV," I said. "Hardly any phone calls. You're right: Michigan inmates don't know what a real prison is like."

Rodriguez nodded and said, "These lightweights here should start their bits at a Level V joint. The numbering of the levels was the complete opposite in Texas from what it is here: minimum security in Texas is Level V, but here it's Level I. And, in Texas, they start everyone out at maximum security working on the hoe squad, then working them down to the lower levels with higher numbers."

A few weeks later, Rodriguez filled me in on the weekend's events on Monday morning.

"Dude got his face burned off while trying to sleep," he said.

"Was it the old Vaseline and water trick?"

"Yeah, but the perp topped it off with a little piss and poop just to add insult to injury."

"Do they use the Vaseline and water in Texas, too?" I asked.

Rodriguez paused, then said, "Yeah, but it seemed like we had a lot more murders of both inmates and officers. The COs were crazy and crooked as hell. I don't think they had very good healthcare coverage or union representation because when one of them got his ass beat, he'd come back the next day with black eyes, broken glasses taped together, and missing teeth. If an officer gets beat down here, you won't see him for a month.

"I eventually worked my way up to the trusty division and was assigned to the warden's property, cutting grass and trimming trees and bushes. I liked to catch grasshoppers and flick them in the pond. I'd watch the fish, especially the largemouth bass, jump to the surface and gobble them up. The warden appreciated me fattening up his fish so that he could show them off to his cronies when they came over to toss in a line."

"Did he live on the prison grounds?"

"The warden and some of the administrative staff lived there. They assigned trusties to keep up the warden's estate: lawn, softball field, volleyball court, horseshoe pit, and a fishing pond."

In Michigan, wardens live off-site, and although they get paid well, their homes differ from the ones Rodriguez described. "The warden's spread in Texas sounds like a resort," I said.

"Yeah, they had it pretty cushy."

"Where did the officers live?"

"Every prison owned an apartment complex nearby for the officers. You could see them from the prisons. The COs would come in and talk about their after-work craziness. Not all of them lived in the complexes, but those who did were cut from the same cloth: unscrupulous party animals. But the warden threw the *real* parties. The local business owners would come to these bashes to land contracts for food, clothing, toiletries, furniture, state vehicles—you name it. I bet the bigwigs got plenty of money, gifts, and favors in return.

"Working on the warden's place was the best job in the Texas system, just like the tutoring gig is in Michigan," Rodriguez continued. "Unfortunately, we weren't paid, but there were benefits. If you overstepped your bounds, though, there was a severe punishment. One slipup and you'd immediately find yourself back on the hoe squad or in the Hole.

"There were other jobs, too. They were flexible about which inmates they let work outside the walls, and the inmates toed the line because the punishment was so tough. If you had farming skills, knew how to repair a tractor, or could mend a fence, you were a shoo-in for a job outside. If you were gate pass-eligible, you might spend a day driving a supply truck from prison to prison on the back roads. That's something you'd never see here. Texas prison regulations were like the Mexican Federales' laws—they make and break their own rules to get what they want."

I asked Rodriguez what the housing units were like in Texas prisons.

"At the lowest-level prisons, the inmates lived in pole barns, like a Michigan Level I. At higher levels, you are locked in a two-man cell. They didn't assign your bunkie by race or religion or what gang you rode with; it was more like how wrestling matches are set up. They matched you up by height and weight."

I asked, "Did they ever match a flyweight Aryan Brotherhood member with a heavyweight Black Gangster Disciple? And then start taking bets?"

Rodriguez stared at me expressionlessly for a beat, rolled his eyes, and turned to walk away.

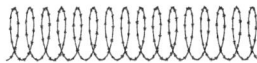

〰〰〰〰〰〰〰〰〰〰〰〰

For a brief period, I employed a tutor who had been incarcerated in the Mississippi State Penitentiary, better known as Parchman Farm. It was somewhat famous for incarcerating Elvis Presley's father in 1938 and the Bukka White song "Parchman Farm Blues." I asked Benoit—a tall, muscular Cajun—to tell me something about Mississippi's prison system.

Benoit replied with a question of his own. "Did you ever see the movie *Life* with Eddie Murphy and Martin Lawrence?"

I had seen the 1999 flick set in Parchman Farm, which gave me a reference and a better understanding of Mississippi prison life. The movie reminded me of the more famous 1967 Paul Newman film *Cool Hand Luke*, set in a Florida prison camp.

It seemed as if Florida, Mississippi, and Texas had similar styles of prison operations. According to the inmates I talked to, the movies were not far from reality. Southern prisons were rampant with sunburned officers on horseback, wielding rifles. They sat watching the workers through their aviator sunglasses while restraining the bloodhounds that were ready to chase down any prisoner who was fool enough to try and bolt.

"I've been down a while in Michigan," Benoit continued, "but when I was locked up in Mississippi they had 32 prison camps, each with its own specialty. For example, as punishment you'd be sent to Camp 29, a cotton-picking disciplinary prison, but there were also camps for raising beef and dairy cattle, pigs, and more. We also worked on the grounds of the warden's house: We mowed, trimmed, cut down trees, made trails, planted flowers, and landscaped. We weren't paid, but sometimes there'd be a cooler full of ice-cold beer on a steaming hot day. I guess the warden sent it."

"How about working in town? Did inmates get loaned out to maintain parks and roadways?"

"Yeah, we were on loan to clean up highways, fire stations, hospitals, and other places. There were four levels of inmates; the lowest-level ones could work inside and outside the fences, but the next level up could only work inside the prison. The two highest levels were maximum security, so their movement was very restricted."

I remembered seeing something on *60 Minutes* about the Mississippi prison system putting on a rodeo for the public. I asked Benoit if they still did rodeos.

"Yeah, they did when I was there. Every year, Parchman held rodeo and boxing matches to entertain the public. If you were asked to be in the rodeo or to box, it was best to do it, or they might throw you in the Hole. They ordered me to be a rodeo clown several times, almost as dangerous as riding a bucking bronco. I was scared shitless, but I did it because I wanted to stay out of the Hole."

"Sounds like a rough place to do time," I said. "Did you at least get visitations?"

"When I was there," Benoit said, "Mississippi had conjugal visits for married prisoners, and if you weren't married, you could slip a guard 20 bucks, and suddenly you were hitched until the end of that visit. The guards were underpaid, so they had a lot of scams going: You could get drugs, booze, and cell phones from them for a price."

Chris Epps was a former Mississippi correctional officer who had been repeatedly promoted up through the ranks. He did a stint as Deputy Superintendent of Parchman Farm and finally reached the very top when he was named Commissioner of the Mississippi Department of Corrections. In 2014, Epps was indicted on federal corruption charges. The judge who sentenced him three years later remarked, "This is the largest graft operation that certainly I have seen, and I have seen a lot." Once again, the scum had risen to the top.

It was intriguing to hear what prisons were like in Texas and Mississippi. The correct way of incarcerating criminals is a problem without an easy answer. It is similar to being a responsible parent. You cannot be too soft on them or too hard on them. There will be negative consequences if you lean too hard in either direction. I do not have all the answers, but I know there are more constructive ways of preparing inmates for reentrance to society than digging ditches and cutting Johnson grass.

CHAPTER 23

A Taste of Jackson Prison

Out of Control

"Inhumanity is the keynote of stupidity in power."
—Alexander Berkman

When Michiganders talk about prison, the first one that comes to mind is Jackson State Prison. Jackson has been the town's nucleus since it opened in 1839. It was the only state prison in Michigan until 1876 when two new facilities were built to ease the overcrowding. Jackson's old cells were tiny: seven feet by three and a half feet. The new ones were a whopping nine by five and a half feet. In 1988, Jackson was divided into four different prisons. Throughout its lengthy history, Jackson has had a negative reputation.

I was getting ready for class one day when I heard two of my oldest tutors discussing their experiences in Jackson State Prison. I have always been interested in learning more about the old Jackson, so I called inmate Beard over to my desk. I said, "Tell me about your first day at Jackson."

"I had just been released from Jackson's RG&C (intake unit)," Beard said, "and was following my sergeant into 8-Block, carrying my duffle bag and paperwork. Suddenly, I see something big falling from the fourth gallery, about 30 feet up from the bottom level. I look up to see it's a damn body. There's this huge crash, and it crushes the podium on the main floor. Papers and pieces of wood are flying all over the place.

I dropped my bag and stared at the body—there was a knitting needle sticking straight through his neck, and his head was smashed in, with a big puddle of blood around it. My sergeant says, 'What the hell are you looking at, fish? You wanna take a picture? Push on. Take that cell right over there.' He points to a cell behind me with an open door.'"

"Holy crap!" I said. "That must have been intense."

"No doubt. My legs were weak, and I felt sick, so I sat on my bunk. The sergeant's shouting, 'Parks, call Control Center and tell 'em to sound the siren for an emergency count! Greenwood, call the State Police 'cause we got a homicide! Johnson, call Healthcare and tell 'em we got another one pushed off the top! Rope off the crime scene. I'll call the fourth gallery to see if anyone saw anything. We'll get a porter to clean up the mess when the state boys are done.'"

"Sounds like the sergeant knew the routine."

"He had to. Things happen now and then. Anyway, I tried not to look at the mangled guy. I kept thinking about how easily that could have been me."

"So…rough first day, huh?"

Beard nodded and said, "And it wasn't over yet. The State Police came and did their investigation, the porters cleaned up, and I got settled into my cell. When the unit opened back up, I headed to the showers. I'm passing a stall in the bathroom, and there's some dwarf with his pants down, standing on an upside-down metal wastebasket. He's bent over, and this dude is giving it to him from behind. That and the podium crusher were the most bizarre and disgusting things I'd ever seen, but that's how it was in Jackson."

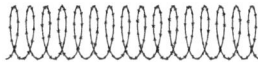

〰〰〰〰〰〰〰〰〰〰〰

When selecting tutors for my classrooms, I preferred inmates who were older or had been down for several years. McIntosh ticked both boxes. At the time of our conversation, Mac had been in the system for about 38 years, consisting of two or three long bits interrupted by some short stretches on the outside. He was what we call "institutionalized" or "state-raised." I wondered how well Mac would do in the real world if he had been released after all those years.

Some inmates locked up for 20 or more years may seem pleasant but are usually hardened underneath. The typical surface impression of a long-timer often differs from the reality of what is happening inside.

I asked him, "How can you have such a good attitude?"

"I've always tried to be a role model," he replied. "Just because you're in a toilet doesn't mean you have to be a turd."

"Did you ever lock at Jackson?"

"Yeah. I went there in '79 before they split it up in '88. It was huge."

"How old were you?"

"Twenty-four. I was only there for three years but felt like I aged decades."

Mac paused for a moment, then confided, "The things that went on there boggled my mind, mainly because the inmates ran the place back then. Since the prison was 140 years old, the cells were in such bad shape that you could open some doors with a little jimmying. The officers let different levels of prisoners mix and let the inmates move between blocks. Can you imagine? The staff completely lost control, and it came to a head with the riots in '81."

"I wasn't with the prison system until '90," I said, "but I've heard stories about the riots."

"The grapevine said that there were a lot of weapons floating around in Jackson. The officers wanted to shake down the whole place and asked the warden to okay it. He didn't. So, on his next day off, the officers went ahead with their plan anyway and started the shakedown at 11:00 a.m., right before lunch. The inmates were already upset about the conditions and were talking about rioting. In addition, they were hungry, so the timing of the shakedown annoyed them even more."

"Yeah, I know I get pretty ornery when I'm hungry."

"They were ready to blow. The siren sounded for the shakedown, and some inmates refused to lock up. They overpowered some guards, took their keys, and went on a rampage, unlocking other prisoners and assaulting inmates and staff. They destroyed what property they didn't steal, raped other inmates, and set fire to 2-Block. When all this hit the media, riots started in prisons in Ionia and Marquette."

"All three prisons involved were over a hundred years old, so they were less secure than the newer joints," I observed.

Mac nodded and said, "They were overcrowded and badly maintained, and the administration was terrible. They were like ships without rudders, so the prisoners took the helms."

I did a little research and found that the 1981 riot was not a first for Jackson. On September 1, 1912, a disturbance started in the chow hall, with inmates throwing their plates against the walls. Many fights broke out, and the riot lasted six days. The mayhem finally ended when the governor called in the National Guard.

In 1952, two maximum-security prisoners in Jackson overpowered a guard and used his keys to release the other inmates in their wing. One inmate was killed, and numerous inmates and guards were injured. Nine officers were held at knifepoint for five days. The 2,600 inmates involved caused $2.5 million in damages, which would be 10 times as much in today's dollars.

Because Jackson is Michigan's oldest prison, many tales exist. I liked acquiring my Jackson information firsthand. The stories of the tragedies that happened there in the past are shared with new hires in the academy for a reason.

CHAPTER 24

Of the Caucasian Persuasion

"What prefix are you on?"

"Two things are infinite: the universe and human stupidity; and I'm not sure about the universe."
—Source unknown, but often attributed to Albert Einstein

Throughout my prison career, I met several inmates from small communities who did not possess a high level of inner-city street smarts. These were primarily White inmates who came from rural communities. J-Man was one of them. The first time he walked into my classroom, he flashed me a smile, and I noticed he was missing just about every other tooth. He was a native Michigander in his early 50s with shaggy brown and gray hair and a scruffy beard. His last name started with "J" and ended with "ski." There were lots of consonants in between, so everyone just called him J-Man. This was not his first trip to prison or the Pugsley facility.

J-Man loved to talk, so I knew I had to get him under control. On his first day in class, he told me, "The last time I was here, I got married in the visiting room." Outlandish as it seems, an inmate wedding is not unusual in prison. Staff do not particularly like the ceremony because it requires additional work. They must shake down the bride, not to mention the minister or other officiant, and they have to run background checks on everyone attending.

The next day in class, J was again getting on the road to babble-on. I asked him to come to my desk for a few minutes. He immediately pulled up a chair and asked, "What's on your mind, Mr. M?"

I told him I was interested in hearing about his pre-prison life but would only lend an ear after he did some work. This attention-seeking trick worked well for several students.

One day, after J-Man had worked diligently for an hour, I asked him to come on down. I said, "I was wondering: What prefix are you on?"

"This is my fourth time down, so I'm on my D-prefix. Why?"

"I'm curious about how you first came to prison."

"Caught my first bit when I was 21. I was in a bar with my buddy, and these two dirtballs were giving him a rash of shit about his harelip. They were saying things like, 'What does a harelipped dog say? Mark! Mark! Mark!' They're laughing and mocking him, trying to make him snap. My buddy kept his cool, but I was getting hot. He turned away from them and started walking toward me. Then, one of them hit him with a kidney punch, and he dropped to his knees. Well, I'd been kickboxing since I was 13, and when I saw the scumbag's leg was planted, I snapped it with a sidekick. My bud knew I was ready to go ballistic on the boys, so he got up, pulled me outside, and said, 'Let's get the hell out of here.'

"We hopped in my truck, and I started driving through the parking lot, and then the other dirtball is running at us and waving a tire iron above his head. I clipped him with my bumper; I found out later that I'd broken his leg, too. Unfortunately, he got my plate number. If I hadn't sideswiped the dude, my bud would have caught that tire iron in the face. Those two started the whole mess, but I caught the case. The judge dropped my sentence from assault with a deadly weapon to simple assault. He gave me one to four years, and I did two on that bit."

"I suppose it didn't look good to the judge that the two guys at the bar each had a broken leg, and you and your bud were fine," I said. "When'd you catch the second bit?"

"Other than a couple of short ones in jail for DUIs, I was out of prison for 10 years. Things were going good until I started dating Betty, this hot little redhead who worked at the party store. One day Betty calls and says our friend Paul needs a ride to the store and back home. I don't think much about it. I give him a ride to the store and tell him I'm gonna catch a bite at the burger joint across the street. I take my food and sit in a booth right when four cops walk in. Two sit in the booth in front of mine, and the other two sit behind me.

"Paul walks in, and I holler, 'Over here, Paul!' Just then, the cops' radios start squawking like crazy, and they all run out of the joint.

"Paul shouts, 'Take me home, now!'

"I go, 'I thought we might hang out?'

"He goes, 'Now!' So, I grab my food and drive him home, though of course I'm wondering why he's in such a big hurry.

"A couple of days later, I'm sitting at home when the cops come and arrest me for driving the getaway car. Turns out Paul had just robbed Betty at the party store at gunpoint before he came into the burger joint. Betty planned the whole thing. The police knew she was up to something when they started to sweat her at the station. They brought her in for questioning, and she told them that me and Paul planned it all. I was lucky—I got a two-to-15 and only did two-and-a-half on my B-prefix."

"What about your third bit?"

"I was clean for 12 years, except for my third and fourth DUIs. Because of the armed robbery case, I couldn't have any guns on my property. Unfortunately, my neighbor saw me stashing them in the safe in my garage. About a week later, the same sleazebag neighbor came over to my house shitfaced at 3:30 in the morning, trying to sell me a stolen chainsaw and generator. I told him, 'Get off my property with that shit!' I guess he didn't like that 'cause when I was working on my buddy's car a few days later, the cops pulled up and said, 'We wanna see what's in the safe in your garage.' Next thing I know, they're arresting me and hauling me in.

"The judge ran the three-and-a-half years I got for the guns concurrent with the two-and-a-half for my fourth DUI. I haven't done as much time as most of these guys: two for the assault, two-and-a-half for the robbery, and three-and-a-half for the guns and DUI—not bad! And, of course, this bit."

"What's this bit about?"

"Me and my brother Jimmy were at a bar downtown, drinking. We were both pretty messed up, spilling drinks and stumbling around. The bartender cut us off, so Jimmy started hollering and causing a scene, and we got kicked out. I'm mad, so when I get outside, I take off my shirt, set it on fire, and throw it back in the bar. The bartender calls the police, and the judge hits me with attempted arson of a building, which is bullshit, 'cause I was mad and making a point, not trying to burn the place down."

Jimmy was J's hero, and their mindless escapades were seemingly endless. Letting J tell his stories not only improved his grades, but when I would say, "J-Man, tell me a Jimmy story," his reaction always told me that talking about his exploits with his brother made him feel good.

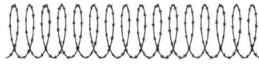

J was looking down and out one day, so I asked him for a Jimmy story. He smiled and launched into yet another sorry tale. "Me and Jimmy were out in his boat pounding beers and fishing. He was having trouble startin' the engine and commenced cussing it out. He finally gets so mad he unhitches it and flips it into the lake. I start laughing, but the next thing we know, the DNR motors up and says, 'Howdy, boys. Where's your engine?'

"Jimmy says, 'We ain't got one.'

"So, the cop rolls his eyes and says, 'Then how did you get way out here?' Jimmy didn't have a good answer, so they towed us in and wrote him up on a few offenses."

"What happened?"

J-Man said, "I went to court for Jimmy's case. The judge says to Jimmy, 'Mr. J, you have been convicted of drinking and driving three times. In addition, you have been arrested for operating a motorcycle, a snowmobile, and now a boat under the influence of alcohol. Please do us all a favor, sir—please do *not* get a pilot's license.' Everyone in the courtroom laughs. The judge gave Jimmy a fine and extended his probation."

"I bet you think about that every time you go to that lake?"

"Yeah, but mostly I think of my little brother Johnny."

"Why?"

"Johnny took the snowmobile out on that lake one winter, but the ice was too thin, and he fell through and drowned."

"Sorry to hear that. Was he drinking?"

"I don't know anyone that don't drink on a snowmobile, 'specially Johnny, Jimmy, and me."

"I'm sorry, but the judge did make a good point about Jimmy. You and your brothers seem to have an issue with drinking and operating motor vehicles."

J chuckled, nodded, and replied, "Yep, we're all pretty much drunks."

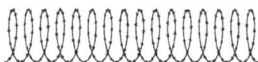

After a weekend off, I asked J-Man if he had any new Jimmy stories.

He said, "I talked with my mom this weekend, and she said Jimmy, his wife, my cousin Billy, and Billy's old lady were driving to my niece's wedding. The floorboard in Jimmy's car was rusted out, so he'd put cardboard and carpet over the holes. But on the way to the wedding, the carpet catches fire and starts smoking up the car something fierce. So, he pulls off the road, hops out, and pisses out that fire."

"I guess that's one time it paid off for Jimmy to drink and drive—so he could be a human fire extinguisher."

J-Man laughed and said, "How come you think Jimmy was drinking?"

I said, "Jimmy was on a road trip, and I haven't heard any story about you or your brothers that didn't involve drinking. I'm guessing Jimmy and his passengers smelled like burnt pee as they sat in church, and that could be embarrassing."

J-Man said, "Oh, you don't know my family."

I thought, *No, but I'm starting to get a pretty good picture.*

I could tell J-Man thought all his felonies should have been thrown out. He was helping a buddy on his A-prefix, just giving someone a ride to the store on his B-prefix, removing the guns from his house as ordered on his C-prefix, and trying to make a point at the bar on his D-prefix.

J-Man, Jimmy, and Johnny were examples of what not to do and why not to do it. They came from a different world than the majority of urban inmates. Although J-Man's stories were humorous, I often felt saddened after talking to him. I thought about the innocent people he and his brothers may have hurt with their drunken buffoonery.

CHAPTER 25

More Europeans

Dog Fights, Meth, a Forked Tongue, and a Street Walker

"We are all born ignorant;
but one must work hard to remain stupid."
—Benjamin Franklin

When I was an officer and had access to the inmates' criminal files, I noticed that the White inmates were incarcerated for a much wider variety of crimes than the Blacks. The Whites were in for Criminal Sexual Conduct, embezzlement, multiple drunk driving offenses, domestic violence, etcetera. The Blacks were mainly there for drug trafficking and violence.

One of my White students, inmate Reynolds, was a hyperactive country boy from southwestern Michigan, near where I was born. My family moved from that area when I was in kindergarten. When I asked him what he was in for, he said, "This time, dogfighting." I knew that hosting or being present at a dogfight was a felony. Knowing nothing about the culture, I asked him, "Where'd you get the dogs, and how'd you prep them for fighting?"

"I bought most of the pits in Arkansas. I'd feed 'em raw meat with gunpowder to git 'em ready to fight. It tears up their gut and makes 'em mad. I'd hook logging chains with weights on 'em to the dogs' collars to build 'em up, and I'd treat 'em like shit to make 'em mean."

"How was the money?"

"Once a month, I'd have five or six fights in one night. I'd make about $500 on each. When I got busted, the cops confiscated all 32 of my pits. Some were in rough shape. They put down the adults and took some pups to the Humane Society."

"Did you ever host gamecock fights?"

"No, but my cousin just got busted for cockfighting. When they popped him, they found 19 dead roosters. He hadn't buried 'em 'cause it was the middle of winter and the ground was frozen.

"We made decent money on the dog and cockfights, but the folks I run with are into meth labs now. Having a dog or cockfight takes a lot of time, trouble, and money. You gotta have a place in the country. You gotta buy the dogs or cocks, feed 'em, train 'em, and have a place to keep 'em. You also gotta have a barn for the fights and a field for people to park in. Then there's the noise, 'cause it can git loud, especially with dogfights. You can't have any close neighbors unless they're all right with what you're doing and will keep their mouths shut.

"The meth game is the way to go; you can git the supplies for about 50 bucks and turn that into $800 easy. Spending $500 on 10 batches of meth gets you about 8,000 bucks, and 100 batches will bring in $80,000. It's best to make big batches like Walter White on *Breaking Bad*. After I cooked it up like Walter and Jesse, I started making bank."

"What kind of ingredients did you need, and where'd you get them?"

"You can pick up everything at Walmart—ammonium nitrate, Coleman lantern fuel, powdered lye or drain opener, and lithium batteries. You gotta be careful opening the batteries 'cause the lithium will blow; it don't mix with water. You shake it up in a two-liter bottle for a small batch and filter it with Roto-Rooter."

"Are you serious?" I said. "No wonder it rots teeth and fries brain— fertilizer, fuel, batteries, and drain cleaner. Who would want to do that to themselves?"

"Hey, a lot of people want it, and once they have it, they want more of it. It gets you buzzed for days." Reynolds started to bob and weave and sang, "I like it, I love it, I want some more of it!" giving a whole new meaning to Tim McGraw's 1995 country hit. "Anyway, meth put cash in my pocket and took my mind away." I thought, *You got that right.*

I have seen plenty of tweakers (meth addicts) walking around in a zombie-like state. They are homeless because methamphetamines, like other drugs, took precedence over their jobs and families. I always wonder about what they could have been. I think about how their moms, dads, siblings, wives, children, extended family, and friends must feel about them. It saddens me. Drugs do not only hurt the users.

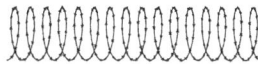

Back at St. Louis Level IV, toward the beginning of my teaching career, I was sitting at my desk when a new student entered the classroom. He was a big White boy, about 6' 5", with a shaved head, broad shoulders, cracker bolt tats on his forearms, and "88" (the eighth letter of the alphabet being H, and 88 being White supremacist code for "Heil Hitler") tattooed on the middle finger and ring finger knuckles of both hands. Both of his earlobes were split down the middle. They looked like a couple of small pink bananas hanging under his ears. Apparently, he miscalculated the size of his earlobe plugs. His short sleeves were rolled up, revealing swastikas on both biceps, and as he walked by, I could see a Confederate flag peeking over his collar on the back of his red neck.

I looked around my classroom, which was about 90 percent Black, and thought, *This should be interesting.* "Mr. Hoffman, take a seat, and I'll be with you shortly to figure out where we will start you on your reading and writing." I looked over his test scores, grabbed a second-grade placement test, and pulled up a chair beside him. I asked, "Mr. Hoffman, do you ever do any reading or writing on your own?"

The young man said what sounded like, "You mean outthide of thcoo-oh?" His speech was muffled like he had a mouthful of cotton. It took me a moment to realize that "thcoo-oh" was his rendition of "school." I asked him if he had something in his mouth.

"Yesth, ith my thung," he said, then stuck out his tongue and wiggled it at me. Hoffman had a split snake tongue, and the fork was flapping, causing little flecks of spittle to fly in my direction. I moved a few inches back and asked him, "What happened there?"

"I thpwit it with a thcapp-oh [split it with a scalpel]," he said, with more saliva flying out of his mouth. The inmates around him laughed as I moved further back to dodge any more spit.

"What made you do that?"

"Thought it would wook wike a thnake's tongue." Every other syllable was hard to understand.

"I guess everyone has their form of artistic expression. You need to take this placement test."

Wondering how Hoffman had landed in prison, I stopped by his unit during lunch hour to look at his institutional file. When I entered the unit office, I asked Officer Bard if we could look at Hoffman's file. I was pleased to see Officer Bard; I had worked with him as an officer at my two previous prisons (Riverside and Mid-Michigan) before this St. Louis facility.

"I have a new student named Hoffman who locks on your unit," I told him. "Judging by his shaved head and tattoos, he's probably with the Aryan Brotherhood. I was wondering if his file shows any violent tendencies?"

Bard said, "I know who you're talking about. He's a hard one to miss. Hold on." He opened a file cabinet, pulled out Hoffman's prisoner file, and started thumbing through it. A minute later, he broke out laughing.

"What's so funny?"

"Hoffman has a long history of bonehead moves," Bard replied. "He walked into a 7-Eleven, grabbed a 12-pack of Milwaukee's Best, set it on the counter, and asked the female cashier for a pack of Marlboro Reds. The clerk asked him for his ID, which he gave to her. When she told him the total, Hoffmann pulled out a knife and said, 'This is a stickup,' but he did not demand any money; he just picked up the beer and smokes, walked out the door, got in his van, and drove away.

"The clerk called the police. When they arrived, she gave them Hoffman's driver's license, which he'd left behind, and the plate number she got off his van. The cops drove to Hoffman's house and found him on his front porch, smoking a Marlboro Red and enjoying one of Milwaukee's Best."

I laughed and said, "Are you for real?"

Bard said, "I'm serious. It's all right here. He's not too sharp, but I wouldn't consider him assaultive. Listen, you haven't heard the best part: This joker's in for attempted arson of an occupied dwelling."

"Yeah, so?"

"So, the occupied dwelling he tried to torch was the police station. Good luck with helping this genius get his GED."

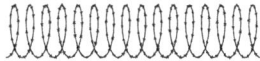

Some inmates have a way of justifying their criminal activities by attempting to make it seem that they are doing society a favor. A chronic-care patient from Riverside 10 Building, where I worked as a CMA, comes to mind. Rydell hailed from Detroit; he was a tall, muscular, mustachioed man in his mid-30s with long brown hair pulled back into a ponytail. He was doing considerable time for kidnapping, extortion, torture, and other crimes. He seemed proud of his exploits and had no problem discussing them. Unlike most White prisoners, he was from the inner city.

One afternoon, I was shooting pool with Rydell when, out of nowhere, he said, "My girlfriend Sapphire was a streetwalker working Woodward Ave. Sexy girl. She got sick of all the johns disrespecting her, so she came up with a plan for revenge. She said, 'Married men with fat wallets and arrogant attitudes need to pay for their cheating ways.'"

Rydell said that his house was buried deep in the hood, almost impossible for anyone to find, and in an area to avoid after dark. A visitor had to weave through a maze of back alleys, between abandoned warehouses and past salvage yards, to reach the dilapidated, century-old, *Addams Family*-looking three-story Victorian that Rydell called home.

While on the job, Sapphire would handpick a wealthy john and signal Rydell, lying low nearby in a white cargo van. When the john was in striking distance, Rydell would burst out of the van, grab him, and stuff him into it. Then, he would cuff, gag, and blindfold his victim before driving to his hideout. He would pull the van around the back, passing through the gate of the eight-foot privacy fence. To prevent his prisoner from running—and probably for his amusement, too—Rydell would wrap a choke chain around his neck to pull him along like a dog on a leash. As he led his victim into the house, they passed the barking, snarling Rottweilers that guarded the property. Then he marched his captive up to his third-floor attic, throwing him into a six-by-four-by-four dog cage.

Rydell would rifle through the john's wallet, then research his family, profession, property, and financial status—he wanted to know exactly what kind of funds he and Sapphire were about to inherit. He would threaten to notify the man's loved ones and ruin his career and reputation unless he surrendered his account numbers, passwords, and PINs. Rydell took his time: The longer the john was caged, the more information he would provide. If he refused, Rydell would choose a tool from the arsenal he had on display: perhaps a big hammer to break a little toe or a pair of pliers that could pinch and twist body parts that most men prefer not to have pinched and twisted. If a hostage did not give him what he wanted, Rydell would threaten to kidnap or kill his family members.

One day, Rydell went to his footlocker and brought out a Detroit newspaper article to legitimize the stories he had told me. I glanced at the paper briefly and handed it back; I did not want to make him think I condoned his behavior or thought he was some hero.

I talked to several of my female acquaintances about Rydell's kidnappings. They said, "The men got what they deserved." To me, their reasoning sounded uncomfortably close to that of Aileen Wuornos, the serial killer and prostitute who slew seven men at point-blank range. Wuornos's rationalization was that she was "angry about the johns."

I got the impression that Reynolds, Hoffman, and Rydell did not feel their actions were worthy of being sent to prison for. In their minds, dog fighting, selling methamphetamines, kidnapping, torture, and arson were all justified. They were just trying to make a living or retaliating for an injustice. This belief was shared by many of the inmates; it did not matter where they came from or their ethnic background.

CHAPTER 26

Crime and Corruption in the United Mexican States

Peruvian Flake and Mota

"Power does not corrupt. Fear corrupts…
perhaps the fear of a loss of power."
—John Steinbeck

In the early 1980s, I worked in a Mexican restaurant where I witnessed illegal immigrants being removed by immigration officials in handcuffs. In the mid-'80s, I lived in Cancun, Mexico, where I was an illegal alien for seven months. These were a couple of reasons I was anxious to learn more about what goes on around the Mexican border.

Felipe Martinez, an inmate and school porter when I was teaching at Pugsley, was small, with close-cut gray-and-white hair and a soul patch. He would come into my classroom after lunch, ostensibly to wipe down the tabletops and dust off the computers, but I got the impression that he just liked talking to my tutors and me. This was an opportunity to learn about the Mexican drug trade in the U.S. When I felt he was comfortable with me, I began by asking him where he was from.

"I'm originally from northern Mexico," he said, "but my family owns land in Texas, just north of the border. I have family on both sides, so it got real…interesting."

"How so?"

Felipe jumped right into it. "The Mexican border cops worked for the drug cartels. They were happy when someone wanted to transport illegal aliens, drugs, or guns into the States because they'd take their slice of the pie."

I heard that Martinez moved a lot of drugs in his time, so I asked him if he was comfortable smuggling contraband across the border.

"Yeah. I was, but I felt sorry for anyone who crossed with a load of fruit, vegetables, or car parts. Those good, honest folks ticked the cops off." Martinez paused, then grinned. "How were they supposed to make a living that way?"

"That's ass-backward," I said.

"Believe me, I know—but it was that way back in the day," Martinez continued. "If you were trying to cross with a ton of weed or 50 keys of coke, you were more than welcome at the border. Whatever game you had going, the border cops loved it because they knew they were in for a treat."

"Sounds like you were making them rich."

"Pretty much. They even made wish lists. They'd say, 'When are you coming back? We want some more Peruvian flake and mota [marijuana] like on the last load, and we'll take some AKs, Smiths, and Colts.'"

"That's pretty bold."

"They knew I didn't want any hassle. If I gave them what they wanted, I sailed right through."

"What about crossing on private land?"

"The farmers would take money to look the other way. The border cops took money, guns, and drugs for their payoffs. If I were moving drugs or guns and ammo, the officials would take a quarter of the load.

"Unfortunately," Martinez added with a wistful sigh, "border security is much tighter today. And things are more intense than when I was in the game. When Reagan started the drug war, the violence began to get out of control. He had the CIA purchasing drugs from Nicaragua to fund the Contra rebels. The U.S. government was doing a lot of dirty deals. Reagan started the crack epidemic and was responsible for putting a lot of Black people in prison."

I heard some of my students make this claim but never asked what led them to such a conclusion. I asked Martinez why he thought Reagan was behind the crack epidemic.

"Crack gets you higher faster than powder cocaine. You pop it in a pipe and light up—no laying out lines on a mirror or mainlining. And it's cheap, so the kids can afford it."

"Okay, but how do you think Reagan put Blacks in prison?"

"Under the federal Anti-Drug Abuse Act of 1986, getting popped with five grams of crack would get you a mandatory five-year minimum sentence. But if you're selling powder cocaine, you'd have to be caught with 500 grams to be sentenced to the same five-year minimum. Blacks use and sell more crack than Whites, who are more into powder cocaine. That law is how so many Blacks ended up in prison, and that was all Reagan's doing. That's why they made that law."

I asked Martinez to tell me more about his experiences moving drugs across the border.

"I bought a pound of Acapulco Gold for $20 in Mexico and sold it for $400 in the U.S.," he said. "If I bought a ton, I could make $800,000, but there was a discount for buying more volume. With coke, I could pick up an ounce for $4,000, cut it five times, and sell it for $26,000, but I wasn't dealing with ounces; I was making more significant buys. Just one kilo would sell for about a million dollars. If I purchased a kilo of Peruvian flake for $1,800, I could cut it five times and sell ounces for $4,800. Selling a few hundred kilos would bring in more money than I could blow in a lifetime.

"After working for a few years and proving myself to one of the cartels, I became the main man who delivered large loads all over Texas. I was selling weed by the ton, delivering 30 or 40 kilos of heroin at a time, and moving hundreds of kilos of cocaine. When I got to the border, I would toss a quarter of my load to the guards without blinking an eye and ask them what kinds of guns they wanted on my next trip."

"Were you just dealing in Texas?"

"The family I was working for liked that I knew how to buy off the border cops on both sides, so they wanted to take advantage of that. Texas is a big state, but the cartel always wanted more—they were looking to go nationwide and place me in charge of the Midwest expansion. I had some serious connections in St. Louis. I loved going there; they treated me like a king because of the volume I was bringing them. They took me to the exclusive clubs' VIP rooms, and I could have anything I wanted." Martinez looked off into the middle distance with his happy memories.

"Did your area include Michigan?"

"Yeah, and Illinois, too. I'd take a bus or fly to Chicago. Then, I'd rent a car, make my Illinois and Indiana deliveries, and drive to Michigan. My regular stops there were Kalamazoo, Grand Rapids, Lansing, Flint, Pontiac, and Detroit."

I asked him what he carried the drugs in.

"A suitcase, but nothing fancy. I'd pick out my luggage at Goodwill. The airport baggage handlers can sense money and sometimes rifle through the higher-end luggage. I would never put drugs or money in fine leather or name-brand bags. Smuggling was a lot easier before drug-sniffing dogs and scanners."

"Was there any money in Lansing? I used to live there."

"There was a *lot* of money there—between MSU, Oldsmobile, and the state capital, everyone wanted to get high. I had a lot of drug houses in Lansing that bought large quantities of product. The problem with some of those houses was that they would give me boxes filled with ones and $5 bills."

"What's wrong with that? It's still money."

"The problem was, I didn't have the time or space to deal with ones and fives, and my boss only wanted $100 bills. So, when I got a box full of ones and fives, I'd throw it into the nearest dumpster."

"What? What about giving the money to the homeless or charities?"

"I wasn't playing Robin Hood. I didn't want to bring unwanted attention to myself—giving away boxes full of money starts people talking. And I couldn't walk into a bank with a grocery bag full of ones and fives, plop it on the counter, and say, 'Change these into $100 bills, please.' In the game I was in, small money didn't matter. It was more important to make sure that there were no questions from anybody about anything. My assignment was to deliver the goods, collect the money, and bring only big bills to the boss."

I could not imagine living life on the edge like that, 24/7. "Did you ever have a chance just to chill?" I asked. "Was there any time when you weren't worried about moving product or carrying huge sums of cash?"

A relaxed smile spread across Martinez's face. "I'd fly to Cancún and stay at the presidential suite at the Casa Maya Hotel. I'd always hire the same taxi driver for my entire stay and put him up in the hotel, too. I'd have him take me and my friends to the Mayan ruins in Tulum or over to see the pyramid at Chichen Itza. Or we'd go snorkeling in the underwater caves in Xel-Há. To me, those are the most beautiful places in the world.

"I'd bring a bagful of tens and twenties that I planned to dump. I handed them out like candy to bellhops, waitresses, bartenders, and my driver. It made me feel great—there's nothing like the gift of giving. If the Federales bothered me for jaywalking or something, I'd pay them off. I didn't bring drugs, and I wasn't there to sell them. I was just there to relax and have fun; part of that was sharing my wealth. Everyone was so appreciative. I gave a few hundred dollars in tens to a little girl on the street who was selling Chiclets."

"Did you splurge on anything?"

"I started buying gold and silver and stashed it in my safe."

I wondered if someone with such a dangerous lifestyle could maintain any relationship, so I asked Martinez if he had ever been married.

"Yes," he said. "A couple of times. I felt bad being on the road so much. I'd come home and give my wives suitcases full of tens and twenties. They would spend it like it was going out of style, buying jewelry, clothes, and whatever else they wanted. I was okay with that because I knew I didn't give them enough time and attention."

I asked him if he had any regrets.

He looked me up and down like I had just fallen off the turnip truck and said, "Haven't you been listening? I lived in a world most people could only dream of. I made and lost fortunes. Sure, I got ripped off by cops, dealers, and buyers, but I still made more money than I could spend. I've been very fortunate to be in the right place at the right time. I've had a good life and am a fortunate man."

No matter how much money I made or where I traveled, going to prison would not be worth it. As Joni Mitchell says in her 1970 hit song "Big Yellow Taxi," "Don't it always seem to go that you don't know what you got 'til it's gone?" In Martinez's case, he would miss the lifestyle, the excitement, and the adventure. I would miss my family and freedom; money cannot buy those things.

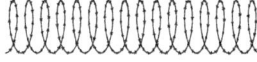

§§§§§§§§§§§§§§§§§

I was fascinated by Martinez's stories about life on the border and wondered if I could get more details from other prisoners. Besides the interest factor, knowing what kind of people you are dealing with is good for safety's sake. I asked around and found that inmate Rodriguez was from that vicinity. By talking to the inmates, I would discover things that were not in their educational and criminal files.

He said, "I grew up in southern Texas and northern Mexico. My cousins and I used to have tarantula fights."

Surprised, I asked him, "How did you catch them?"

"There were lots of tarantula burrows around my aunt and uncle's place. We'd wait for the spider legs to come out of a hole, then shove a stick behind them so the spider couldn't go back; it could only move forward. Then we'd grab it between its head and torso and toss it in a jar. When we caught another, we'd put it in the same jar and watch them fight."

"Would the winner fight the next one you caught?"

"No. After the winner buried its fangs or whatever into the other spider and killed it, we'd pour gasoline on the spiders and set them on fire."

"So, win or lose, both spiders were toast?"

"Yeah, but it was cool because the tarantula's torsos exploded, so they went out with a bang!"

"Mmm, deep-fried tarantula guts. So, was that a gateway to watching cockfights and then bullfights?"

"I guess—both cock and bullfights are Mexican traditions." I recalled that cruelty to animals is one of the three indicators of probable future criminal behavior in the "homicidal triad."

While I lived in Mexico, I visited a fair that featured cockfights. The spectators screamed, jumped up and down, and waved pesos as they placed their bets. I did not stick around to see the battle. I heard that the birds' owners strapped razor blades to their claws.

From what I had witnessed, heard, and learned about Mexico's rampant crime and corruption, I wondered who they even bothered sending to prison. So, when I overheard one of my tutors, Reuben Desoto, talking about his friend who had spent time in a Mexican prison, I invited him to my desk to tell me what prisons south of the border were like.

Desoto said, "Mexican prisons aren't run like any prison in the States. My friend Tito was living in Mexico by the border when he was busted trying to move a couple tons of weed to the U.S. He found out too late that paying the border cops off was a thing of the past."

"So, he got popped at the border?"

"Yes. The Federales wanted to know who his supplier was, but Tito wouldn't talk, so they tied him up, packed his mouth full of ice and duct taped it shut, plugged his nose, and beat him without mercy. When he tried to breathe, the feds would unplug his nose, pour hot sauce in a bottle of mineral water, shake it up, and shoot it up his nose. They busted a half-dozen ribs, knocked out his front teeth, and broke his nose.

"Tito played dead, which wasn't too hard—he was halfway there already. He was lying in the back of the feds' vehicle when he heard one of them say, 'He's dead; let's dump him in the desert.' When they looked closer, they saw that Tito was still breathing, so they took him to a jail; he was transferred from there to a prison and was locked up for four years."

"Did he get any medical attention?"

"I don't think so," Desoto said. "I don't know if he lost too much oxygen or had a closed-head injury from the beatings, but mi amigo was never the same man after that."

"So, how was prison for Tito?"

"He did okay, but you won't get anything if you don't have some support inside or outside. There is no classification placing you in a job. No quartermaster hands out sheets, blankets, or pillows. No officer on the intercom calls your unit to chow because there's no chow hall. Food is hard to come by: You must buy, grow, beg, borrow, or steal it. You gotta get a hustle immediately if you want to buy toiletries and food, or you'll be one stinky, starving hombre."

"Survival of the fittest, eh?"

"Yep. In a Mexican prison, you need to sell cigarettes, drugs, booze, weapons, food, clothing, or whatever else people want to buy. The prisons are real moneymakers for a lot of inmates and dirty guards. The prisons in the States give you everything you need to live, but in Mexico, you have to figure it out on your own."

Much of Mexico and its Central American neighbors are stricken with crippling poverty. Trafficking in drugs, arms, and humans is rife and extraordinarily violent. For these reasons, among others, there is a steady flow of documented and undocumented immigrants who risk their lives to cross the border into the United States, their Promised Land. There is no easy answer to this challenging situation.

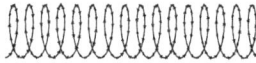

◊◊◊◊◊◊◊◊◊◊◊◊◊◊◊

Reyes was another inmate at Pugsley who lived in Texas by the Mexican border for many years. He told me, "Every year at harvest time, the farm workers in our area would drive around the perimeter of the sugarcane fields, playing a recording over a megaphone. In Spanish and English, the tape said, 'We're not the police or immigration. We will burn the sugarcane from the outside to the middle, so you must exit the field *now!*' This is part of the farming process. It does two things: It kills the microorganisms living on the plants, and it exposes the stalks to make them easier to harvest."

I remembered seeing the smoke from big fires when I went to Florida in the winter. Until Reyes clued me in, I did not realize it was probably coming from sugarcane fires. Live and learn.

Reyes said, "The sugarcane is too sturdy for the farmers' ATVs to drive through. Illegals cut out a small area to hide and sleep. The cane is thick and doesn't grow in rows like other crops. The aliens need to be alert because when the farmers start up the flamethrowers, they may be unable to escape, which is why they have found a lot of charred bodies."

Reyes said, "When Texas became a state in 1845, my family's property value increased. They and all their descendants became U.S. citizens, and there were suddenly lots of ways for them to make money. Some farmers on the U.S. side would allow coyotes [smugglers who aided the passage of undocumented immigrants] to cut across their ranches for

$500 a person. A truck packed with 40 illegals could make a farmer $20,000. That sounds like a lot of money, but it was nothing compared to the smuggler's take. A coyote might charge the illegals $12,000 each, so he could make $480,000 from them before paying out the 20 grand, a drop in the bucket."

There are many possible ways that illegals might perish on their pilgrimage to the United States. Countless citizens of Mexico and Central America head north when their lives are in danger from their country's gangs or drug cartels. Some Hispanics will participate in illegal activities to afford the high price of crossing the border. Talking with the inmates about their experiences surrounding the border gave me a better understanding of the problems with immigration today. There is no easy answer to the border crisis.

CHAPTER 27

The Gangs Are All Here

The Color of the Clothes You Put on in the Morning

"Everyone's a gangster until a real gangster
walks in the room."
—Al Capone

hroughout my career in corrections, I have encountered numerous gang members. For many inmates, belonging to a gang on the outside is how they ended up involved in crimes that brought them to the inside. Once they entered, they could hook up with their gang. Occasionally, they might take a break from gangland, which is easier said than done.

One day at Pugsley, a 5' 4", 122-pound 23-year-old man arrived. On his arm, he had two lightning bolts tattooed. These resembled the letters SS, a symbol for the Nazi organization the Schutzstaffel. Unsurprisingly, the Aryan Brotherhood (AB) tried to recruit him immediately. Although few of its members were housed at Pugsley, they have a significant presence in America's prisons regarding murder and mayhem. The young man told them he just wanted to do his own time; he fashioned a shank when they did not leave him alone. When he was approached again by some AB members, he lifted his shirt to show the weapon sticking out of his waistband. A CO witnessed this, confiscated the shank, wrote him a ticket, and placed him in segregation. Grand Traverse County

Judge Tammi Rodgers sentenced him to an additional 15 to 30 months for weapon possession.

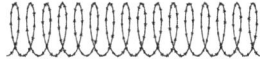

〰〰〰〰〰〰〰〰〰〰〰〰〰

A new prison hate group has recently emerged. Like other prison gangs, they use religion as a cover. Christian Identity followers believe in race separation, claiming Whites are God's chosen people. Michigan's prison system has been ordered under federal law to allow the Christian Identity to hold religious services. The law protects the religious freedom rights of this anti-government, White supremacist group.

I do not think the MDOC should recognize or allow any hate groups of any kind to assemble. Their meeting as a group only stokes the fire for more hostility and violence. When gangs are involved, rather than just a couple of individuals, there is the potential for riots to break out, which in turn will cause injuries to inmates and staff.

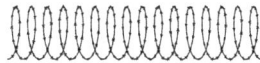

〰〰〰〰〰〰〰〰〰〰〰〰〰

On the subject of gangs, I told Derick, a new student, that I wanted him to write an essay on a topic he felt strongly about. The young man said he felt strongly that he never wanted to belong to a gang. I said, "Usually, I don't allow students to write about gangs, but I'm okay with it because you would not be glorifying gangs." This young man would be describing the negative aspects of gang life.

His essay was entitled "No Peace." He was from the east side of Detroit, where there were a lot of gangs that were constantly involved in fights and shootouts. Derick said the members never knew if today was the day to kill or be killed. There would be enemy gang members who want to kill you for something one of your gang members did. He said you could be shot because of the color of the clothes you put on in the morning if those colors represented the wrong gang. Some rival gang members would take you out to prove their gang was more powerful than yours.

Derick said, "When you're in a gang, there is always a fear you are going to go to jail or prison. You also fear for the safety of your friends and loved ones. The rival gangs may take out one of your family members as a warning to you."

These were the reasons Derick said he avoided joining a gang. In his neighborhood, there was a lot of pressure to become a gang member, but he said he would not join because once you are in a gang, there is no peace.

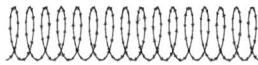

〰〰〰〰〰〰〰〰〰〰

One afternoon I was in my classroom talking with Stan, a fellow teacher, about when my wife, Molly, volunteered for us to get "bumped" on a flight to Florida. In addition to helping out the family of five that would have to be split up, Molly had an agenda. In return for our bump, we received two $500 vouchers for future plane tickets, a night at the Ramada in Newark, New Jersey, and $60 in airport or hotel restaurant food coupons.

The lady at the counter had said, "We'll get you on the first flight out in the morning."

Molly answered, "No, we'd like the last flight out at night. I want to spend the day in Chinatown."

The following day, we hopped on a bus to Manhattan, took the subway to Chinatown, and ate lunch at a very crowded Vietnamese restaurant. A friendly New Yorker allowed us to share his table with him. After an enjoyable afternoon, we made our way to the airport for our 8:30 evening flight, and we were pleasantly surprised to find that the agent booked us in first class.

While telling Stan this story, my students filed into the classroom after lunch. When Stan left, a student named Lopez approached me and said, "I heard the tail end of your Manhattan story. I love Chinatown during the day, but I'm always out of there before midnight."

"Why's that?" I asked.

"'Cause that's when the Flying Dragons and the White Tongues come out."

"Gangbangers?"

"Chinese Mafia—serious gangsters. They shake down all the businesses you saw and probably the restaurant where you ate. They don't care whom they extort money from. They'll hit up Chinese, Japanese, Vietnamese, and Taiwanese restaurants and grocery stores. If the owners don't give up the money, someone will get hurt bad, or their place will be destroyed. They're ruthless.

"The Flying Dragons' boss, Johnny 'Onionhead' Eng, got 24 years for 14 counts of running heroin. He shipped it into New York, hidden inside stuffed animals. Word is that Onionhead's cousin is running the show now."

I asked Lopez if he lived in Manhattan.

"Hell no!" he said. "I can't afford that. I'm from Brooklyn."

"What gangs run Brooklyn?"

"I don't know who runs it now. Things change; I haven't been there in a while."

"How long have you been down?"

"About 14 years. Back when I lived in Brooklyn, there were Crips, Bloods, and the Jamaican Smoke Posse, but it was mainly controlled by Latino gangs: La Familia and the Latin Kings were pretty much in charge."

"Were you in a gang?"

"No! I have a son. I had to get him out of there. He's bipolar, ADHD. The kid says anything that comes into his head. He wouldn't last a weekend on the streets of Brooklyn. I moved him and his mom up toward Boston, out of the city."

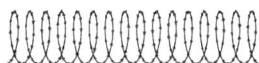

〰〰〰〰〰〰〰〰〰〰〰

When listening to NPR, I learned that Chicago was experiencing more gang-related deaths than New York and Los Angeles combined. I asked Chi-Raq to take a seat in front of my desk and said, "I want to know more about the south side of Chicago and what the projects were like."

"Have you heard of Cabrini Green?"

"Sure," I said. Cabrini Green projects earned a national reputation for their rampant lawlessness. "So, was your place in the Ida B. Wells Project like that?"

"It was off the hook."

"Lots of crime and gangs?"

"Yeah."

"Did the gangs wear colors?"

"I've been down a minute, but I think that's more of an '80s thing. Since I'm color-blind, I'm not the best guy to ask anyway. Every gang in Chicago knows where they can and can't go—and at what time—whether they're wearing colors or not. The best rule is don't be in any gangland after midnight. That's when the bangers are high on crack or buzzed up on tequila and are ready to start some stuff."

"You're the second inmate that mentioned the danger of being in a big city after midnight. I'm guessing that rule applies in most cities. What gangs would you find from State to the Lake?"

"Very good, Mr. Myette. You're picking up the lingo of the hood. There'd be GDs, Vice Lords, Four Corner Hustlers, Latin Counts, Latin Kings, Dragons, Maniac Latin Disciples, Latin Disciples, Y-Low-Ds."

"Wait, what does Y-Low-D stand for?"

"Young Latin Disciples."

"Sounds like a lot of Hispanic gangs. Are there many Black gangs?"

"A couple I mentioned and probably a lot I didn't, like the Black Gangster Disciples and the Mickey Cobras."

"Any White gangs?"

"Yeah—the Playboys, Gaylords, and Two Sixes."

"How big's their turf?"

"There's different gangs every couple of blocks. Some of them hook up and ride together because they're tired of fighting with each other, plus the more members, the more money—and that's the hokey pokey."

"Money from selling what kind of drugs?"

"It changes with time, but when I was there, it was heroin, crack, weed, and ecstasy. Then there's money from the old standbys: prostitution and robberies."

"What about coke or meth?"

"Powder cocaine wasn't happening back then. And meth was for country boys."

"How'd you decide which gang to join?"

"It's mostly about where you live. Sometimes your family are already members. It's like you go to a certain school because that's where you live. You might join a gang for protection if you're getting beat up all the time, or maybe you don't have any family, so you join a gang to feel the love."

"Do you get beat in when you join?"

Chi-Raq said, "Depends. In some gangs, you must take a beating—that's their way of testing you. If the police pick you up and take you down to the station to question you, your gang wants to know you can take a beating and won't crack. Then some gangs bless you in, giving you a load of drugs or 10 grand. They want to give you a taste of the good life."

"Do gangs ever do anything positive for the neighborhood?"

"Yeah—they close off the street and have block parties or throw the party in the community center. They always have a back-to-school party where the kids come with their mothers or grandmothers, and the gangs give away backpacks full of school supplies. They also throw Christmas parties where they give away tons of toys to all the kids. Their parties always have games, food, and drinks, and they're always a lot of fun."

I was surprised and glad to hear about the generous and legal things that Chicago gangs did for their communities, as the news usually covers just the negative aspects of everything.

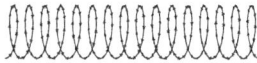

§§§§§§§§§§§§§§§§§§

One of my more entertaining St. Louis students was Lieutenant Riggs. He was married with children and claimed that he took good care of his family. He said he was a deacon in his church, coached his son's basketball team, and was an upstanding member of the PTA—all impressive accomplishments considering that he had a third- or fourth-grade reading level, at best.

Riggs was a drug dealer who sold to many gang members. Sometimes, he needed to lay low, so he would tell his wife that he was going away on business—then take a train to his safe house in Gary, Indiana. I recall driving past Gary when visiting a good friend in Chicago. Heading south, I could smell Gary well before seeing the steel mills by the water to the highway's right. On the left were rows of cookie-cutter houses where the steelworkers lived—and the safe house that belonged to Lieutenant Riggs.

Riggs said his house looked like all the others on the street, but the doors were steel reinforced, and the windows were bulletproof and secured by decorative bars. Video cameras were mounted in critical positions inside and outside. The lieutenant had a hidden staircase leading to a soundproof basement with a three-quarter bath, a kitchenette, and a sofa bed to sleep on when he needed to disappear completely. A safe in the basement housed an arsenal of weapons, a stash of emergency cash, and several phony IDs in case he wanted to go totally off the grid. This guy was more than a little paranoid: He had a panic room in his safe house.

When he was at the safe house, he went by a different name and carried himself in a different manner than he did back home, and he got around in a spare vehicle he kept in the garage. Riggs played dual roles in keeping everybody ignorant. In Gary, the lieutenant would wave to his neighbors and exchange pleasantries. No one from his Chicago life was aware of his secret other life—not his wife, children, extended family, or even girlfriends.

He kept the safe house up, trimmed the bushes, and mowed the lawn, trying to avoid any suspicion or complaints from the neighbors. Despite these precautionary steps, he must have slipped up somewhere because he was in a high-level prison for a significant amount of time.

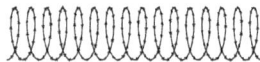

〰〰〰〰〰〰〰〰〰〰〰〰〰

I asked the class if anyone else was from Chicago, and a student named Rico, who was of Puerto Rican heritage, said, "I am."

I said, "Come up here for a minute." Rico rose, walked to the chair in front of my desk, and sat down. "Tell me, what side of Chicago are you from?" I asked.

"The northwest side—the Humboldt Park district."

"Are there any gangs there?"

Rico laughed at the naivete of my question and said, "When I was there, Humboldt Park was controlled by Puerto Ricans, and the strongest gang was the Latin Kings."

"Who were the others?"

He smiled and said, "There were so many gangs; it would be easier if I just wrote them down."

"Please do."

Rico started writing on a piece of paper. A few minutes later, he said, "Here you are, Mr. Myette. I'm sure I missed some, but you'll get an idea of how many gangs there were in my hood."

This was Rico's list:

Spanish Cobras, Insane Dragons, Maniac Latin Disciples (MLDs), Spanish Lords, Latin Lovers, Latin Eagles, War Lords, C-Notes, Milwaukee Kings (on Milwaukee St.), Harrison Gents (on Harrison Ave.), Unknown Kings, Puerto Rico Stones, Family Stones, O-A (Albany Orchestra on Albany St.), Y-Lo Cobras (Young Latin Cobras), Y-Lo Disciples (Young Latin Disciples), Imperial Gangsters, Latin Jivers, Insane Deuces, Latin Brothers, and Los Puchucas.

I looked Rico's list over and said, "Are you for real? I never imagined there could be so many gangs in one area. Are they all Hispanic, or do they allow Whites and Blacks to join?"

"Some gangs allow other races because the more members, the more money and power. But the muscle behind the gangs comes from the Mexican Mafia, and they have gotten into many of the neighborhoods and are backing the local gangs—money beyond their wildest dreams."

"I heard there were 18 gang-related killings in Chicago last week," I said, citing a statistic I heard on the radio on my way to work.

"Sounds about right. Money changes people's priorities. The gang-bangers grew up with nothing, and now they have more cash than they know what to do with. They want to flash it in the faces of their friends and family. They'll be sporting $300 shoes and $2,000 leather coats. Anyone who tries to take away their freedom will be looking down the wrong end of a gun."

In 2021, more than 800 people were murdered in Chicago; the killings were concentrated in the city's most impoverished areas and were mostly gang-related. Aristotle was right when he said, almost 400 years before Christ was born, "Poverty is the parent of crime."

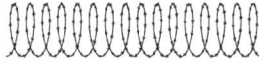

My tutors shared the classroom with me for about eight hours of my 10-hour day, so there was plenty of time for conversation. Murphy, a tutor with multiple incarcerations totaling over 20 years, hailed from Saginaw, or, as they say in prison, Sag-a-nasty. I asked him how someone would join a gang in his hometown.

Murphy said, "You're beat in—the gang members whale on you for five minutes."

I asked him what gangs were in Saginaw when he was there.

"In the mid-'80s, there were about 25 gangs. There was a rivalry between the Clicks and the Crazy Eights. There were also the Six Fours, 7th Street Players, Burt Street Crew, the War Lords, Brother Doggs, Jr. Doggs, Mafia Kings, and even an all-girl gang called the Golden Girls. All of them sold drugs and fought with rival gangs. Most of the violence was on the east side."

"Were women allowed in the gang's clubhouses?"

"The gangs were very promiscuous in the '80s. Members shared their girlfriends, and some even bragged about their mothers being sluts."

Gang names change with mergers and takeovers. Recently, the names have not been terribly original, with the North Side Gang, the East Side Gang, and the Sunny Side Gang, which occupies the city's south side. As in most cities, gang violence is mainly limited to inter-gang warfare within their territories.

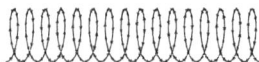

After I learned a little about street life in New York, Chicago, and Saginaw, I thought it was time to question someone about Detroit. I recalled attending a department educational seminar where I stayed downtown at the Renaissance Center on the Detroit River, about a five-hour drive from my home in northern Michigan. I checked into the Marriott at 10:00 p.m., tossed my bags onto the extra bed, opened the drapes, and looked out from my 32nd floor window. I could see the reflection of lights on the river from the casinos across the water in Windsor, Canada.

I decided to go downstairs to socialize with the other seminar attendees. At the time, I was the only academic teacher at Pugsley; my fellow educator, Jim Walker, had passed away.

I hoped to see some of the teachers from the St. Louis prisons where I used to work and others I met at previous seminars. I entered the glass elevator, looking at the panoramic view as I descended to the lobby.

While I was perusing the hotel's bars, I did not see any familiar faces. Wanting to experience *some* nightlife after the long drive, I walked over to the Greektown Casino to play a couple of slots and a few hands of blackjack. I am not much of a gambler, mostly because I know the odds are with the house. Around midnight, after losing a few bucks, I walked back to my hotel. Passing a strip bar in a shady area, I recalled my conversations with Lopez and Chi-Raq, and thought, *Maybe I shouldn't be here at this hour.*

After returning to my classroom, I asked one of the inner-city Detroit students about the witching hour. "Mr. Johnson, would you walk from Greektown to the Ren Cen after midnight?"

"Mr. Myette, if you be out in downtown Detroit or my hood at that time, someone's goin' to be checkin' you out. They gonna be buzzed up and feelin' cocky. They be lookin' at how you dressed and if you look like you got any cash. They be lookin' at how big you are, how strong you look, how you be walkin'. If they think they can get some money—if they think they can kick yo' ass—they gonna give it a try.

"They'll test you first—you know, see how you act. They'll roll up on you, ask you if you know what time it is so they can check out yo' watch, or if you got any spare change or a smoke. They want to throw you off yo' square, see if you act scared. But then again, if you try to play tough guy, you might be in trouble 'cause they probably packin' heat. Thieves rob pimps, hos, dealers, or anyone dumb enough to be out at that hour in the city. In the ghetto after midnight, you better carry a gun—'cause everyone else has one."

I asked, "What do you think about the casinos in downtown Detroit?"

"These days, with the casinos, the high-end hos don't need to hang out on Woodward no mo'. Now, Woodward be for the skanky-ass hos, drag queens, and dope fiends."

"Thank you for that update on the solicitation circuit, Mr. Johnson."

"Oh, I know more than that about Detroit. It's got about a million people, mostly Black. Dearborn is the Middle East, and the Arabs got all the gas stations and party stores sewed up. The Indians, you know—the kind with the red dots, got all the cheap motels—but you get around enough to know that. It ain't just in Detroit, right?"

"You're correct on most of your Detroit stats, except the population."

"Ain't there about a million peeps?"

"No," I said. "There used to be, but now the population is under 700,000. After the riots in '67, many Whites bailed out to the 'burbs, and, in the '80s, when the car companies closed plants and laid off all the workers, thousands more left town. Other than that stat, Mr. Johnson, you are a veritable plethora of knowledge."

"Why, thank you...I think."

My conversations with my students and tutors about the gangs on the streets and in our prisons helped me to be more aware of my surroundings. On the outside, I notice graffiti on buildings and boxcars that are sometimes gang-related. I am aware that those wearing clothing supporting professional sports teams could be representing a particular gang affiliation.

In prison, I looked at the inmates' tattoos, listened to their greetings with each other, and paid attention to their conversations, for they sometimes indicated which gang they were riding with. Prison employees need to be aware of the presence of gangs because they are behind the majority of violence that takes place. Employees must attend classes concerning prison gangs for their safety and the safety of others. I attended the training sessions and did some research on my own.

CHAPTER 28

Problems with Gangs

Rock and Pockets

"The vilest deeds like poison weeds
Bloom well in prison-air:
It is only what is good in man
That wastes and withers there"
—Oscar Wilde

When I was considering hiring new tutors, at each interview I usually asked the candidate to tell me about their prison experience. This allowed me to get to know them, see their communication skills, and check if their responses matched the files I had previously read. Selecting the correct tutors was extremely important to running a classroom. They had to have the right mix of academic knowledge, patience, and personality. Inmates could have all these attributes and still bump heads with the wrong group of people.

On one occasion, I asked a 37-year-old inmate nicknamed Rock if he had run-ins with his bunkies. He said, "It would be amazing if I didn't. I've been down for 14 years."

He continued, "On one occasion, I questioned my new cellmate about blaring his TV at night rather than using his headphones after midnight when I was trying to sleep. He instantly jumped to his feet and rushed toward me. He placed his hand on my forehead, squeezing my temples with his thumb and pinky, saying, 'What choo gonna do, bitch? I will butcher you!'"

Rock said, "I stood up slowly, brushing his hand away. My bunkie said, 'You need to fear the wrath of my brother-men.'" By this, he meant the Melantic organization he was a member of. The Melantics were a notorious Black so-called religious group known for committing severe violence against other inmates and corrections officers, particularly Whites.

I said, "The MDOC formally dissolved that group after the U.P. prison riot in 1999. I heard they're still around, even though they can't have formal meetings. Did you have run-ins with any other gangs?"

Rock said that two young Black men from the Nation of Islam (NOI) tried to recruit him.

They began to impart their religious beliefs to him, which were those of their leader, Louis Farrakhan. He said the NOI took it for granted that he was on board and agreed with all their teachings.

They began to instruct him to carry out assignments as a warrior and mandated that he adhere to their grooming practices. They asked him to post up (stand guard) for the Grand Sheik, the leader of the prison's Nation of Islam group. They wanted him to put his life in harm's way by acting as a bodyguard, following the head honcho around.

He began questioning the reasoning of the two recruiters and other members of their fold. The more he learned, the more he knew he disagreed with their beliefs. He told them he wanted to part ways, which did not go over well.

It was common knowledge in the housing unit that the Nation of Islam intended to do Rock harm for offending them. He said he learned to play a dual role, hiding his fear and insecurities, which every inmate must do to survive. He had to muster enough courage to go about his daily routine.

Then, while on his way to breakfast one dark winter morning, he observed a swarm of NOI members violently stab a man multiple times and leave him for dead. The incident caused such a ruckus that the administration ordered all members of NOI to be transferred to other prisons.

I asked Rock if he felt prison had changed him. He said, "Many prisoners go through the system and come out molded negatively. A pervasive malignant spirit demoralizes their souls if they are not strong. If someone's eyes are open, observing and reflecting on what is happening around them, they may be released into society as a much wiser, more socially conscious individual."

Rock lived up to his name, not wavering in his dedication to his belief system. He was more thoughtful and articulate, seemed to have higher moral standards than the average inmate, and fit the bill for my tutor team. He completed a couple of years at a Michigan university and probably would have graduated with a degree in psychology if he had not caught his case. He enjoyed working with people, had a positive outlook, and continually tried to improve himself. I observed Rock daily, and he was unflappable in the two years he was tutoring in my classroom. He said prison made him ponder his past and helped him on the path to self-improvement.

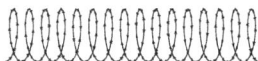

〰〰〰〰〰〰〰〰〰

Pockets, another tutor I hired, was a computer hacker from the Saginaw area who copped a plea for five-to-20 years on two counts of breaking and entering. The B&Es stemmed from six computer fraud cases in which he stole massive amounts of cash from ATMs and transferred the money into offshore accounts. Pockets was a 36-year-old man who acquired his nickname because it was said on the streets that he had deep ones.

Pockets was 19 when he was sentenced. He was sent to Riverside's RG&C and then placed in general population there. I asked Pockets if he had any problems with any of the prison gangs during his stay.

He responded, "I swear everybody in prison is affiliated with some gang or religion; everybody but me, that is. I don't hang with the gang-bangers, because there isn't any money in it, nor am I into religion.

"I remember an old White dude who rode in with a carton of Pall Malls. A Black religious group, the Moorish Science Temple, approached him and requested to buy the box. The old man refused the offer, saying he enjoyed smoking. The group respected his decision and left him alone, but a couple of days later, they saw the old man offering cigarettes to some of his friends. They took this as a sign of disrespect, which is not overlooked in the joint.

"The U.P. winters are always long, and the ground is usually covered with snow before Halloween and doesn't clear until Memorial Day. We could get several feet of snow in a week, which created many blind spots. The snowbanks along the sidewalks between buildings were several feet above your head. The inmate snow removal crews were the best. In prison, the sidewalks are scraped down to the cement without a sign of snow or slush. The snowbanks on the side of the walks are cut at a 90-degree angle.

"The emergency siren blew one day, which was odd because we usually got a heads-up. Occasionally, an inmate would overhear staff talking about the upcoming practice mobilization. On this afternoon, the old guy with the Pall Malls was found beaten down and stabbed multiple times. He had been lying there so long that he was frozen to the pavement in an iced puddle of blood. That's an example of the trouble a carton of smokes can bring in the slammer."

I asked Pockets, "What do you think of the Black prison gangs?"

"My bunkie was one of the Melantic leaders. The power structure of the group was out of whack, with the members fighting and stabbing each other over trivial bullshit. Many of the Black religious groups in prison are just prejudiced, violent gangs. They are not to be downplayed; prison gangs are no joke. They all try to recruit so they can grow and stay strong just as they do on the streets."

I said, "Did you have any run-ins?"

"Oh, yeah. I had this old, ornery Black guy who, unfortunately, happened to be my bunkie. He was a bit crazy, and it took its toll on me after a while. I had dreams about offing the old coot, so when I was finally able to move to another cell, I was elated. This angered the old man for some reason. I suppose he missed his whipping post. Truth be told, although I try to present it differently, in prison, I'm not considered dangerous. I try to play the tough guy, but most of the time I'm walking around scared shitless.

"One day, after I returned from the yard, I attempted to get in the unit's only shower, but it was terrible timing. My ex-bunkie, the old man, decided he would cut in front of me. This whole situation was entirely my fault because I'd been allowing the old man to get away with a lot of garbage for weeks. These were things that I would not let anyone else get away with.

"I would be sitting in the TV room watching *60 Minutes*, and the old fart would stroll in and change the channel, just to piss me off. I didn't say a friggin' thing. I just walked out, biting my lip and feeling like a castrated kitten. At other times, I'd be in the card room playing cards, and he'd walk right up behind me and yell, 'He's got the killer hand!' He was trying to trip my trigger, and it worked. I'd get up and walk out rather than call him on it. The more I allowed things to happen, the more they kept happening.

"So, anyway, there I was, attempting to get my shower, when the old fart cut in front of me. I finally spoke up and said, 'You have pushed me for the last time. I'm going in the shower next!' The old man got in my face, put his index finger on my forehead, and said, 'Bitch! No, you're not!' For me, that was the point of no return. Prison Rule #1 is: Don't put your hands on anyone. If you do, expect them to put their hands back on you. And that's exactly what I finally did. Everything the old man ever did to me built up to that point, and I hauled back and hit him in the temple as hard as I could. I knocked him out cold with a serious right hook, and then I did my best to beat the breath out of him. That was when the turmoil started.

"I found out a day later that the old man was a member of the Moorish Science Temple of America, so I was in trouble with the entire Muslim community. I was in a dangerous position. I think this was the first time I was okay with someone writing a kite to the bigwigs on my behalf.

In fact, it may have saved my life. The Level IV prison in the Thumb was all abuzz; they knew I was going to get stabbed like a pincushion. It seems like when the Grand Poobah gives the thumbs down on someone, all the warriors in the religious group want in.

"I was continually the subject of a conversation I did not want to be in. The administration had summoned everyone in my cellblock to the gym so the officers could shake down the unit for shanks, which were probably meant for me. This was all because I beat down the wrong person. Being in the gym with my entire unit was not good because there was nowhere to run or hide. While there, I was called in front of the Moorish Science Temple's council to tell my side of the story. They only believed my story because one of their members had seen the complete shower altercation, and, fortunately, he said I was justified in my actions. He saw the old man drill his finger into my forehead and call me out. Having a witness come forward probably saved me from being butchered."

Although Pockets and Rock are Black they found themselves in adverse situations that became more complex because of the politics behind Black prison gangs. The conflicts these men had gave me a glimpse of the challenges all inmates will experience, even when trying to stay in their own lane.

Inmates and staff must always be cautious around other inmates and staff. I am not being paranoid. I have been burned by both.

CHAPTER 29

Papa Smurf

There's Federal Law; There's State Law, and Then...

"If you forgive the fox for stealing your chickens, he will take your sheep."
—Georgian proverb

When I was a church camp counselor, a student teacher, and a park director, the kids I remember the most drove me crazy. It was the same way when I was an officer and a teacher in prison. I will never forget the ones that tried to push me over the edge.

Inmate Porter entered my room with a big, toothy smile, 30 minutes late on his first day of class. He was a boastful, 6' 1", broad-shouldered and light-skinned man in his mid-30s. After I got to know Porter better, he told me that, years ago, he had been in a car accident and was knocking on heaven's door for a couple of minutes. His friends at the scene told him he turned an alarming shade of blue before the EMTs started CPR. After he returned to the land of the living, they nicknamed him Papa Smurf.

I told Porter, "You're a half-hour late. You have a detail [a document that states where the inmate is supposed to be] for school, and you're expected to be here on time." He ignored my comment and talked about nothing to anyone who would listen. When he eventually found a seat,

I said, "Mr. Porter, you need to take these locator tests so we can get you started on the correct level of material, which will help you work toward your GED."

He laughed and said, "I don't need your GED. I make more money on the streets than any GED can earn me."

It was obvious to my students and me that Mr. Porter would be a royal pain in the keister. He did not do any work that day or come to class for the next three days, so I hit him with three major out of place tickets.

He stormed in late and irate on the fourth day, interrupting my presentation of Words of the Day. I tried to keep my composure when I exclaimed, "Mr. Porter, sit down! I'm trying to teach students who actually come to class on time and want to learn!" Porter snarled at me and took a seat. After his ticket trifecta, he finally started coming to class and coming on time. Knowing he loved to talk about his criminal exploits in Detroit, when he did some reading or mathematics, I would invite him to sit in the chair in front of my desk. I would boost his ego by asking him questions about his favorite subject: his criminal capers. This reward system worked well with many of my students.

Once, I asked him to come up to my desk at the end of class and said, "Mr. Porter, the way I hear you spin stories, I think you may have the makings of an excellent writer, but I haven't seen any real proof. Why don't you write a paper on what you want to be when you grow up?"

Porter snapped back, "I'm a grown-ass man, and I am what I want to be. I have a Ph.D. in B&E."

"I understand they call it home invasion now. Not exactly an honorable way to make a living, hmm?"

"Hey, I don't mess with people's homes. I hit businesses, and I'm not out to hurt anyone. If there's a possibility of someone getting hurt, I'm out of there. I rip off businesses that rip people off!"

"Or maybe you're ripping off honest business owners?"

"There is no such animal. They're all on the take."

"Now, that's a pretty broad generalization. Tell me, how did you break into the business of breaking into businesses?"

"You have to be creative. It all depends on the kind of barriers you have to get through. Tell you what I mean. I cased out a leather store filled with coats, vests, pants, and purses. We're talking nice stuff, like

Yves Saint Laurent, Brunello, and Gucci. The coats were selling from $1,200 to $5,500. All the drug dealers wanted them for themselves and their ladies."

"So, how'd the heist go down?"

"The problem on that job was the security gate that blocked my access to the back of the building."

"How'd you solve that problem?"

"U-Haul. They come in handy for B&Es."

"You rent them?"

Porter let out a laugh. "No, I borrow them. The people who turn the trucks in after hours leave the keys under the floor mats, in the ashtrays, or above the visors."

"You stole a U-Haul?"

"No—you're not listening. I *borrowed* a couple of them. If the customer leaves the keys in them, and U-Haul doesn't snag them until later, they're basically offering a public service."

"How nice of them. Why two trucks?"

"We used the lead truck as a battering ram on the security gate. When I got through the gate, I pulled around and floored it right through the back wall to get inside the shop. When we were ready to leave, we left the first truck where it was, with its nose buried in the back of the building, because it would have drawn too much attention on the street. I used truck number two to take the goods to my safe house; then I ditched it a few miles away."

I said, "Sounds like a good night. One B&E, thousands of dollars of stolen merchandise, destruction of property, and a double grand theft auto."

"Hey, U-Haul will come out ahead in the end," Porter said. "That truck had a ton of miles on it and was in pretty rough shape before I took it off their hands. And the leather store has insurance, so they'll come out all right, too."

"Yeah, they both probably wanted to send you thank-you notes."

I asked Porter once if he usually brought a partner to his heists.

"Not usually—always, and usually two. I wanted one inside with me, and I'd have the other patrolling the neighborhood, looking for cops. We kept in touch with walkie-talkies. You have to be very selective when you choose your partners."

"I'm sure they're all high-class, man-of-the-year-type model citizens."

"Okay. I admit I made some mistakes," Porter said. "Once, I was robbing a bar in the downriver area of Detroit. The register only had chump change, so I told my inside partner to grab the hooch. He loaded the cargo van with booze while I checked out the safe in the office. Usually, I'd split the take evenly with my partners, but when we got to the safe house to divvy it up this time, I saw that this fool had taken only the booze from the bottom shelf, which is where they put the liquor for well drinks, the cheapest crap they can find. He didn't look up to see the Glenlivet and Glenfiddich, Johnny Walker Blue and Patrón. He snagged the all cheap-ass house liquors like Popov vodka, Five O'Clock gin, and Kessler whiskey. I was so pissed I told him, 'You can keep that bottom-shelf bullshit as your cut. Any drinker can tell you that every liquor store and bar places the high-call hooch up top. That's why they call it top shelf!'"

"So, maybe your partner wasn't a drinker. Maybe you need to be *more* selective. You should know you can't trust a man who doesn't drink. Where did you sell the high-call liquor?"

"People I know. After-hours clubs and bars always try to cut corners and save a dime. There's never a problem unloading high-end booze."

"You mentioned checking for a safe. Are you a safecracker?"

Porter smiled and said, "A safe is welded together, and, like a woman, it has a sweet spot. You've got to find it, and when you do, if you hit it long enough and hard enough, it'll be yours for the taking. Small safes—I take them with me and open them later. A larger safe, you take off the hinges and pound wedges around the door."

"When breaking into a place, do you split if the alarm goes off?"

Porter snickered. "No, just the opposite. If I don't hear an alarm, I'm off like a prom dress. No alarm means someone's home, and I ain't goin' in. Remember, I don't want anyone hurt, especially me. If there's an alarm, it's a welcome sound. I locate the system and clip a few wires. It's usually close to the door, so I can get to it quickly."

"If you don't have a U-Haul, how do you get in? Pick the lock?"

"I'm not a cat burglar." Porter rolled his eyes.

"I'm serious; how do you sashay into these places in the wee hours of the morning?"

"First of all, Papa Smurf don't *sashay* anywhere. Secondly, I have the friggin' key to the city. My trusty four-foot crowbar! I don't kick in the door—I *remove* it, frame and all. And then I *strut*—not sashay—through the hole."

"So, you go for the cash register, the safe, the booze…anything else?"

"Of course; I go for it all. One night, we weren't having any luck. Every place we wanted to hit, there was a reason not to hit it; a cop was parked nearby, a wino passed out by the back door, or a dog was barking. Finally, it was almost sunrise, and we rolled up on this dive bar that looked like a possibility. It had a security door, so I used the crowbar to rip the frame off, and the door fell in. This place had a bunch of those Megatouch video gambling machines that sit on the bar. With those things, you get a double whammy because you can sell the machines after you take the wad of bills inside. I love it when the bar owners let the money build up. On that haul, I got 30k. Then I sold the 10 machines for $1,500 apiece to a couple of bar owners on the other side of town. Used machines are usually about $1,900; new they're about $5,000, so both of my customers were happy, and I made another 15k.

"Then there's the bar offices—they can be little goldmines. The owners always try to be big shots, inviting waitresses in for a quickie, to do a few lines, or maybe burn a fatty. It ain't unusual to find primo booze, fine wine, all kinds of drugs, jewelry, Cuban cigars, and other goodies inside the office. The owners and their special guests are usually the only ones who go in there.

"One time, I was sniffing around a bar office, and my partner stepped in and said, 'You smell that? Smells like weed. It's in here somewhere.' I'd already shaken the place down and found nothing. I glanced up and saw a tile in the acoustic drop ceiling that was a little askew. I pick up a broom standing in the corner and give the tile a little shove to the side—and a kilo of weed hits the floor with a thud. We both just started laughing and high-stepping. It was a beautiful thing.

"We took 10 kilos from the overhead hideaway. The bar owner had a hell of a side business. I wondered if he made more selling the booze or weed."

ⱰⱰⱰⱰⱰⱰⱰⱰⱰⱰⱰⱰⱰⱰⱰⱰ

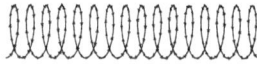

On a particularly disagreeable winter morning with the winds of a merciless blizzard howling, I finished shoveling my way out of my driveway. Once again, I drove to work through snowdrifts on the unplowed back-country roads of Grand Traverse County. Fortunately, I had put snow tires on my Honda Accord to help me struggle through the 18 inches of fresh snow. On a good day, a four-wheel-drive truck might have left a path of tire tracks I could take advantage of. I had to keep a steady pace if there was a foot or more of snow, like this morning. But not too slow, or I would get stuck in the middle of nowhere: Pugsley Correctional Facility was 10 miles from the nearest town and 28 miles from my home.

After crossing the prison yard, I unlocked my classroom and shook off the cold. Porter entered the class as I removed my gloves, coat, and hat. He was early for once. He laughed and said, "I thought you were gonna be a no-show, and I'd have to hit you with a major out of place ticket!"

"Oh, now *you* got jokes?" I said. "Hey, I was listening to the news on the way in and heard about a Verizon store that got hit. Do you have a crew out there working for you?"

"Yeah. Where'd it happen? 'Cause I got a girl I trained in the city. She hits cellphone stores and sells the goods to the Arabs. They sure do like their phones. I hit a few myself, and when I did, I called up this Arab who owns a store, and he'd buy everything I had any time I called. He'd drive in the middle of the night to pick them up with cash money. This guy loved to hear from me, and I loved to do business with him. Once, I stumbled onto a place where I lifted 50 $500 phones, and he bought them for $250 a piece. He turned around and sold them for $500 a pop, and we each made twelve-and-a-half grand."

"Ever rip off a train?"

"Who do I look like—Jesse friggin' James? No trains or stagecoaches for me, cowboy. I wouldn't touch a train. I don't want anything to do with the feds. I can deal with the state because I keep a stash of cash around for my lawyers, then I'll cop a plea, but I don't do planes, trains, or automobiles."

"Anything other than B&Es?"

"I was into the dope game for a minute. I dealt crack and powder. I wasn't selling the crack; my assistants took care of that. I'd find abandoned houses, pay someone to install security doors and board up the windows. I'd kick on the power by going to the utility box and removing the cheap-ass lock; then I'd twist the glass bubble and push it in. I'd pay a brother 50 bucks to flip the cable switch on; then I'd pay someone else to sell my goods."

"That sounds familiar," I said, recalling Tippy Toes's similar tale.

"It should. Everyone does it."

"What kind of money did you bring in?"

"I'd drop off the crack, my pushers would each make $500 a day, and I'd make $2,500 a day on each of my four houses. I also sold powder—kilos, ounces, halves, quarters, and eight balls. But the crack was the most bang for the buck because you could stomp the crap out of it." (Stomping is slang for "cutting" a drug: mixing it to increase the weight and thus the dealer's profit.)

"Why'd you quit if it was so lucrative?" I asked.

"I stepped aside when they started indicting people close to me. I was due for a career change. You can catch a lot of time for slinging dope, but with a B&E, if you have a good lawyer and a couple of bucks, you're only gonna do a short bit."

"What kind of time?"

"One to five, but a good lawyer would plea bargain it down."

"What if you have a gun?"

"I leave those at home. A gun'll get you eight-to-15 on a robbery. Armed robbery ain't no joke. Just carrying a gun around is a two-year flat sentence. So, if I'm gonna rob a place, I don't carry. I got popped one time but wasn't too worried. I knew a guy who had money friends."

"What's a money friend?"

"A money friend is someone that can make things happen. When people asked, 'How you gonna take care of that?' my man Cash Money would hold up a wad of bills and say, 'I've got friends!' This dude knew some folks in all the right places, and mysteriously, some prosecution files on my case came up missing."

"So, if I understand you right, Cash Money is the big roller, and he knows all the right people, who're called 'money friends.' And, with a little moolah, these people can make files and evidence—or, I'm guessing, even people—disappear?"

Porter said, "Bingo, Mr. Myette. Justice is up for sale in America. Everyone's on the take: cops, judges, and especially lawyers."

"Maybe only the sleazeball lawyers that would take on *your* cases?"

"Hey, I hire the best. Those who know people and will do anything you want for cash."

"Yeah, like I said. So, do you only work in Detroit?"

"I step outside the Big D if the heat is on or if I used up my home-town options. I always do my homework: I case out the town and the spot I'm targeting. I check out the escape routes because I need to know how to get out fast, by car and by foot."

"You're lucky you have people you can trust."

"I've learned not to trust anyone. I trusted this smokin' hot chick, took care of her lock, stock, and barrel, and even bought her a brand-new Honda Civic. We argued once, and she said, 'I'm going to tell the cops about your heists.' I couldn't believe it. I paid for her apartment, bought her clothes, jewelry, car insurance, and even took care of her kid. All she had to do was breathe. She'll never get that again. Lightning doesn't strike twice in the same spot."

"Mr. Porter, you mentioned jewelry, and it got me thinking. Do you buy jewelry or throw a brick through the window and take it?"

"There you go again, funny man. In my hood, they don't leave the merchandise in the windows at night, or if they do, it ain't worth stealing. Most of our store windows have bars over them. After closing time, the good stuff is in a safe, usually a friggin' *big* safe that's locked up in the back room."

"I'm wondering, during the holiday season, do you go Christmas shoplifting?"

"You're getting funnier and funnier, Myette."

"Seriously, how long do you see yourself in this business? Will you ever go legit?"

"Of course I will. I'm gonna get into the cellphone business. That way, I'll get familiar with the phone warehouses, and then I can send out a crew I'm training so they can steal the phones. Then my sales will be pure profit."

"That's not legit. Plus, you'll have to pay the crew, so that's not pure profit."

"Yes, it is. The crew I'd send would be my protégés. I'm teaching them a craft, an art, and that's priceless. The skills are a gift passed down from generation to generation, so I don't have to pay them—they're like my interns. My grandfather taught me the ropes but didn't pay me when I was learning. He taught me to be independent and to carry on the business when he was gone."

Some people's grandfathers teach them to tie a hitch knot, play "Chopsticks," or fish. Porter's taught him to be a professional thief. What a legacy.

"Seriously, how many times have you been down?"

"This time makes three," Porter said matter-of-factly.

"What'll you do when you get out?"

"I'm not going to shit you, Myette. I'm going right back to the game." Porter stood up and walked away.

I thought about a poster I once saw. It read: "We cannot force someone to hear a message they are not ready to receive, but we must never underestimate the power of planting a seed." I never gave up on planting seeds with the inmates, including someone as pigheaded as Porter, because I felt satisfaction when I saw the seeds germinate and the plants begin to take root and grow.

I do not think I changed how Smurf would operate in the world, but after our talks, he will be aware that not everyone sees things from his perspective. I hope he ponders the questions I raised that day and reevaluates Smurfy's Law, which seemed to be "If you don't get caught, you deserve everything you steal."

V:

GENERAL EDUCATIONAL DEVELOPMENT TEACHER AT PUGSLEY CORRECTIONAL FACILITY

CHAPTER 30

Crusade Against Education and Inmates' Success

I Build Them Up, and They Knock Them Down

"Hurt people hurt people."
—Yehuda Berg

In the classroom, I attempted to motivate students, provide a positive atmosphere, and build self-confidence. However, the administration, classification, and my principal at Pugsley Correctional Facility appeared to be against students graduating. The reason behind this mindset was simple: graduation ceremonies required extra work. Each ceremony celebrated the work the students, tutors, and myself invested, and we were proud of our accomplishments.

Attitude is responsible for success at anything: ball games, elections, job interviews, and even earning a GED. Teachers who are clear with instructions, consistent in enforcing the rules, have high expectations, and are enthusiastic about teaching will have a profound positive effect on their students' motivation, self-image, and performance. In my classes, I often talked about having a positive attitude, self-fulfilling prophecies, and Maslow's hierarchy of needs.

These concepts were the opposite of those practiced by an officer at Pugsley. Although Vincent Weasley was a guard, he envisioned himself as the warden in charge of the entire facility and carried himself accordingly. The academic teachers and inmates who entered the school building on his shift felt his need for control.

One of the first times I crossed paths with Officer Weasley, he stood in the hall outside my classroom at a podium, talking with a Black inmate. As I keyed the door to my class, I overheard him say to the young man, "That's the difference between me and you. I'm smart, and you're dumb. I'm wearing a black-and-gray uniform, and you're wearing and singing the prison blues." Weasley let out a chuckle that I can only describe as…well, weaselly.

He loved to hear himself talk and impart his lack of wisdom to everybody. He constantly lectured others on how they should think, act, and live their lives. Weasley was a stickler for rules and loved when they were broken. Rule violations allowed him to jump on people verbally or snitch out staff behind their backs so they might be written up. Weasley was thrilled when the administration punished or fired someone that he ratted out. I imagined that he kept a scorebook of people he had taken down.

I walked into Pugsley's Programs Building one day and heard him say to Webster, a Black inmate, "Ya know how the state could save some serious money?"

"No, sir. How's that?"

"Nine hundred and fifty-eight bullets. That's how."

"I don't know what you mean, sir."

"I mean, that's how many worthless, piece-of-shit scumbags are locking here. A bullet in each of your heads would save the department a lot of money." Webster stood speechless as Weasley smiled, enjoying his discomfort. Officer Weasley was trying to push the inmate over the edge. Weasley hoped the inmate would snap so he could call the yard officers to place inmate Webster in the Hole.

Officer Weasley was a blast from the Jim Crow past and probably still is. Since it appeared that no one had a problem with his attitude, words, or actions, I would bet that he continues to behave in his racist manner. The deputy warden was made aware of Weasley's statements and conduct. Still, nothing was done to curb his behavior. Such negligence communicates to staff and inmates alike that anything goes, and the employees begin bragging about how they demean and abuse inmates and colleagues, knowing there will be no repercussions.

This is one reason the recidivism rate is so high. The inmates, who need to build their self-esteem, are conditioned to despise authority figures such as COs, parole officers (POs), police, and employers. Once an inmate is out of prison, if he does not have good relationships with these folks, he will likely bump heads with them and increase his chances of returning.

Weasley often tried to take me down, sometimes directly, but often in a roundabout way. A rule prohibited students from wearing hats or do-rags in the academic classrooms, but it was inconsistently applied and confused the students. Headgear was allowed in the library on one end of the Programs Building and the Building Trades classes on the other, but not in the academic classrooms in between. So, a new student entering the building would see plenty of inmates wearing hats and do-rags and would naturally think it was all right if they wore one, too. Officer Weasley enjoyed and exploited this uncertainty among the new students, which gave him a chance to harass and degrade them or write them tickets for breaking the school rules.

In the winter, my students bundled up to cross the yard. They entered the building and made their way to my classroom, stomping the snow from their boots, removing their gloves, unzipping their coats, and removing their hats—a natural order for removing winter gear.

Sometimes, a student would forget to remove his hat at the end of this process. When that happened, I would remind him to remove it, and he would comply. But, if Weasley were there and saw an inmate still wearing his hat when he hit my door, he would fly into my room like Kramer on *Seinfeld* and yell, "Take off your hat!"

He would then run to Richard, the principal, like an elementary school tattletale, trying to make it look like I was not enforcing the rules. He would write the infraction in red in the school logbook, which sat on the podium in the hallway, drawing attention to the incident so that the sergeants and lieutenants making their rounds would notice when they signed the book. Soon enough, Richard would tell me, "I understand you're not enforcing the rules." The hat game seemed to give the principal and Weasley much satisfaction. Each time it happened it was very irritating, but I tried not to spend too much time worrying about their games. Enough about those two!

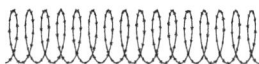

$$\text{000000000000000000}$$

When students approached me and said, "I'm never going to get my GED; I can't do it!" I replied, "You're right!"

Their jaws would drop, and they would say, "What do you mean? You aren't supposed to say that. You're the teacher."

I would tell them, "I believe what Henry Ford believed. If you think you'll succeed, you're right. If you think you'll fail, you're right. Either way, you're correct. It's your choice."

I heard on National Public Radio that we talk to ourselves 150,000 times a day and that 87% of that talk is negative. We are all products of what others tell us and what we tell ourselves. Therefore, we need to control our self-talk, avoid or tune out negative people, and seek out those with positive mental attitudes. I always told my students, "It's impossible to be depressed when you're thinking about something pleasant." To give my students a positive boost, I showed all my classes a video by motivational speaker Les Brown. He proposed the question: What do you want others to say about you at your funeral?

I want others to say: "He was a great father, husband, brother, uncle, and friend. He always helped others and was quick with a joke and a kind word." Whatever someone wants others to say, they must live accordingly. A prison is a place that gives people the time to evaluate their life. It is a time to think about their accomplishments, relationships with others, and who they are.

A prisoner can ask himself, "Did I tell those I love that I love them, and why? Did I help those who were in need? Did I do anything to benefit humankind?"

I continually attempted to build students' knowledge of the world. My Words of the Day time was a way of improving four out of five (Science, Social Studies, Writing, and Reading) subject areas of the GED. Once, one of my Words of the Day was "Stonehenge," so I asked my second-hour class, "What is Stonehenge?" When there was no response,

I drew a quick sketch of the site on the blackboard and said, "Stonehenge is a frequently visited tourist attraction in England. Incredibly, 13-foot-tall stone pillars weighing 25 tons each were brought from Wales, 150 miles away from the site, to build a sacred circular monument four or five thousand years ago."

A new student raised his hand, and I said, "Yes?"

He blurted out, "Why are you making up this bullshit?"

I asked, "Why would you dispute these facts? You can easily find information about Stonehenge in the encyclopedia on the shelf."

The student said, "I say this is BS because I know there wasn't no friggin' whale—even a prehistoric one—5,000 years ago that could drag 25-ton stones for 150 miles through the ocean!"

I chuckled at his confusion and used the opportunity to discuss homonyms like Wales and whales and geography—where the countries of Scotland and Wales lie in relation to England, and so forth.

Once a week, in each class, after Words of the Day, I had one of my tutors select an inspirational quote for our Thought for the Day. The quotes were from famous people, such as Benjamin Franklin, JFK, Ralph Waldo Emerson, and Martin Luther King Jr. My favorite quote by Emerson is: "What lies behind us and what lies before us are tiny matters compared to what lies within us."

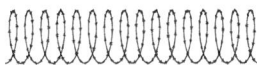

◊◊◊◊◊◊◊◊◊◊◊◊◊◊◊◊

I played music in my classroom for the six years I taught at the Level IV prison in St. Louis. At Pugsley, I got permission to do the same, and it was a great success with the students, keeping them calm and focused. After about four years, my principal, Richard, told me that the music was disturbing my students' concentration and that I had to stop playing it immediately. It was a sad day for my students and me. I hauled my entire selection of jazz and classical music, which we all enjoyed so much, out to my car and took it home.

I could not picture any of my students complaining about the music; they all seemed to love it. The impetus for my principal's demand most likely originated with the officer who set me up before, Vincent Weasley.

The day the music died was in 2010, when I was the only academic teacher at Pugsley. That year, I had 56 graduates, the most of my entire career. Unfortunately, the following year, 2011, I had the lowest graduation rate of all my years teaching GED classes.

Did my playing smooth jazz and my graduation rate correlate? I believe so. I saw the effects of music in the classroom for over a decade in two prisons. The students appreciated it and said they looked forward to coming to class to hear the music. Warning: Exposure to music must be used with extreme caution because it may inspire joy and happiness and spark energy and creativity.

After killing my music, Richard tried to slaughter another of my most popular and successful tools: He said that Words of the Day were a waste of time. My St. Louis principal, Ron, encouraged Words of the Day, knowing that it expanded the students' knowledge of the world, enhancing their reading and writing abilities.

He knew that comprehending what one reads depends on familiarity with the vocabulary. Few of these men were read to as children. It is doubtful that their parents discussed politics. Most students were not involved in Boy Scouts, did not attend summer camps, and never visited any state or national parks with their families. These men needed help filling in the blanks so they could pass the GED and prepare for life in the outside world.

I promoted group participation and encouraged students to become more proactive and self-directed. I needed to recognize the vast spectrum of adult learning styles and cater to each.

When an adult inmate truly cares about getting a GED, it is no longer just a goal to help him obtain parole; it also provides a sense of accomplishment that gives him a stronger self-image and a thirst for more knowledge. When a student realizes that education will help him get a job in the real world, it is a good day for him, me, and our society.

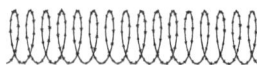

When the St. Louis Correctional Facility school opened in 2000, my friend and fellow teacher, Dave De Vries, hired inmate Powell as a mathematics tutor. Powell would come over to my class under the pretense that De Vries needed to borrow supplies, but in reality, the tutor just wanted to shoot the breeze and listen to the jazz CDs.

Years later, when I was working at the Pugsley facility, Powell was transferred there, and I hired him as a tutor. He did well for me for about a year before Jeff Lilly, the classification director, suddenly yanked him out of his position without a warning.

Lilly reassigned him to a work crew that picked up trash and cut brush out of ditches. Powell informed Lilly that he had a bachelor's degree, enjoyed his tutor job, and refused to go out on the work crew. Lilly placed Powell on "00" status, meaning that he was unemployable, which was ridiculous; he was employed when Lilly removed him from his job.

One day, Powell flagged down the deputy warden on the yard and asked, "Do you think cleaning shrubs out of ditches is more important than helping students get their GEDs?"

"You will work where the facility's needs dictate," the DW answered coldly.

Plenty of other inmates were qualified to work on outside crews. However, few matched the qualifications I wanted in a tutor: a Black inmate (like most of my students) with a bachelor's degree from a major university and prior tutoring experience. It was rare that I found someone who possessed all three of these attributes.

Powell upset the administration somehow, and pulling him from a job he enjoyed was their payback. Knowing Powell, I figured his response was to file grievances against Lilly and the deputy warden. He had been in and out of the prison system and knew how things worked. Powell was granted parole and shipped to a community corrections center in Grand Rapids with a work-release program. The administration handled him just as they might a problem employee; since they could not force him to conform, they promoted him right out the door.

I once asked, "Powell, how long have you been down?"

"I'm doin' life on the installment plan," he said with a smile.

"What?"

"A 20-year sentence is considered life. I've passed that, but I'm doing it one bit at a time."

"Clever expression, but I'm disappointed with you for not staying out of prison."

The writer and motivational speaker Wayne Dyer said, "Our lives are the sum total of the decisions we have made." This explains why some of us sit in the catbird seat and others remain in a cage. Sometimes, staff deliberately destroys inmates' agenda; other times, they take care of that themselves.

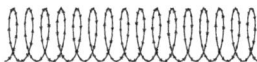

ΩΩΩΩΩΩΩΩΩΩΩΩΩΩΩ

Leading the students in class discussions was more effective than giving lectures. People learn best when they are engaged and feel ownership of their education. To provide students with practical writing experience, I would allow them to write letters to their friends and family, but only if I could help them edit their work. My letter-writing rules were: no foul language or mention of illegal activities, sex, drugs, or anything gang-related. Although I found these taboo topics interesting, I had to place limits on the subject matter.

Inmates rarely wrote letters before taking my class because they were not confident in their writing abilities. I talked to them about the format of a letter, it was very similar to the GED essay. I had students turn in a rough draft, helped them clean it up, and they were proud to send it off in the mail. I counted the letter as a writing assignment.

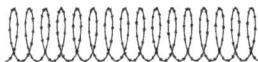

ΩΩΩΩΩΩΩΩΩΩΩΩΩΩΩ

At Pugsley Correctional Facility, I decided to apply a teaching technique I had utilized in St. Louis. I encouraged my tutors to teach specific subject areas to the class using the blackboard, which built confidence in the tutors and the students. When Richard saw my tutors using the blackboard and engaging the students in conversation, he pulled me out of the classroom and instructed me to stop, saying that the department was paying me, not my tutors, to teach.

This was unfortunate because the students became involved in learning, and their self-esteem and grades improved. The principal had a "keep the convicts down" mentality. I explained to him that strengthening students' self-esteem and giving them ownership of their education increases their chances of obtaining their GEDs. I said that my teaching style was designed to impart manners, respect, and civic responsibility to the inmates.

He responded, "You *will not* allow your tutors to use the blackboard or lead discussions." I could not say or do anything to change his mind.

For a prison to run smoothly, the administration must work with staff at all levels. A "Good job!" occasionally improves employees' performance and attitude. Staff will work harder if the head honchos listen to their suggestions and praise them when they do well.

When teachers praise their students and tell them they are smart, their academic work improves. Conversely, a teacher who persistently doles out negative comments will damage the students' progress. A teacher's expectation influences the students' work and ability to succeed.

The same approach holds outside of the classroom. When an inmate was going to be released on parole or was maxing out, I often heard COs say to him, "You'll be back!" This gives the inmate the impression that he is a screw-up and cannot make it in the real world. Those ideas can become engrained in the inmates' minds, especially if they were already there before the officer's cruel comment. Such words frustrate and infuriate inmates. When prisoners are released, they should be encouraged, not peppered with antagonistic remarks. We should want them to succeed, so the last words they hear before walking out the gate should be, "I know you'll do well!"

Several students informed me that they looked forward to coming to class for the words of the day and said the music helped them study because it was relaxing. It all comes down to a straightforward law: What we put out comes back to us. This law applies to everyone, including prison inmates and staff.

Graduation

Behind the Eight Ball

"Education is the most powerful weapon which you can use to change the world."
—Nelson Mandela

As youth, many of my students were expelled from every school in their district for absenteeism, fighting, or selling drugs. It was also common for them to be bounced from household to household and to crash wherever possible. Some inner-city kids lived in a culture of drugs, violence, and murder. Others had siblings and parents who had been in prison or served time. Some were disruptive, hyperactive, and angry at the world when they found themselves in my class. But their pasts were of no consequence to me; I only expected them to apply themselves and succeed in the present.

Young men everywhere suffer from depression and anger. They drop out of school for various reasons, usually concerning their home lives or external circumstances. Some typical reasons on the GED survey are that "I had to get a job to help pay the bills," "I got my girlfriend pregnant," "My mom was sick, and I had to take care of her," "My family moved a lot," "My parents never finished high school and didn't care if I did."

Other reasons for non-attendance of school: "I didn't feel safe there," "I was embarrassed because I flunked a couple of grades," "I didn't get along with teachers [or other students]," "I cared more about partying than schoolwork," "I was expelled."

Given these roadblocks and numerous others, it is not hard to understand why so many inmates did not make it to the twelfth grade. According to the 2022 Kids Count Data Book, Michigan ranked 32nd among the 50 states in overall child well-being. The conservative estimate reports that over five million U.S. children have had a parent in jail or prison at some point.

The Annie E. Casey Foundation compiled a nationwide Kids Count report indicating that about one in 10 Michiganders has had a parent incarcerated in their lifetime, most commonly for crimes associated with substance abuse; this is among the highest rates in the nation. The report makes a strong case that a child's education suffers when a parent is incarcerated. Many of these parents would be far better served by drug rehabilitation than by years of incarceration.

As a prison teacher, my feet were firmly planted in both arenas: corrections and education. My students were unsuccessful in school on the outside, but those who applied themselves thrived in my class-room. They were provided with a teacher and tutors who wanted them to succeed: computers, workbooks, pencils, and paper. For a student who wanted to obtain his GED, my classroom was an optimal place to accomplish the task.

I substitute taught at some inner-city schools that were crumbling, unsafe, and drastically short of supplies. Teachers burn out from dealing with discipline problems, violence, and lack of parental support. These were the schools that the majority of my students came from. However, if they did not get a proper education before prison, they would at least have a chance inside the walls. Education reduces recidivism and is our best tool to stop the penal system's revolving door—and costs—from spinning out of control.

In the 2022 National Assessment of Educational Progress (NAPE), Michigan ranked in the bottom five states in eighth-grade math per-formance among Black students. As a Michigander, I am embarrassed about this sad and exasperating situation.

During my 15 years of teaching in the department, the GED tests were administered on paper, but in 2014, just before my retirement, the testing was changed to computer-based. During this period, the state purchased new computers for the academic classrooms and a new server for the department-wide education network. The server, however, continually crashed when students attempted to take the test. The information technology department requested more money to upgrade the system with technology that could accommodate such basic requirements. At that point, the state denied any further purchases, maintaining that the mistake was the fault of the prison education department.

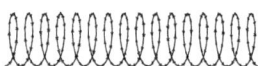

$$\text{VVVVVVVVVVVVVVVV}$$

When my students filled out the paperwork for the GED test, I told them, "Make sure that when you put your name down on the form for each portion of the test, it's the same every time. You can't use a middle initial or 'junior' one time, and not the next, or your new GED test scores won't be combined with your previous scores because the paperwork won't match."

One of my students, inmate Williams, was filling out his GED paperwork and sheepishly asked, "Mr. Myette, what if my real name isn't the same as the one on my prison ID?"

"What do you mean?"

"When I got arrested, I told the police I was my cousin Andre Williams, not Darnell Johnson, my real name. My prison ID says Andre, so do I get my GED in my cousin's name or mine?"

"We need to straighten this out, Mr. Johnson…or Williams…or whoever you are. If your cousin doesn't have a high school diploma or a GED, maybe you should keep it in his name to pay him back for giving him a criminal record."

Johnson blurted out, "What?"

I said, "Just kidding."

Some criminals use multiple aliases to confuse the authorities when they get arrested. Many inmates did not know their Social Security numbers; they never needed to because they never had legitimate jobs. When an inmate was incarcerated under an alias, getting the GED paperwork straightened out was challenging.

Before I started teaching at Pugsley, I was excited that I would be helping students earn their GEDs. I enjoyed teaching ABE classes at St. Louis but was ready to have the students see the fruits of their labor and hand them their diplomas.

Unfortunately, the Pugsley principal was not as interested in the number of students graduating as he was in the number of students enrolled. Then I remembered what my boss at St. Louis once told me: principals received kudos for the number of students in school because it reduced what they called the "idleness rate."

Every student who graduated meant one less in school—and another seat to fill. Giving principals praise based on the number of students enrolled in class allowed their egos to take precedence over the students' graduation rates.

For students to graduate, the principals needed to arrange for them to be tested, and then the paperwork had to be sent to Oklahoma to be scored. When students pass the GED, the principal and teaching staff must plan for graduation. They must locate motivational speakers and coordinate the ceremony with custody and administration.

Because graduation ceremonies require extra work, they were few and far between at Pugsley. When we did have one, it was bare-bones. In contrast to the ceremonies at St. Louis, Pugsley graduates were not given caps and gowns or allowed to invite their family and friends.

Since the ceremonies were so rare, students who passed the test often asked, "When are we going to have a graduation?" or "When are we going to have our pictures taken in caps and gowns?" It was common for Pugsley's graduates to transfer to another facility without having been formally recognized for their accomplishments.

GED graduation ceremonies in prisons increase inmates' self-esteem, perhaps more than any other experience. For most of them, their general education diploma was the only time they set a goal, accomplished it, and were recognized for doing so.

The graduation program was run quite differently at the St. Louis Level IV facility, where, whenever about 25 students recently passed the GED, we would hold a ceremony in the visiting room. We had about four such ceremonies yearly, with six teachers producing around 100 graduates annually. Our school consistently ranked at or near the top of Michigan's prison schools in the number of graduates.

Education staff, tutors, students, and the students' families were excited about graduation at St. Louis Level IV and Mid-Michigan Level I. After all, why were we teaching? Our goal was to help students obtain their diplomas, bringing them closer to *their* goals: getting paroled, obtaining jobs, and functioning better in the world. I considered that the number of graduates we produced gauged our success.

Unlike at Pugsley, Ron, the St. Louis principal, allowed each graduate to invite two guests from the outside world to the ceremony. The teachers were allowed to invite their academic tutors to attend because we all felt they were worthy of recognition.

I brought my CD player to the ceremony to play Elgar's *Pomp and Circumstance* when the graduates entered the visiting room in caps and gowns. The warden welcomed everyone, and the principal introduced the teachers, who presented their tutors and received a gratifying and well-deserved round of applause.

The principal presented the guest speaker, who shared words of encouragement and inspiration with the graduates. Among the speakers featured at our ceremonies were a local school district superintendent, a state representative, and one of my favorite professors from Central Michigan University. Our upper-level GED teacher, Joe McGuire, asked his father—who retired after serving as principal at Jackson prison for 20 years—to speak. It was a special treat for me when *my* dad—a minister for 40 years—addressed the graduating class at one ceremony, with my mom in tow as a guest. He told them they should be proud of their accomplishments and that he was glad they had started on the road to success.

To close the ceremonial part of each event, the class valedictorian was asked to say a few words. After the Level IV ceremonies, I played smooth jazz CDs while everyone enjoyed cookies, punch, and coffee. The graduates and their guests socialized and had their photos taken by an inmate photographer.

The security requirements at the Mid-Michigan Level I facility next door were less stringent than the Level IV. So, the administration allowed an inmate band to play mellow jazz before and after the ceremony. Live music from a guitar, bass, keyboard, and the singer added much more to the celebration.

The hype surrounding graduation motivated students to work harder. Those who did not have their people in attendance were proud to have diplomas and graduation pictures to send home to them. Watching the graduates walk across the yard in their caps and gowns, the other inmates got caught up in the buzz of accomplishment and appreciation. I was delighted because the procession was a beautiful demonstration of the power of education.

When producing graduates at Pugsley, one of the most important motivational tools I had was the "Graduate Wall of Fame." At the top of my walls, encircling the classroom, I put up, in bold print, the name and prisoner number of each of my graduates, along with the dates they passed the GED. After I presented them with their certificates, my students would stop back into my classroom to see their names posted on our wall.

When a graduate stopped in, I would greet him and announce to the other students, "Gentlemen, this is so-and-so, Pugsley's latest graduate," and the students would applaud. The graduates would leave my classroom with big grins and walk out with their heads held high. A GED or high school diploma is nothing special to most people, but to these young men, it was incredibly important. I heard numerous students say, "I'm the only one in my family to get a GED or diploma, and they're very proud of me."

VI:
THOUGHTS ABOUT MY TIME IN PRISON AND RETIREMENT

CHAPTER 32

A Couple of the Best

In Search of Good Prison Employees

"Do what you can, with what you have, where you are."
—Theodore Roosevelt

When I think about superior officers, Ken Carnegie and Roy Banister come to mind. I went through the Corrections Academy and was assigned to Riverside Psychiatric Prison with them. These men were 10 years my junior but repeatedly proved themselves in dangerous situations. We were fortunate to have the psych units as our original training ground.

A few months after I retired, I was shopping at a local grocery store when I ran into Lt. Ken Carnegie. He is a short, balding, jolly fellow who almost always has a smile on his face. As my wife, Molly, listened, Carnegie and I exchanged prison stories. Carnegie recalled, "I was playing Euchre at Riverside once, and inmate Bellinger came to the table and asked me for a light. I give him one, and I set my Zippo on the table. After the game, I got up and started to walk away, then remembered to pick up my lighter—but it was gone. I grabbed another CMA, and we headed to Bellinger's cell. We put on our gloves, asked him to step out into the hall, and shook his room down, but we came up with nothing.

"As we started to leave, Bellinger said, 'I didn't take the lighter.'

"So, I say, 'I never mentioned a lighter. Bellinger, take your pants and underwear off. Bend over and spread 'em.' The lighter must have leaked fluid because there was a red ring around his brown eye. I said, 'All right, Bellinger, I know it's up there; now give me some strong coughs and squeeze it out.' So, Bellinger coughs, and the Zippo pops out of his rear and hits the floor—clink. The other officer and I laughed hysterically. I picked up the Zippo, but I never used it again."

Molly said, "Well, Ken, thanks for sharing that delightful story. It was nice to see you. We'll have to have you and your wife over for dinner so that you can share more lovely tales of your time at Riverside."

I am looking forward to that dinner party, for I know that Ken Carnegie will have plenty of anecdotes to tell; he had a long career after leaving Riverside. When Carnegie was laid off, he interviewed and was offered a job at Pugsley, where he worked for the next 20 years. He was promoted to sergeant, then lieutenant, before the state closed the facility in 2016. By then, he already had 25 years in the department. Still, he was too young to retire, so he transferred to the maximum-security facility in Manistee and worked there until he reached the official retirement age of 52. Ken was fair and consistent when dealing with the inmates. He was one of the good officers who was promoted on his abilities rather than for being an obsequious ladder climber.

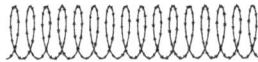

~~~~~~~~~~~~~~~~~~~~~~

In 2022, I was down in Lansing to see some old high school friends playing in a band when I heard someone call my name. I turned around to see Roy Banister, a slim 5' 8" man I had not seen in a decade. He retired in 2019, giving him 29 years in the department.

I told Roy I was writing a book about my time in the prison system and wondered if I could call him to discuss some of his experiences. I asked him what prisons he worked for after Riverside. He said, "Freeland, by Saginaw, I-Max in Ionia, and St. Louis Level IV, where you worked, but I think you moved on to Pugsley shortly after I arrived."

I told him I was an officer until 2000. I asked when the state started using Tasers to subdue inmates. When I was an officer, we just tackled inmates, cuffed them, and put them in leg irons.

Roy said, "The department didn't start using Tasers until 2012, and I used them often. I was a rover in St. Louis, which involved escorting the two units from our building across the yard to the chow hall. The brass issued me a Taser because the yard and the chow hall are two main places where things hop off."

I asked Roy to tell me about his scariest experience in prison. He said, "Lincoln, an intoxicated inmate at St. Louis, got into an argument with a sergeant in the chow hall. The sergeant left the chow hall, and I heard over my radio, 'Officer needs assistance; I've been stabbed!' I ran out of 4 Building to the yard in time to see Lincoln wielding an ice pick. A group of officers surrounded Lincoln, and a slew of inmates began to gather. A couple of fights broke out between the onlookers, and I was working on crowd control. I tried to keep the inmates back, ordering them to disperse. Our main objective was to secure the weapon and to remove the assailant, which happened when I hit Lincoln with the Taser, and he dropped. After the siren was blown and the yard cleared, several officers went to the hospital, besides the one initially stabbed. After completing my Critical Incident Report, I checked the prisoner's file. He was in for murdering someone with a sword and maiming another. You can't know the background of every inmate, but sometimes it helps."

I said, "My wife says I have PTSD. I would be surprised to hear of anyone who worked 25 or 30 years in prison, especially in high-level facilities like us, that didn't have nightmares, causing them to thrash around. I bet you've had your share of bad dreams. I remember you being attacked at Riverside by the strongest inmate I've ever seen. You know who I'm talking about?"

"Oh yeah! Wolfgang went off his meds and threatened to hurt staff. The nurse ordered us to place him in seclusion but later told me to take him out to the airing porch for a smoke break, which I thought was a bad decision. I removed his handcuffs so he could smoke and reached into my pocket to get my lighter; as I brought it up, I saw his fist coming at me. He broke my nose, and I became unhinged! I lunged at him, lifting him up, and body-slammed him. I swung at him, but he nodded his head down, and I broke my hand on his forehead.

"Because of the goose egg on his noggin', I was raked over the coals by the nurse and psychiatrist. I explained that I was in fear for my life.

I'm not a big man. When you believe you might die, you're capable of more than you think possible. Sometimes, it's not under your control. You react.

"I was crossing the yard a week or so later, and Wolfgang called me over. I wasn't sure what to do. If I had kept walking, he might think I was scared. So, I approached him and said, 'What's up?' He says, 'I'm sorry I broke your nose. You never gave me a reason to do that. I hope you'll accept my apology. I was wrong.'"

I asked Roy if it was okay to bring up these memories, and he said, "For your book, yes, but I don't talk about this stuff with your average Joe. People don't *realize* what we went through, so maybe the book would help them understand."

I said, "Since we're getting deep, I wonder if you ever saw anyone murdered in prison?"

"Yes, I did, and I kind of saw it coming."

"How so?"

"There was this big White guy that the Bloods were continually approaching, so I pulled him aside and asked what was up. He said the gang wanted him to move drugs around the prison for them, but he told them to get fucked. I decided to keep a close eye on him because it's dangerous to disrespect a Black gang member. I was standing 10 feet from this guy in the chow hall when this huge Black dude came out of nowhere and hit him with a tremendous uppercut to the jaw. The White guy hits the floor backward, and I swear I heard his melon pop. He started twitching and bleeding out his ears, which was not a good sign. I took the Black dude down and cuffed him. Then I looked over and saw the White guy lying there motionless and thought, *That man is dead.*

"Incidents like that make me think there should be mandatory counseling for employees who experience such brutal assaults. You might not think it affected you at the time, but you'd be wrong. That hit haunts me to this day."

Roy is another one of the good ones. He and Ken Carnegie were stand-up guys. Although they were some of the smallest officers I knew, I would take them as backup any day. In prison, it is not how big you are but how you handle the situation. We all learned a lot about ourselves, each other, and human nature from working in the Riverside psych wards.

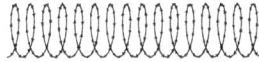

◊◊◊◊◊◊◊◊◊◊◊◊◊◊◊◊

Once, while teaching at Pugsley, I was summoned to the warden's conference room. A half dozen of us were there to be recognized with lapel pins for our longevity in the department. The deputy warden was asked to honor those of us who had 10, 15, and 20 years of service. As we sat at the long table, the DW said, "For 10 years of service in the Michigan Department of Corrections…blah…blah…blah; for 15 years…blah… blah…blah." When it was my turn, he said, "For 20 years of service, I present this pin to Jack Mayotte." I said, "It's pronounced My-ette." He looked at me and said, "Here's your pin, Mayotte."

Five years later, my principal passed me in the hallway, stopped, said, "Oh, Jack, I forgot to give this to you at the meeting today," and handed me my pin for working for the Michigan Department of Corrections for 25 years. Then he turned around and continued walking down the hall. There was no announcement, no handshake, no congratulatory words, nada.

These experiences gave me an idea of how the inmate graduates must have felt when they were not adequately recognized for earning their GED, a significant event in their lives.

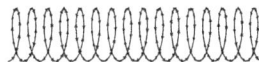

◊◊◊◊◊◊◊◊◊◊◊◊◊◊◊◊

After I had been retired for seven years, I went to the Northwest Michigan Fair and saw Jeff and Frank, a couple of COs I knew from Pugsley. They were in their correction officer uniforms, tending a booth where they were attempting to recruit new employees to work for the Michigan Department of Corrections. Like so many other businesses, Michigan prisons are short-staffed, which increases the danger.

These two men were hired after 1997 when the state stopped offering pensions to employees. I always felt terrible for those who missed the cutoff date because they did the same job as me. They put their lives on the line but would not receive a pension. As I approached the booth, I thought, *What could these two guys possibly say to entice me to return to work in prison as an officer or teacher?*

Jeff said, "Jack, you hired in before 1997, so if you came back as an officer, you'd still have your medical benefits and pension, plus you'd get officers' pay on top of that."

I said, "But I don't want to work full-time."

Jeff said, "You don't have to. You can dictate how much you want to work. You tell the facility what days and shifts you want. When they call, you decide whether you will accept the assignment."

I said, "You are joking, right? Why would they be so flexible?"

Frank said, "For several reasons. First, you've already gone through the corrections academy, so they don't have to train you. Secondly, you've got your benefits, so the state doesn't have to shell those out. Thirdly, if someone calls in sick and you pick up their shift, they don't have to pay someone else overtime."

I said, "That does make sense, but I'd probably be ticking off the other COs who want the overtime."

"Oh, plenty of overtime is still available," Jeff replied.

I said, "Why's that?"

Frank said, "Because no one wants to work these days. Just like outside of prison. We live in a different world than when you or I grew up."

I said, "Ain't that the truth."

Jeff said, "If you want to make some real money, you should come back as a prison teacher."

I said, "When I was teaching, I was making about captain's pay."

Frank said, "Well, that was then. Now you can make a whole lot more."

Jeff said, "They have a hard time finding prison teachers, but the inmates are still required to get their GEDs. So, the MDOC subcontracts teachers and pays them almost twice what you were making."

"Holy crap! That's well into a six-figure income. Any other perks?" I jested.

Jeff said, "Yup. You know how we get paid every two weeks?"

"Yeah, so?"

He says, "Well, if an employee doesn't call in sick in their pay period, they get an extra $250 in their check."

"What? You mean if you don't call in for the month, it's an extra $500 in your pocket?"

"That's right. Handing out the bonuses is still cheaper than paying overtime."

I said, "You know I used to sell timeshare, and what you two are telling me sounds like what we called in the business, 'pitching heat.'"

"Hey, we're not making this stuff up. We're out here recruiting because we need people. Like other businesses, the state is doing everything possible to attract new employees. They're also going to be giving everyone a 5 percent raise. Just think about it and tell others about the perks the department is offering."

CHAPTER 33

Prison Reform

"That's all I have to say about that."

"No one knows a nation until one has been inside its jails. A nation should not be judged by how it treats its highest citizens but its lowest ones."
—Nelson Mandela

The department's incentives were enticing, but 25 years in an alternate universe was good enough for me. My perspective was of Michigan prisons, but much of the United States penal system needs reform. The changes must come from the top. Leadership positions should be examined and evaluated, and employees who do not meet expectations should be required to be trained in their deficient areas. If improvement follows in a timely manner, the employees in question should be retained; otherwise, a career change may be in order.

Capable employees need to be recognized for their efforts. They should receive bonuses and be promoted for competence, not because they are obsequious informants or part of the good ol' boy system. Seeing strong, capable, honest management at the helm would be refreshing.

The state must consider alternative forms of incarceration. Norway's prisons are designed to give the inmates a feeling of community and foster independence. They wear their own clothes, cook their own meals, and work at jobs that prepare them for employment on the outside. Norway has the lowest recidivism rate of any country in the world, at 20 percent, as opposed to the U.S., which has the highest rate, at 76.6 percent.

Studies in the U.S. have proven that education reduces the recidivism rate, so we need to educate efficiently. The educational computer network and software programs must be scrutinized vigorously. Previously, the server was deficient, and the educational software programs were flawed. Once again, those at the top should be held responsible.

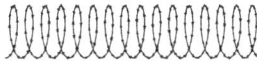

$$\textcolor{black}{\text{〰〰〰〰〰〰〰〰〰〰〰}}$$

It takes work to strike a fair and equitable balance between what should be demanded of prisoners and what privileges they are entitled to. Even employees working at the same prison disagree. Those on the outside generally want society to be tough on crime, but they often do not want to spend the money on food, clothing, housing, medical needs, education, and programming that the laws dictate.

Many employees take the old "They ain't got nothin' comin'" attitude, ignoring the necessities and privileges the inmates are legally entitled. When inmates' rights are ignored, taxpayers will be burdened with funding the lawsuits that will follow. Inmates should be expected to work, attend school, learn a trade, and be productive. They should be allowed to participate in leisure activities like playing sports, watching TV, and reading. We want them to be of sound mind and body so they can obtain jobs and pay taxes upon release.

Society should want to improve the inmates' state of mind. We should want prisoners to become successful and productive citizens. Without programs and positive experiences, many return to the outside world with the same ignorant, angry, and anti-social ways they brought in.

I have heard complaints from prison staff and civilians about inmates having TVs and cable services. These people are unaware that the state does not provide the TVs; the inmates purchase them, and the Prisoner Benefit Fund (PBF) pays for the cable. The money in the PBF comes from various sources: the vending machines in the visiting room, a surcharge on the inmates' store orders, and a percentage of the sales of prisoner-made hobby crafts. So, the TVs and cable do not cost taxpayers anything. TVs keep inmates in touch with what is happening in the outside world.

The prison library is another source of an inmate's connection to the world beyond the walls. At first, I wondered if the state had paid for all the reading material. Later, I learned that many books had been donated and that the PBF purchased newspapers and magazines.

The recreational activities offered at the lower-level prisons are therapeutic. Once the equipment is purchased or donated, softball, basketball, volleyball, handball, and horseshoes are not an expense. If these games were not allowed, thousands of inmates would not get sufficient exercise, and the doctor's bills would pile up. To improve the inmates' functioning, we should try to instill good work ethics, keep them fit, and enhance their social skills. The Prisoner Benefit Fund pays for Michigan prisons' sports and weight-pit equipment.

In answer to the question, "Do prisoners have something coming?" I say, "Yes, they do." Research has shown that people locked in cells without stimulation will often descend into madness. And, since the cost of finding placement for the mentally ill is much higher than housing the sane, it makes sense to give them recreation and other diversions rather than to throw them in a cell and lock the door. We do not want to increase the number of people with mental problems before releasing them into our communities.

I have heard people complaining about inmates being paid to attend school in Michigan prisons. In most facilities, they cannot work and go to school simultaneously. When I was teaching, students were paid 59 cents a day, so if they attended four days a week, they would earn less than $10 a month. If they were not paid for their schooling, they would have no source of income, and the state would be required to provide them with toiletries like soap, toothpaste, and deodorant. Paying them minimal money teaches inmates how to apply their budgeting skills, which helps them learn to make choices and take responsibility.

People appreciate things more if they have to work for them. Anyone who works hard toward a goal and achieves it has earned bragging rights and should be proud. I once talked to a man who ran a homeless shelter. He said they used to provide their clients with free food and clothing, but the indigent clients complained about how terrible the food and clothes were. Then, they decided to charge a token fee for both, and the compliments started rolling in.

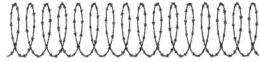

ⅩⅩⅩⅩⅩⅩⅩⅩⅩⅩⅩⅩⅩⅩⅩⅩ

The United States' problems with the mentally ill, the homeless, and prison overcrowding are intertwined. Mental illness is plaguing jails and prisons across our nation. In Michigan, closing state hospitals in the late 1980s accelerated the problem. The best way to reverse this is to turn back the hands of time. A solution to the problem is to reopen the state mental hospitals and have them and our prisons run as in the old days. The Traverse City State Hospital was self-sufficient and made a profit in the late 1800s. It would be nice if the bigwigs could figure out how things were run about 140 years ago.

COVID changed the way many businesses operate. Now, much of the workforce operates out of their homes, leaving office buildings across our nation empty. Many of these structures are still available and could be used for homeless shelters, low-income housing, halfway housing for parolees, or state mental hospitals. The empty buildings that some see as a problem, others with foresight might view as a blessing.

Michigan has closed or consolidated over 20 prisons since 2005. These facilities would need some renovations, but they are already in place with administration buildings, chow halls, athletic facilities, housing units, etc. The State of Michigan already owns them; why not constructively utilize these empty prisons? Housing the mentally ill and homeless in these facilities would reduce the prison population. The old Traverse City State Hospital is a perfect example of how a closed-down facility can be repurposed from empty structures to something useful once again.

The MDOC could use a financial boost, for it employs almost one-third of the state's workforce. Michigan prisons use 20 percent of the general fund, which is $2 billion annually. If today's prisons had competent staff, were again self-sufficient, and had strong educational and vocational programs, the state could turn the Michigan Department of Corrections around. Accomplishing these goals could free up a couple of billion dollars for the state's infrastructure, public schools, police and fire departments, and state parks.

CHAPTER 34

"A purpose to fulfill"

Calling It a Day

> "Either write something worth reading
> or do something worth writing."
> —Benjamin Franklin

When I started with the department, I did not know what situations I would encounter. I made up my mind that, whatever the hardships were, I would stick it out for 25 years. People look forward to retirement for decades, but when it approaches, some begin to fear the concept, partly because others tell them, "You can't retire! You won't have enough money. You'll be bored. You'll have to find supplemental work." These people are expressing *their* fears. They often add, "I'm going to work until I drop. The longer I work, the more Social Security I'll get. I've done the numbers." When family, friends, acquaintances, and near-strangers said that to me, I thought, *Working until you drop might suit you, but I want to experience as much as I can while I'm still able to get around.*

I would say, "I think I'll be all right. I won't have to buy work clothes, drive back and forth to work, pay union dues, go out with others to lunch, or put money in my 401(k). I have lots of things to keep me busy. I'll write songs, play guitar, travel to new places, and maybe even write a book."

When thinking about retirement, I contemplate my dad's dad, Arthur Eugene Myette. He began working for the United States Postal Service as a mail carrier in Burlington, Vermont, in 1907. When he started, he was paid $300 a year and had to provide his horse and cart. It was estimated that he had walked the equivalent of the earth's circumference five and a half times during his 40 years with the USPS. He retired in 1947 and died in 1951 before my parents were married, so I never had the pleasure of meeting him. Maybe if he had called it good after 30 years, he would have had at least one decade to enjoy his retirement—he certainly earned it.

We live our lives in chapters, and each one has a purpose. My father said, "My dad enjoyed his job because he loved talking to his customers along the way. Unfortunately, the last chapter of his life was too short."

My father spent nearly 40 years as a minister for the United Methodist Church, marrying, burying, consoling, and counseling people in nine different churches. Dad played an essential role in the lives of thousands of people. Happily, he lived a couple of decades longer than his father.

Growing up around the various congregations, I witnessed Dad touching many lives. He only lived a fraction of his life in Traverse City, but local parishioners and ones from previous parishes showed up at his funeral in droves. The church was packed. I gave the eulogy, but I was a bit nervous and choked up; I do not remember exactly what I said other than telling the assembled what a big heart he had and some humorous stories about him. He was one of those guys that cracked people up, even when he was not trying to be funny.

In his last years, Dad and Mom lived in a guest house behind the house where I lived with my wife, Molly, and my son, Max. Dad would take a walk almost every day at the same time. My father, John Stephen Myette Sr., died on May 5, 2012.

Soon after, with summer approaching, I was working in our front yard when a man I did not recognize approached me and said, "Where's your dad been? I haven't seen him around." After a few minutes, a woman approached me and asked, "How's your dad?" And so, throughout the summer, I encountered a parade of people my father had touched.

When I told these folks that he had passed away, they would offer their condolences and say they missed him; I responded that we did, too. They told me that Dad used to walk by their houses almost daily and would stop to talk with them. Because he would make his rounds at about the same time nearly every day, some would even come outside, hoping to catch him. They said he seemed to care about what was going on in their lives and always made them feel good about themselves. Everyone described him as a friendly, positive person—a truly good man. It made me proud that he was my father.

I thought my dad's walks were about getting fresh air, escaping Mom's nagging, and staying in shape. I was wrong. His time on Earth was not about him. It was for all the lonely people who needed someone to talk to—people who were thankful for someone who would listen to them. Everyone wants to think there is someone who appreciates them and cares about them. My father shared his wisdom through his sermons and articles for numerous newspapers, so his spoken and written words reached thousands.

Dad used to say, "We all have a purpose to fulfill on earth, and if we are working on that purpose, it does not feel like work at all." I like how Mark Twain put it: "The two most important days in your life are the day you were born and the day you find out why."

I felt unfulfilled when working in various sales jobs. I was taking rather than giving. Although my jobs as a corrections medical aide, corrections officer, and prison teacher were very stressful, there was an unequivocal gratification from helping fellow human beings. Interacting with lost souls helps them feel more human, less hated, and more hopeful about their lives.

I initially accepted a job with the Michigan Department of Corrections because I wanted a steady income, medical benefits, and a pension. These are three critical things that most people want. However, my journey has taught me so much more.

As an officer, I learned how to prevent prisoners from physically hurting themselves and others. I learned how to protect myself and how to use de-escalation techniques. I also helped inmates with their communication and socialization skills.

As a teacher, I taught students to read, write, and do math. I helped them reach their goals, which improved their self-esteem. I learned about a completely different world through my conversations with the inmates.

Helping others made me feel better about myself. The more the prisoners improved, the more satisfaction I gained. I saw a transformation in the prisoners and felt it within myself. My career in corrections gave me a better understanding of myself and others.

My quarter bit, my 25 years in prison, was the purpose I needed to fulfill.

Glossary

This glossary is a compilation of abbreviations, slang, terms, and phrases often heard in the Michigan prison system.

AB – Abbreviation for *Aryan Brotherhood*, Alice Baker, The Brand, or One-Two. The AB is the nation's oldest prominent White supremacist prison gang. Founded in 1964 by Irish bikers, the 20,000 members can be found in prisons and on the streets.

Area of Control – The location in the prisoner's cell or cube for which he is held responsible. For example: "The shank was found under his mattress, which is in the prisoner's *area of control*. He was written a ticket for possession of a dangerous weapon."

Bat Cave – Slang for one's house outside prison, a.k.a. on the street.

Bit – A slang term for the time a prisoner was sentenced. "I'm doing a five-to-15-year *bit*."

Black Tag – At one time, a corrections officer who had completed their year of probation would qualify to wear a *Black Tag* with their last name on it. Now, all officers wear black name tags from the beginning of their careers.

Bone Hawking – A slang term used for the assignment of corrections officers running showers for the inmates.

Buck-50 – A slang term for an inmate being slashed from their mouth to their ear, requiring about 150 stitches. The scar is meant to brand the recipient as a snitch forever.

Bug – A derogatory slang term that refers to a mentally ill patient/inmate or sometimes staff who are perceived as having mental problems.

Bunkie – A slang term for an inmate who shares a bunk bed with another.

Catcher – A slang term for the submissive sex partner in a male prison.

Cracker Bolts – The SS or cracker bolts are a Nazi symbol derived from Schutzstaffel, an elite military unit of Hitler, responsible for the murder of six million Jews. In prison, the tattoo is a White supremacist/neo-Nazi symbol worn by gang members. The gangs are known to be behind the assaults and murders of other races and those of a different belief system.

Doing all day – A phrase referring to a life sentence without any chance of parole.

Dress out – A slang prison term used for an inmate throwing urine, feces, and/or semen on unsuspecting staff. In federal prisons, the preferred term is "being slimed" rather than "*dressed out.*"

Fish – A derogatory slang term for prison staff or inmates new to the correctional system.

Flop – A term meaning the inmate's parole was denied by the parole board. The denial is usually a result of negative behavior and an accumulation of tickets by the inmate. A typical flop is for 12, 18, or 24 months. The inmate will hear from the parole board again after their flop is up.

Gangbanger – A slang term for a member of a criminal gang, especially one involved in violence.

G-Ma – Slang term for grandmother.

GP – Abbreviation for *general population* prisons, as opposed to a psychiatric prison.

Goon Squad – Slang term for a four-member response team in riot gear summoned to perform room rushes or control violent, out-of-control inmates. A more politically correct term, SORT (Special Operations Response Team), has recently been used.

Green Tag – Previously a new corrections officer who had completed the Corrections Academy but had not reached their one-year probation period. The Red and *Green Tag* system has been discontinued.

In the Car – A slang phrase meaning the employee is in favor of the upper echelon, placing them on the fast track to promotions, i.e., "CO Johnson is a shoo-in for the job; he's definitely *in the car.*"

Key – 1) A term used for unlocking doors in prison. In older prisons, officers must manually *key* or open cell doors for the inmates rather than push a remote button. An inmate will ask, "CO, will you key my door?" 2) A term used for pushing the button on a mobile radio to talk, i.e., "He *keyed* his radio mic and shouted, 'I need assistance! Fight on 11-2-East!'"

Lock – A common term for where a prisoner's cell is located. A CO may ask, "Inmate Jones, where do you *lock*?" Inmate Jones's response, "I lock in C Unit, 118."

Lock-in-a-Sock – A literal description of a common weapon. A padlock is placed in a sock and usually swung at another inmate's head. The lock may also be attached to a belt and used similarly.

Mug – *Mug* is a euphemism for motherfucker, i.e., "It's cold as a mug out today."

OJT – Abbreviation for *On-the-Job Training.* A new hire must complete two months in the prison where they will be assigned, in addition to their classroom training at the Corrections Academy.

Pitcher – A slang term for the dominant inmate's role in a sexual relationship in a male prison.

Porter – Term used for an inmate worker in a janitorial position. *Porters* are employed to clean the prison units and the rest of the facility. Lower-level inmates may be used as porters in and around higher-level prisons.

Punked Out – A slang term for an inmate used as a sex slave. The inmate is often sold or traded to other inmates to perform sexual favors.

Quarter Bit – An amount of prison time. A prisoner might say, "I did a nickel," or "I'm doing a dime." A quarter bit is equal to 25 years in prison, which is what I did for the MDOC.

Real World – A common prison phrase inmates use to refer to the outside world because prison is unlike the "real world."

Red Tag – Corrections officers used to wear red tags when starting their probation period, including their first OJT assignment. The Red and Green Tags are no longer used.

Rode Out – Prison term for an inmate transferring to another facility or being released. *Rode out* is the past tense of ride out. For example, "My bunkie rode out yesterday, and I'm scheduled to ride out tomorrow."

Shake Down – A procedure used when an employee searches an inmate, an inmate's area of control, or a section of the prison to find contraband, weapons, or drugs.

Shank – A slang term for a handcrafted bladed weapon, usually made of metal, resembling a knife.

Shiv – A slang term for a non-metal sharp, pointed object used as a knife-like weapon. They may be made of a glass shard, plexiglass, or a sharpened toothbrush handle. Shivs became more popular when prisons began using metal detectors.

Short-Timer – An inmate with little time left on their sentence or bit. An inmate is said to be short or a *short-timer* when they have less than a year to go on their sentence.

Snow Train – A slang term for when a prisoner gets transferred from a prison in Michigan's Lower Peninsula to an Upper Peninsula prison, i.e., "They put me on the *snow train* to the Kinross facility in the U.P."

Spital – A slang contraction of the word "hospital." Coincidentally, the actual word for "hospital" in Albanian is *spital*.

Spot – A slang term for the place someone may go after the bars close to continue partying. A *"spot"* is unmarked, but the people in each inner-city neighborhood know where they are.

Spud – A slang term used for homemade alcohol. Its name is derived from the fermentation of potatoes. Inmates more commonly make *spud* from fruit or juice. They speed up the fermentation process by adding sugar and heat.

Stinger – A device made by cutting off the electrical cord from a lamp or small appliance and stripping the end of the wires. When the cord is plugged into a wall socket and the wires are touched together, inmates can light cigarettes without matches. The *stinger* is also used to speed up the fermentation process of spud by dropping the exposed wires into the juice and plugging the other end into an outlet to heat the liquid.

Trap House – A slang term for a crack house.

The Hole – A slang term for a punishment cell that is also called the box or solitary confinement.

Acknowledgments

Special thanks to Dorothy Hanson, Jackie Payne, Dr. Michael Wells, the Plantation Writers Guild in Leesburg, Florida, and the fine folks at Mission Point Press in Traverse City, Michigan, who made this book a reality.

About the Author

As an art major with a minor in speech and drama, Jack Myette was an unlikely candidate to work in the prison system. He graduated from Central Michigan University with a Bachelor of Science in Education in 1980 but spent the next decade working in the restaurant business and the sales field. He sold everything from computers, major appliances, cars, and trucks to resort property in Cancun, Mexico.

When immigration came to Cancun and started deporting illegal aliens, Jack decided to return to his roots and move back to Michigan. Although it was a giant leap in another direction, in 1990 he accepted a job working with the criminally insane for the Michigan Department of Corrections. While he was an officer in a psychiatric prison in Ionia, Michigan, he received the N.A.P.P.I. Award for his Non-Abusive Physical and Psychological Intervention in a highly dangerous situation and was selected as a Special Operations Response Team member summoned for crisis interventions.

In the mid-1990s, the psychiatric prison in Ionia closed, so Jack spent the next five years as a corrections officer at a general population prison in St. Louis, Michigan. During his 10 years as an officer, his teaching certificate expired. He returned to school, renewed his certification, and earned a Master of Arts in Educational Administration.

Jack spent his next six years teaching Adult Basic Education (ABE) at a high-level prison. During his last nine years in the department, he taught General Education Development (GED) classes at a low-level facility. His principal informed him that at one time, he had the highest graduation rate of any teacher in the Michigan prison system. By helping inmates obtain their GEDs, he felt he was doing his bit to help reduce recidivism, save taxpayers money, and satisfy something inside himself.

Fortunately, from his first week in the Michigan Department of Corrections, Jack kept meticulous notes. Spanning 25 years, these allowed him to write the book now held in your hands. His story is told through his and the inmates' eyes, incorporating details from the many conversations he had and interviews he conducted as an officer and a teacher.

Now, Jack enjoys reading, writing, photography, playing guitar, singing around the campfire, listening to live music, riding bikes, and traveling. He says, "Travel is the most intense educational experience one can have, and the more diverse, the better."

www.ingramcontent.com/pod-product-compliance
Lightning Source LLC
Chambersburg PA
CBHW052015030426
42335CB00026B/3155